Yale Southeast Asia Studies, 8

Southeast Asian Transitions

Approaches through Social History

Edited by Ruth T. McVey

with the assistance of Adrienne Suddard

New Haven and London, Yale University Press, 1978

Published with assistance from the foundation
established in memory of Philip Hamilton McMillan
of the Class of 1894, Yale College.

Designed by John O. C. McCrillis and set in IBM Press
Roman type. Printed in the United States of America
by The Alpine Press, Inc., South Braintree, Mass.

Published in Great Britain, Europe, Africa, and Asia
(except Japan) by Yale University Press, Ltd.,
London. Distributed in Australia and New Zealand
by Book & Film Services, Artarmon, N.S.W., Australia; and in Japan by Harper & Row, Publishers,
Tokyo Office.

Library of Congress Cataloging in Publication Data
Main entry under title:

Southeast Asian transitions.

   (Yale Southeast Asia studies; 8)
   "Essays written to honor the late Harry J. Benda."
   Includes bibliographical references and index.
   1. Asia, Southeastern—Politics and government—
Addresses, essays, lectures. 2. Asia, Southeastern—
Social conditions—Addresses, essays, lectures. 3.
Benda, Harry Jindrich—Addresses, essays, lectures.
I. McVey, Ruth Thomas. II. Suddard, Adrienne.
III. Benda, Harry Jindrich. IV. Series.
DS511.S58   309.1'59   78-4171
ISBN 0-300-02184-4

To Harry J. Benda

This seal was presented to Harry J. Benda by his colleagues
in token of appreciation for his help in founding the Institute
of Southeast Asian Studies in Singapore. The characters *ming
te* may be read either as "brilliant and virtuous" or as a
transliteration of "Benda."

87

Contents

Acknowledgments

This book owes its existence as much to the affection in which Harry J. Benda was held by his colleagues and students as to their respect for his scholarship and profound influence on Southeast Asian historiography. Their voluntary efforts, upon which the venture was entirely dependent, had a spontaneity and selflessness that transcended professional commitment. Such dedication is a private matter bringing private meed, but let a few of the many who helped accept public thanks. Karl J. Pelzer, Harold C. Conklin, and James C. Scott, successive directors of Yale University Southeast Asia Studies, made office facilities available and absorbed countless small expenses. R. William Liddle of Ohio State University was a major participant in the original planning. Eva Benda followed progress with a warm interest and several very valuable suggestions. Robert L. Williams, director of the Yale Map Laboratory, undertook personally to translate some rather rough sketches into fine maps. Others whose concern for the success of the venture was made manifest in singular ways include Charles R. Bryant, Lance Castles, Christopher S. Gray, George McT. Kahin, Sartono Kartodirdjo, Truong Buu Lam, and Milton Osborne. At Yale University Press the manuscript became a book by the expert intercession of Marian Neal Ash, who like the rest of us cherishes memories of H. J. B.

Introduction
Local Voices, Central Power

RUTH T. McVEY

Before World War II, historians of Southeast Asia engaged themselves principally in accounts of Western penetration and rule or in reconstructing the great civilizations of the precolonial past. After independence, they turned their attention to the rise of anticolonial movements and the emergence of new intellectual and political leaderships. This involved a considerable shift in orientation; indeed, the whole locus of scholarship moved, from the former metropoles to, in the first instance, the United States. In another sense, however, things did not change. Anticolonial spokesmen, imperial administrators, and kings all had one thing in common: their thoughts and deeds were in some way a matter of record. Inscriptions, chronicles, company accounts, governors' reports, newspapers, and inflammatory tracts gave evidence of these actors' existence, and, duly interpreted, their doings became the significant past. On the historical scene which thus emerged, notable individuals and significant groups moved against a backdrop of political assembly, colonial office, or court. Everyone knew that this action took place only on the proscenium, and that behind it the historical stage was vastly populated; but how to discern those masses which only showed themselves for confused and violent instants before the documentary lights? For sure, they were talked *about* by the principal actors, but could one know if their perceptions, let alone their accounts, were accurate? Moreover, even those characters most loquacious on the subject of "the people" noted very few aspects of their existence, the doings of lesser folk not being, except in limited and ritualized ways, generally worthy of recount.

The problem was most acute for the history of the past century. Understandably, not much could be said about the structure of societies in historical periods on which there was little material; at the same time, precisely because scholars of precolonial Southeast Asia had

1

relatively few records to work with, and those not immediately congruent to the categories of Western scholarship, they were emboldened to extrapolate on what they found, and so did at times venture social generalizations. The students of better documented areas and times feared to claim such privilege; the archives lay upon their imaginations like incubi. Moreover, though the records were abundant they dealt only haphazardly with the common people, who, when they were not statistics, appeared as objects for improvements, causes for concern, or choruses for a new elite. Then, too, the available local-level evidence was discouragingly inconsistent; the exhausting study needed to reconstruct developments in one place might give the scholar very little authority to argue about any place else. On the whole, it was sensible to stick to aspects that could be well documented and were on a "national" and thus significant scale. The result was the paradox that we seemed to know more in a general way about precolonial Southeast Asian societies than about those of the more recent past.[1]

From the early 1960s this self-limitation of modern historiography came increasingly into question. It was charged that in concentrating on Western rulers and their Westernized successors, dealing with them in categories and through materials recognized as valid by the West but not necessarily by the societies concerned, scholars were describing what might well be mere epiphenomena of the Southeast Asian experience.[2] It was asserted that we need to know more about the charac-

1. The evident exception to this is Thailand, which did not undergo a direct colonial experience and which boasted notable scholars of indigenous culture and history. The divergence is only partial, however, for the extreme bureaucratic centralism of the Siamese polity and the high birth of its native historians strongly influenced the nature of the information available and the problems studied. Foreign scholars of the time tended to interest themselves in the country's modernization as a nation-state, the traditions of its court, and the accomplishments of its rulers. Some studies of contemporary village life were made, but very little work was done on the linkage between the world of the village and that of the capital, or of the way in which the modernizing initiatives from above actually affected the course of life below.

2. A highly influential contribution to this self-criticism was John Smail's "On the Possibility of an Autonomous History of Modern Southeast Asia," *Journal of Southeast Asian History* 1, no. 2 (1961): 72–102. Arguments along this line had been introduced by earlier historians of the region, notably J. C. van Leur, "Enkele aanteekeningen met betrekking tot de beoefening der Indische geschiedenis," *Koloniale Studiën* 21 (1937): 651–661 (translated as "On the Study of

ter and persistence of indigenous value systems, about the changing nature of the relationship between political center and periphery, and about how ordinary people perceived and experienced their world. There was, in consequence, a move toward studies which brought out the autochthonous aspects of national experience or which tried to look into the experience of actors outside the Westernized and thus recorded elite.[3] This trend was greatly spurred by the emergence of a significant body of Southeast Asian scholars trained in modern historiographical methods, sensitive to indigenous cultural nuances as foreigners could not hope to be, and concerned to establish the relationship of their societies to their precolonial past. Moreover, historians in general were increasingly turning their attention to the lower levels of society both as intrinsically significant arenas of experience and as essential base-points for understanding social change.

Southeast Asia's marked instability in the decades after World War II also drove home the suspicion that existing approaches to the past were inadequate. International power games aside, such flux was surely part of a fundamental social shifting which had begun well back in time. The historian must attempt to trace it, but how could he do so without generalizing wildly? The result was a reassessment of the potential of small-scale histories. It might be true that each local experience was distinct, but this need no more deter the historian from considering its wider meaning than field experience in one village need keep the anthropologist from attributing to his conclusions a broader significance or the medievalist from making suggestions about society on the basis of a single manor's accounts. The results are propositions, not certainties; but without them we cannot begin to understand the possibilities of the time, let alone its actual course.

Indonesian History" in *Asian Trade and Society* [The Hague: Van Hoeve, 1955], pp. 145–156). Such essays came before their time, however, in part because World War II and subsequent independence struggles kept attention fixed on national-level events.

3. To date, the most comprehensive effort at writing Southeast Asian history along these lines is David Joel Steinberg, David K. Wyatt, John R. W. Smail, Alexander Woodside, William R. Roff, and David P. Chandler, *In Search of Southeast Asia* (New York: Praeger, 1971). This admirable work treats the period from the eighteenth to the mid-twentieth centuries, for the most part on a country-by-country basis. It includes a very useful bibliographical section.

Accordingly, Southeast Asia historians began to engage in the reconstruction of small worlds, arming themselves not only with the tools of their own craft but also, increasingly, with techniques, theories, and information from other disciplines—most notably anthropology and sociology, but also economics, political science, and the study of literature. Choosing areas on which there was relatively great documentation and which they thought historically significant (that is, meaningful to rather than typical of a larger process), they could hope to discern the relationship between the various parts of society, and particularly between peasant mass and local elite, much more clearly than could be done through studies on a grander scale. Within the smaller compass the process of social transformation could be traced, and from the observations thus obtained the potentialities of change elsewhere could be extrapolated. Out of this, eventually, a picture of Southeast Asia's recent past might emerge which would not only delineate the transfiguration of its societies but make more visible that vast portion of humanity which bears history and is so rarely expressed by it.

Harry Benda, to whose memory this book is dedicated, was a prime mover in this enterprise. His work centered on the region's social history; in particular, he concerned himself with the impact of foreign ideas and systems on indigenous social structures, whether through the introduction of Islam, European colonialism, or wartime Japanese occupation.[4] He was especially interested in the way these innovations

4. Benda contributed importantly to the revision of the Europocentric approach to Southeast Asian history through his essays on "The Structure of Southeast Asian History: Some Preliminary Observations," *Journal of Southeast Asian History* 3 (1962): 106–138; and "Decolonization in Indonesia: The Problem of Continuity and Change," *American Historical Review* 70 (1965): 1058–1073. See also his exchange with Herbert Feith on the meaning of modernization and the colonial experience in "Democracy in Indonesia," *Journal of Asian Studies* 23 (1964): 449–456 (Benda); and ibid. 24 (1965): 305–312 (Feith). Benda also contributed, with John Bastin, to the general historiography of Southeast Asia through *A History of Modern Southeast Asia: Colonialism, Nationalism, and Decolonization* (Englewood Cliffs: Prentice-Hall, 1968); and, with John Larkin, *The World of Southeast Asia: Selected Historical Readings* (New York: Harper and Row, 1967). Benda's major articles are collected in *Continuity and Change in Southeast Asia,* Yale University Southeast Asia Studies Monograph Series No. 18 (New Haven, 1972); the articles referred to in these footnotes may also be found there. See pp. 303–306 of that volume for a list of Benda's other works.

reflected and affected elite-mass relations. What happened, as a result, to established sources of leadership?[5] Did new ones arise, and if so what was their relationship to the population and to their times?[6] What brought the masses into movement, and what were the inherent limits to their action?[7] And—since Benda was highly conscious of the weight of the past upon the present—what did these changes in Southeast Asian social structures imply for the region's future?[8] Dissatisfied with the impressionistic generalizations which existing studies offered the student of social change, he came to see a particular need for small-scale studies which linked the specifics of local change to a larger concern for social pattern. He turned his own research in this direction and encouraged his colleagues and students to work along these lines.[9] The studies collected here are one product of this effort.

5. See especially his "Political Elites in Colonial Southeast Asia: An Historical Analysis," *Comparative Studies in Society and History* 7 (1965): 233–251; "Christiaan Snouck Hurgronje and the Foundations of Dutch Islamic Policy in Indonesia," *Journal of Modern History* 30 (1958): 338–347; "Decolonization in Indonesia: The Problem of Continuity and Change"; and "The Pattern of Administrative Reforms in the Closing Years of Dutch Rule in Indonesia," *Journal of Asian Studies* 25 (1966): 589–605.

6. See, in addition to the above, *The Crescent and the Rising Sun: Indonesian Islam under the Japanese Occupation* (Bandung and The Hague: Van Hoeve, 1958); "Non-Western Intelligentsias as Political Elites," *Australian Journal of Politics and History* 6 (1960): 205–218; "The Beginnings of the Japanese Occupation of Java," *Far Eastern Quarterly* 15 (1956): 541–560; "Indonesian Islam under the Japanese Occupation, 1942–45," *Pacific Affairs* 28 (1955): 350–362; and "Continuity and Change in Indonesian Islam," *Asian and African Studies* 1 (1965): 123–138.

7. See his introduction, with Ruth T. McVey, to *The Communist Uprisings of 1926–1927 in Indonesia: Key Documents* (Ithaca: Cornell Modern Indonesia Project, 1960); "The Communist Rebellions of 1926–1927 in Indonesia," *Pacific Historical Review* 24 (1955): 139–152; "Peasant Movements in Colonial Southeast Asia," *Asian Studies* 3 (1965): 420–434; and, with Lance Castles, "The Samin Movment," *Bijdragen tot de taal-, land- en volkenkunde* 125 (1969): 207–240.

8. See especially "Communism in Southeast Asia," *Yale Review* 45 (1956): 417–429; and "Reflections on Asian Communism," *Yale Review* 56 (1966): 1–16.

9. Benda embarked on a study of Javanese rural change which he intended to develop, in the first instance, through a major work on the Java War. His early death prevented the project's completion. The only study of local history which appeared before he died was "The Samin Movement," an investigation of a rural Javanese sect written with Lance Castles.

These essays deal with the time of intensive contact between Southeast Asian societies and Western colonialism. They concern themselves
with liminal periods in the relationship—the first three with the years in
which colonialism made its different ideological assumptions and
economic demands felt at the local level, and the last two with the
collapse of colonial power and institutions. In considering these transformations, the essays look especially at the relationship between local
leaders and populace in order to show the direction of social change
and the evolution of those discontinuities which continue to mark most
Southeast Asian societies.

Very roughly, the time of intense contact between colonial power
and the local level of Southeast Asian societies begins in the latter part
of the nineteenth century, following the opening of the Suez Canal
in 1869. This was the period of high capitalist development, when
patterns of modern Western extraction and administration were massively imposed on populations that had had no direct experience of
Western power and, in many areas, little familiarity with any effective
nonlocal control. This periodization must be used with caution, however: colonial power spread very unevenly in the region, and many parts
were affected much later or to a much lesser degree. A case in point
in this collection is the Malay state of Trengganu, which came under
colonial control only in the twentieth century and which did not
experience a major reorganization of its peasant economy. Nor were
early and later methods of extraction so distinct when we look at their
local effects. Such earlier policies as the Cultivation System in Java
and the tobacco monopoly in Luzon tended to rely on methods used
by existing indigenous elites, while later exploitation preferred methods
more directly linked with Western enterprise and capitalist production.
However, when we see what actually happened to local social and
economic relations in areas which were objects of particular colonial
interest in the earlier period—such as Cagayan in Luzon and Madiun
in Java—we observe that a very considerable distortion of local socio-
economic patterns took place and there was considerable imposition of
nonindigenous standards for economic and bureaucratic performance.

The point is not only that colonialism differed between intent and
practice but that it was experienced differently at the macro- and

microhistorical levels. If we view this phase of Southeast Asian development solely from above, whether from a colonialist or national standpoint, we are unlikely either to appreciate its full social meaning or to understand the popular response. In all but the simplest precolonial societies, the world appeared very differently to the common people and the great, and, as we shall see, this gap tended to widen under colonialism.

The essays presented here aim at showing some of the relationships between ruler and ruled, between the view from above and the view from below. They have been arranged in an order which roughly reflects their relative time in the process of colonization and not their relative chronological time. The first study, an investigation by Heather Sutherland into the establishment of colonial rule in the Malay state of Trengganu, considers the ideological, administrative, and economic system of a precolonial state and the early effects on it of the imposition of colonial rule. The second, Edilberto de Jesús' essay on the workings of the Spanish tobacco monopoly in a province of Luzon, discusses the impact on peasant society of an early form of colonial exploitation for the international market. Onghokham's investigation of colonial relations in the Madiun district of eastern Java focuses on the changing role of the supravillage elite under early and high colonial development. In John Larkin's essay on the Philippine province of Pampanga, the emergence of a new indigenous elite under colonialism is seen through its cultural celebration of itself. Finally, Dorothy Guyot's consideration of the communual violence which followed the collapse of British rule in the Burmese delta describes the results of the colonial transmogrification of social structure and of attempts to find a new social unity through revolution.

As may be apparent from this summary description, the subject matter of these essays is sufficiently close for their links to be seen by reading through the studies themselves. I shall not therefore bore the reader and do injustice to the contributors' arguments by trying to point out their relationship in a general way. Rather, I should like to make free with their contents in another manner, taking only one of the themes they present and considering its implications for the general pattern.

My theme arises from a problem in the definition of "local" which will no doubt strike the reader as he makes his way through this book. It lies in the fact that we understand the term through two measures, scale and subordination. First of all, something local should be small and relatively simple. As noted earlier, by considering comparatively uncomplicated and autonomous environments we can get an overview of a whole social pattern and can suggest themes applicable to less easily observable states.

The second criterion is subordination: something local can be seen as existing in relationship to something central, and we must therefore be able to identify a center for our locality. Moreover, if this implication is pursued, we may argue that a locality only has meaning in relationship to a center: it cannot be autonomous in any real sense but, to use Redfield's term, forms at best a "part-society."[10] From this viewpoint we study something local because it offers a glimpse of the lowest levels of society—the ordinary folk whose lives would otherwise be buried under layers of economic, cultural, and political distinction—and also because we may learn from the way in which a particular subordinate unit is integrated into the whole something concerning the parts to which it relates.

Now if we look at the first essay in this volume, Sutherland's study of Trengganu, we shall see that it fits the first measure very well but not the second, and if we look at the last essay, Guyot's investigation of the lower Burma delta, we shall find it matches the second criterion but not the first. Trengganu before the British had a modest popula-

10. Robert Redfield, *The Little Community and Peasant Society and Culture* (Chicago: University of Chicago Press, 1960), essay on "Peasant Society and Culture," esp. pp. 23–39. Redfield sees agrarian communities being drawn from primitive autonomy largely through the workings of a developing market, in which process they become increasingly subordinated to urban values. The resulting peasant society occupies a halfway position in a process of civilization which involves integration into a much wider, urban-dominated world on the basis of abstract rather than personal relationships. He thus shares some of Durkheim's evolutionary assumptions which we shall discuss below. In Redfield's definition only primitive communities, which have no meaningful market relationships and measure themselves against no outside high culture, can be really autonomous. I am applying the term here to more complex social groupings, which include bearers of a high culture, on what I think is Redfield's core criterion: whether the community is capable of functioning, ideologically and otherwise, on its own.

tion, largely confined to the lower course of adjoining rivers and the seacoast between. It had a self-sufficient and simple economy and a ruler who styled himself sultan but who was in various ways little more than a paramount chief. But to what center does Trengganu relate? True, it offered the gold and silver flower to Siam, acknowledging that kingdom's suzerainty, but what significance did that have in terms of Trengganu's political, economic, or cultural structure? Virtually none, as you will see. Trengganu did have more meaningful links to other entities—the Malay states surrounding it, the larger Muslim world—but the relationship was by our familiar standards diffuse, and it is difficult to say where the precise center of these other spheres of action lay.

The problem is that we are used to thinking in terms of the nation-state, whose power dominates all other kinds of power, so that religious, economic, and all other meanings come together at the level of the state, whose claims subsume, overshadow, or at least strongly affect them. In some of the great premodern Southeast Asian states this was also the case, above all in the areas near the capital; certainly their rulers tried to make it so, both by their pretentions to divine kingship and by their assertion of rights over all economic activity.[11]

11. The classical statement is Robert Heine-Geldern, *Conceptions of State and Kingship in Southeast Asia*, Cornell University Southeast Asia Program Data Paper no. 18 (Ithaca, 1956), a first version of which appeared in *Far Eastern Quarterly* 2, no. 4 (1942): 15-20. Most major studies of premodern Southeast Asian states have concentrated on this tradition: see among others G. Coedes, *The Indianized States of Southeast Asia* (Honolulu: East-West Center Press, 1968); B. J. O. Schrieke, "Ruler and Realm in Early Java," in *Indonesian Sociological Studies*, ed. B. J. O. Schrieke (The Hague: Van Hoeve, 1957), 2; Soemarsaid Moertono, *State and Statecraft in Old Java*, Cornell University Modern Indonesia Project Monograph Series no. 43 (Ithaca, 1968); and Akin Rabibhadana, *The Organization of Thai Society in the Early Bangkok Period*, Cornell University Southeast Asia Program Data Paper no. 74 (Ithaca, 1969). In recent years historical interest has developed in societies whose organization was less complex and whose rulers' claims were more chiefly than divine. See for example Leonard Andaya, *The Kingdom of Johore, 1641-1725* (London: Oxford University Press, 1975); and Anthony Reid and Lance Castles, *Precolonial State Systems of Southeast Asia*, Malaysian Branch of the Royal Asiatic Society Monograph no. 6 (Kuala Lumpur, 1975). A good bridge between the two types is provided by the studies in Kenneth R. Hall and John K. Whitmore, eds., *Explorations in Early Southeast Asian History: The Origins of Southeast Asian Statecraft*, University of Michigan Papers in South and Southeast

But this was rather a small part of Southeast Asia territorially, and much of those rulers' boastings were aimed at claiming through ideology what they had not the means to bring about in any other way. For Southeast Asians generally, the state was not all; often it was not very much. A man's overlord was something, and so was his clan, his religious teacher, the man to whom he was in debt; and these all represented larger worlds of activity and authority. These linkages were not necessarily overlapping, perhaps not even touching, but all were political in the sense that they were power relationships, and it was from the tugging and pulling of them that a man made up his mind where he stood, whom he served, and with whom he went to war. Above all, these were relationships understood in terms of people; even religious loyalties were determined, whatever the doctrinal implications, largely in terms of loyalty to this or that leader, and it was his opinions and alliances that moved men to action.

Now if we look at the lower Burma delta on the eve of World War II, we see something very different. There was only one center, British-run Rangoon, and nothing local had meaning except in relation to that. When that center was removed by the Japanese invasion, the local social structure shattered into fragments that were separate but not autonomous, engaged in furious struggle to discover both their own intrinsic meaning and to locate a new center outside. The contested relationships were not personal but collective: people thought in terms of ethnic and religious group identity, of economics, education, and generation. Older ties had been lost or were no longer effective motivators; they had come to have meaning only insofar as they were recognized by some larger order, and that order had had its locus at the level of the now extinguished colonial state. Only those who had been least integrated into the colonial order produced leaders who required no legitimation from outside to make themselves the center of action. These, however, were equally estranged from a local society which thought in terms of meanings derived from or sanctioned elsewhere: hence, though in a sense more liberated, they appeared and

---

Asian History no. 11 (Ann Arbor, 1976). It may be hoped that this trend into the investigation of still simpler societies will continue and that there will be cross-fertilization with anthropological investigations of Southeast Asia, which so far have generally lacked an orientation toward time.

were understood largely as outlaws.[12] Some semblance of meaning was restored only by the imposition, under new auspices, of Rangoon's authority.

We cannot study the Burma delta as an autonomous entity; it was not an entity, only an aspect of something else. Trengganu, on the other hand, could exist in and for itself—it had no indispensable external center. So, as we shall see, could the East Java locality of Madiun before the Dutch assumed control. Though Madiun was closely linked to the royal center of Mataram, it had little trouble acting as an independent state during the Java War when Mataram's hold was weakened. It was subordinate to a center but also replicated it, and thus could emerge as a center of its own. Its linkage with the other parts of the kingdom was mechanical, in Durkheim's term, as was the relationship of most units in premodern Southeast Asian states. But lower Burma's linkage was what Durkheim would have called organic; that is, it was integrally part of a larger society, and when the directing center was removed it could no more function on its own than could a creature rendered headless.[13]

12. This situation is by no means always clear-cut, however, for (leaders of) such alienated groups can adopt "outside" ideological claims to legitimize their own position. We can see something of this in the local groups that proclaimed themselves units of the Burma Independence Army. This may be simply window dressing or it may be, or turn into, the formulation of a new group consciousness. Hence the familiar problem of distinguishing bandits from revolutionaries in the early stages of the breakdown of a social order. Groups which have adopted such an ideological orientation may find allies in the belief's proponents at the center or they may find themselves in competition with an emerging alliance between local and central elites—in which case, if they do not abandon the ideology, they will tend to take a more antihierarchical interpretation and appear as a radical threat to the emergent order. This contrast need by no means reflect a simple left-right division. The literature on the Indonesian revolution is particularly relevant to this problem; see especially Benedict R. O'G. Anderson, *Java in a Time of Revolution* (Ithaca: Cornell University Press, 1972); Henri J. M. Alers, *Om een rode of groene merdeka* (n.p.: De Pelgrim, 1956); Anthony Reid, "The Birth of the Republic in Sumatra," *Indonesia* 12 (1971): 21–46; and John R. W. Smail, *Bandung in the Early Revolution,* Cornell University Modern Indonesia Project Monograph Series no. 23 (Ithaca, 1964).

13. Durkheim's argument is set out in his classical study of *The Division of Labor in Society* (De la division du travail social), first published in 1893. He considered that as society moved from primitive to complex organization, the relationship between its members became less the association of people with like

It is no accident that the first of our two criteria is met by the initial essay of this volume, and the second by the last; for what colonialism did was to destroy the autonomy of small communities, transform the position of local elites, and cause spheres of action to be reshaped or rendered irrelevant until all meaningful power relationships followed the pattern of the state. Let us now consider how these essays delineate that process in terms of the changing relationship between local and central power.

I should like to suggest that, from the viewpoint of colonialism's effect on such small-scale social arenas as villages, chieftaincies, and petty states, the most salient difference between early and late colonialism was not a change from indirect to direct rule, precapitalist to capitalist extraction, or any other qualitative alteration of economy or administration, but rather a change in the weight of outside rule, expressed primarily in a shift of power from local to central political units. This was not simply a matter of transferring power from one center to another, but of an increase in the power available to any center at all. Indigenous rulers' claims were often absolute but their

---

background and functions and more a structure of specialized and interdependent units. He saw this reflected particularly in the increasingly large-scale and complex economic relationships of the industrializing Europe of his day, and in this sense he was dealing with the same phenomenon which was affecting Southeast Asia through the medium of colonialism and involvement in the world market. Not only did Southeast Asian societies experience few of the benefits and most of the burdens of this monumental change, but they were being integrated into an organism whose "head" was both physically distant and culturally alien. Seen in this light, the nationalist enterprise was aimed at fashioning a new and more familiar directing center; but because it grew out of a fundamentally altered structure and reflected those social elements which were most completely the products of change it tended in the end to replicate the imposed values rather than to restore earlier ones or create something completely new. It is no accident that colonial boundaries, however artificial, have been preserved by the states of Southeast Asia, as by much of the rest of the ex-colonial world: this is the structure that appears natural to national leaderships, children as they are of the imposed order. Their problem has been to give coherence to this framework, for the fact that the colonies were geared to an industrialization taking place elsewhere meant that they did not really develop the new solidarity which Durkheim saw binding European societies. Instead there were great discontinuities, with highly specialized vertical linkages rising from the midst of an unspecialized and unintegrated but profoundly disturbed "native" society.

capabilities were usually feeble, and colonial forces at nearly every stage possessed superior strength and organizational ability. At first in local alliance and later on their own, they were able to impose their will on native leaderships and to back cooperative ones effectively against lower-level resistance. They thus did a great deal to shift the balance of power away from local interests, even when they destroyed indigenous claimants to centralized power. The colonial forces moved in this direction almost from the very beginning, but having neither the means nor the will to impose themselves uniformly they restricted their attentions and their effect to areas of particular economic interest—such as, in our collection, Cagayan and Madiun. It is this which makes the changes which took place in the social structures of those areas under the tobacco monopoly and the Cultivation System similar in many respects to those which occurred more massively during the high colonial period from the late nineteenth century.

Let us consider this first of all from the viewpoint of its effect on the position of the supravillage elites. In several of the small-scale studies presented here we can get a good idea of how those leaderships related to the populace before colonial rule and what structural and ideological effects the colonial presence had on them. For the *bupati* of Madiun in Java—half-chief, half-governor under the precolonial system—the Europeans appeared initially as a source of backing but not as serious competitors for power. Dutch support could prevent the resurgence of the bupatis' princely overlords and enchance their own control over their subjects; but inasmuch as the Europeans were totally alien to the society they could not—so the bupatis reckoned—hope to reach peasant producers save through the indigenous elite. This was in fact not far from the Netherlanders' own estimate of the situation at the time, and they resolved to make the bupatis the key to their rule.

The Dutch did indeed destroy the power of the Javanese princes; the position of the bupatis was regulated and their posts were made, in principle, hereditary. In the process of pacification and economic development, population increased and became more fixed; the bupatis no longer needed to worry about peasant flight or defection to a rival lord. Moreover, they had a share in the new production for the international market, and this meant additional wealth. From this viewpoint all went as they had hoped, but the trouble was that as the colonial system imposed itself it began to transform the society in its own image, and in the process the traditional sources of leadership were changed from social linchpins to anomalies.

Exactly how this came about in Madiun can be seen in the essay on the Brotodiningrat affair, but for our argument here it is useful to note some salient developments. In the first place, certain of the mechanisms by which perennially weak traditional rulers had sought to prevent defection or usurpation of power by lesser chiefs were not found necessary by the much more powerful colonial authorities once they had established their control. This particularly affected the practice of increasing the number of *kabupaten* in a realm in order to keep royal relatives employed and prevent any one territorial chief from acquiring too much power. In the course of time, as the Dutch desire for efficiency in extraction and administration grew and their need for the mediating power of the bupatis declined, the colonial authorities began to reduce their number, in spite of an initial undertaking to make their positions hereditary. The few who remained were, in theory and in ritual, much grander than their forefathers had been, but their distance from ordinary folk was less a sign of strength than of weakness, reflecting as it did a loss of the chiefly role which had been the source of much of their independent power in precolonial days.

In the colonial period, Dutch backing made it less necessary for the bupatis to cultivate sources of popular support, and colonial demands for European-style performance made it less easy for them to meet local expectations for patronage and appropriate chiefly behavior. In the end, what kept a bupati in power was not his ability to command the loyalty and service of his people but the good opinion of the colonial government, and, as colonial administration began to put down roots toward village-level society, its representatives found it less and less necessary to take the bupatis seriously. Their own reaction—beyond the cautious enthusiasm of a few for educational modernization as armament against the Dutch—was toward a cultural involution which, precisely because it rested on a consciousness that they were the custodians of a dying world, only strengthened their isolation and irrelevance.

We can see a variation on this development in the study of Trengganu, which concerns itself in part with the isolation and fossilization of indigenous leadership under colonialism. Nor was there, in the end, very much difference between the directly and indirectly ruled regions of Southeast Asia, for the dissolving pressure of colonial rule was such that autonomy became a matter of form, save in the most isolated areas. The major large-scale exception to the discrediting of the established indigenous leadership was rather in the development of the Philippines, where increasing involvement in the nineteenth-century international economy was accompanied by a decline in the strength of the metropolitan power. The long evolution and relatively simple administration of the Spanish presence in the Philippines had combined with the lack of an elaborate precolonial civilization to allow the emergence of an elite with both modern economic and traditional patronage roles.

This elite was considerably influenced by a mestizo element, which combined European and sometimes Chinese blood with that of indigenous notables. Eurasians elsewhere in colonial Southeast Asia were marginal men; though favored above the purely native population, they were kept at a distance by white communities as the latter grew in size and stability, and in turn indigenous elites viewed them both as competitors and oppressors. But in the Philippines, where the metropolitan style formed the only effective high cultural model and where there were fewer barriers to miscegenation, a mestizo population emerged which found a place not on the fringes of foreign rule but at the core of an evolving indigenous elite. Together with the powerful homogenizing influence of Catholicism, this provided an effective link between indigenous tradition and exogenous modernity which made for a relatively smooth transition between old culture and new and for relatively strong links between the emerging modern elite and the peasant mass.

As a result, in spite of the considerable pressures undergone by local leaders in such areas of intense exploitation as Cagayan, there was an overall continuity between traditional and modern Filipino leading groups which one does not find on a large scale elsewhere in Southeast Asia. We can see its effects in the emergence of a self-confident indigenous elite in Pampanga at the time of the overthrow of Spanish rule. This is not to say there were no gaps of perception and interest between elite and mass—there were, and serious ones—but indigenous leadership was not sharply divided between traditional and modern either in role or cultural orientation.

The more usual prospect for indigenous leadership was clearly perceived by the Trengganu rulers of this volume, who were able to observe the position of colleagues in the neighboring Malay states at the end of the nineteenth century. They had no desire to trade independent power for the cosseted irrelevance of British protection, but the problem was how to avoid it. They attempted to do so by imitating administrative and fiscal "reforms" which the British had imposed elsewhere in the peninsula, in the hope that this would both mollify the Europeans and provide themselves with enough centralized strength to resist outside force. In addition, they sought to renew their cultural armament, looking in particular to Islam as a source of ideological strength and a modern alternative to Western thought.

In Trengganu's case, the revitalization effort was not overwhelmed by military advance or economic inundation but by structural and ideological dilemmas. On the structural side, the ruler found it impossible to transform the sort of center-periphery relations typical of a traditional Southeast Asian state into those characteristic of a colonialized one. To create the sort of infrastructure which would permit the administrative and extractive efficiency of a modern state meant that the ruler needed many more resources than he could acquire under the old system. Once the new order was established, it would provide the center with much more economic and political control than before; but it acquired greater inputs too—money to pay salaries in place of prebends, police in place of chiefs' men to provide order, collectors of the taxes which replaced tribute, and soldiers to enforce the ruler's will on lesser leaders who had no more desire to become cogs in the sultan's bureaucratic machine than he did to become a cog in the British. For a colonial government this initial input was no great problem: the financial and technical resources came from outside. For the ruler attempting it on the basis of internally available resources, the likelihood was the collapse rather than the reinforcement of central power; and this is what happened in Trengganu.

The introduction of Western education and practices as part of the Trengganu leaders' effort to combat imperialism with its own weapons only speeded the decline, for it threw the ideological basis of the old order into question and provided younger and peripheral leaders with a "modernizing" justification to increase their role with the cooperation of the British and against the ruler. We can see the importance of this aspect if we diverge for a moment from our reference to the examples in this book to consider the Siamese government's efforts in the second part of the nineteenth century to achieve the same goals as Trengganu's in the face of Western pressure. The modernization of the Thai bureaucratic system was ultimately achieved only with significant inputs of foreign resources and the silent acceptance of British hegemony. Even so, Chulalongkorn's reorganization faced very considerable internal resistance, arousing serious revolts by chiefly elites in the outlying parts of the kingdom. And in the end, through the substitution of Western education and bureaucratic standards for indigenous ones, it undermined the legitimacy of the absolute monarchy itself, bringing its overthrow by a military-civilian bureaucratic elite whose attitudes, behavior, and goals have not been greatly different from those of postcolonial elites elsewhere in Southeast Asia. Had the Trengganu ruler succeeded in the reforms he essayed, there is every chance he or his heirs would have suffered a similar fate.

Though the Trengganu effort at renewal failed, it is worth devoting attention to it not only for the light the attempt sheds on the dilemmas which European encroachment presented to indigenous elites but also for its creative ideological aspects. Elsewhere in Southeast Asia there were analogous attempts to renew or reform indigenous culture to meet the foreign challenge, which historians have tended to overlook in favor of more large-scale, successful, or clearly modern efforts. It is important that they be considered, not only because they contribute to the richness of the region's history but because they bring us more clearly than the study of overtly Westernizing (including Marxist) movements to an understanding of how Southeast Asians conceived their world. It is altogether too easy, looking at "modern" movements, for Western or Westernized scholars to see only those things which are familiar and to dismiss the anomalies as remnants of dead tradition.

So far we have considered the impact of accumulating colonial power on the supravillage elite; let us turn now to its effect on peasant society. We have already noted that colonialism shifted the balance of power more decisively from the village level to that of indigenous chiefs and territorial officials, and thence to the colonial governments. With the

ending of intra-elite feuding and the beginning of effective economic
regulation it was less easy to flee or find an alternative patron; new
security and development measures caused population to rise rapidly
in the areas of colonial economic interest, and the possibility of finding
usable empty land declined. As indigenous elites lost their chiefly
aspect and became more dependent on and acculturated to the foreigners, they became accustomed to reckon prestige in terms of command over material possessions and European approval rather than of
command over men; many of the old patron-client relationships that
had attached village notables to the supravillage elite thus decayed.
Other such connections were forced underground by colonial authorities wary of native officials with too much popular influence, and the
result was a growing distance between the peasants and those who
ruled them.

Though precolonial Southeast Asian peasants were commonly engaged in a subsistence agriculture from which any appreciable surplus
was appropriated to support the ruling elite, traditional peasant society
was not a uniform mass, and colonial pressure therefore affected
village structures in different ways. We can see one of the possibilities
in the case of Madiun, where it appears that a relatively highly differ-
entiated peasant society was subjected under the Cultivation System to
considerable leveling. Because of that system's demand for still-scarce
labor, and the bupatis' growing dependence on Dutch rather than rural
notables' support, a tacit alliance was struck between the lower strata
of the peasantry and the supravillage elite, which broke the village
leaders' control over labor and moved peasant society toward the quasi-
egalitarian, communal practices that were to shape the stereotypical
image of traditional rural Java.

Although the power position of the peasantry generally declined
through the colonial period and, particularly as land became more
valuable than labor, their economic well-being markedly deteriorated,
this was by no means a uniform process. For one thing, in some areas
the peasantry profited, at least for a time, from the switch to export
cultivation; in the Cagayan case, for example, the problem for the
peasants was not the fact that they were forced to cultivate tobacco
but that under the monopoly system the authorities periodically
forced them not to. Similarly, in twentieth-century North Sumatra
the Dutch felt it necessary to suppress burgeoning smallholder competition with plantation production of rubber by setting elaborate

standards for quality. In many cases relative prosperity and independence were short-lived, succumbing to population pressure or large-scale
production, but they left lasting ideological, organizational, and
economic imprints in the communities where they had existed.

Aside from a general trend toward peasant impoverishment and
dependency, rural Southeast Asia was marked, particularly in the later
colonial period, by what Harry Benda liked to call a "revolution of
rising irritations."[14] The increasing gap between peasantry and officialdom was bridged for one-way traffic by a succession of rational bureaucratic regulations, demands for taxes and fees, and requirements for
labor on projects deemed of general benefit. The motivation and
usefulness of these were rarely appreciated by the villagers; indeed,
nothing could be more disastrous to workable rural arrangements
than the efforts of an improving colonial administrator, as the account
of Trengganu shows. Moreover, not only did the peasants find such
new forms of extraction as taxes less legitimate and amenable to
traditions of reasonable exaction than were the old forms of tribute,
but they frequently added to rather than replaced their existing burdens. Indigenous officials, liberated from the need for peasant support
and · aspiring to Western as well as local standards of display, clung to
the old forms of appropriation as they benefited from the new. They
had perhaps a better idea of the burden their practices imposed than
did the European administrators, but the widening cultural and intelligence gap between officialdom and countryside considerably blurred
their vision. The result was that often enough officials simply had no
idea what it was they were asking the peasants to accomplish.

Faced with unacceptable demands and skeptical of their official
superiors, peasants turned to evasion, sabotage, and rebellion, as we
see illustrated in the Javanese and Malayan examples. Rural folk were
certainly not inexperienced in this, for princely wars, hard times, or
oppressive chiefs had undoubtedly brought disaffection often enough
before colonial days. Now, however, the choices were fewer: flight
was ceasing to be a viable alternative, while the effective centralization
of power meant that officials looked only upward for support, elimi-
nating villagers' chances of finding a champion among rivalrous members of the elite. The best that rural folk could do was look to the

14. "Peasant Movements in Southeast Asia," p. 433 in *Asian Studies;* p. 234
in *Continuity and Change in Southeast Asia.*

protection of some traditional leader who was at odds with the Europeans, as with the bupati Brotodiningrat in Madiun. These faint hopes being invariably dashed, peasants eventually abandoned them, and in the last colonial decades we find rural revolts which, though often ideologically highly traditional, did not appeal to leadership from the established supravillage elite.

If it had earlier been rare that a village leader could force himself by strength of arms and following into the official hierarchy, now it became impossible. Nor would rival chiefs, trying to add more than genealogy to their claims on an incumbent's office, seek to raise a following with claims of divine inspiration and calls to peasant ideas of just rule. The old appeals which excited rural support were forgotten: the vocabulary of supravillage leadership was addressed to itself and to the Europeans. As a result, the language and techniques of protest lost all connection with the official elite and instead became restricted to other sources of leadership, in the first instance religious. Here colonial secularism and fears of religious mobilization against Western rule combined with popular alienation from traditional officialdom to create or deepen divisions between native religious and secular leaders. Religious renewal, which hitherto might be embraced by persons aspiring to princely power or asserting their rights against a suzerain, became almost exclusively a matter of opposition to the customary ruling class, and messianic appeals now were uttered not, as might happen, by leaders seeking to revitalize a decadent system but only by the totally alienated. As elite images of the ideal future turned more toward Westernism and modernity, the ideals of disaffected villagers often moved in the opposite direction, toward the utter rejection of nonvillage works and ways.[15]

15. This was an emphasis of Benda and Castles' study on "The Samin Movement." It was also developed in one of the earliest major studies approaching Southeast Asian social change through local history, Sartono Kartodirdjo's *The Peasants' Revolt of Banten in 1888,* Verhandelingen van het Koninklijk Instituut voor Taal-, Land- en Volkenkunde, no. 50 (The Hague, 1966). Peasant uprisings—or movements whose rebellious tendencies were feared—are a principal recorded source of knowledge about rural perceptions of the world. A few notable prewar studies resulted from official investigations of the social sources of revolt: see especially B. Schrieke, "The Causes and Effects of Communism on the Westcoast of Sumatra," in his *Indonesian Sociological Studies* (The Hague and Bandung: Van Hoeve, 1956), vol. 1; and the "Banten Report" in Benda and

All this contributed to the increasing opacity of society's lower depths, in spite of the new means for investigation and control which the colonial apparatus possessed. Modern administrators, foreign or otherwise, were even less able to understand local society in its own terms than were members of the coopted traditional elites. Almost invariably they assumed that peasant society was basically immobile; when a self-generated movement occurred it was viewed as unnatural and dangerous. Inasmuch as peasant movements took unforeseen directions, expressed what appeared to be wholly unrealizable demands, and had no chance against the force arrayed against them, they were seen as "primitive," "desperate," or "fanatical," with little reference to their material occasion and none to the world of thought which produced them.

McVey, eds., *The Communist Uprisings of 1926-1927 in Indonesia: Key Documents.* The movements noted in Sartono Kartodirdjo's *Protest Movements in Rural Java* (Singapore: Oxford University Press, 1973) indicate the great range of such manifestations which still await study.

Historians and anthropologists have given some attention to similar phenomena in the Philippines; among the historical studies are David Sturtevant, *Popular Uprisings in the Philippines, 1840-1940* (Ithaca: Cornell University Press, 1976); David Sweet, "The Proto-political Peasant Movement in the Spanish Philippines: The Cofradía de San Jose and the Tayabas Rebellion of 1841," *Asian Studies* 8 (1970): 94-119; Milagras Guerrero, "The Colorum Uprising, 1924-1931," *Asian Studies* 5 (1967); 76-78; Richard Arens, "The Early Pulahan Movement in Samar and Leyte," *Journal of History* 7 (1959): 303-371. Movements in mainland Southeast Asia remain largely undescribed, but see E. Michael Mendelson, "The King of the Weaving Mountain," *Royal Central Asian Journal* 48 (1961): 229-237; and idem, "A Messianic Buddhist Association in Upper Burma," *Bulletin of the School of Oriental and African Studies* 24 (1961): 560-580; John Murdoch, "The 1901-1902 'Holy Man's' Rebellion," *Journal of the Siam Society* 62, no. 1 (1974): 47-66; Tej Bunnag, "Khabot phu mi bun phak isan," *Sangkhomsat parithat* 5, no. 1 (1967): 78-86; idem, "Khabot ngiao muang phrae," *Sangkhomsat parithat* 6, no. 2 (1968): 67-80; Charles F. Keyes, "Millennialism, Theravāda Buddhism, and Thai Society," *Journal of Asian Studies* 36 (1977): 283-302; Anthony R. Walker, "Messianic Movements among the Lahu of the Yunnan-Indochina Borderlands," *Southeast Asia* 3, no. 2 (1974): 699-709; and Yoneo Ishii, "A Note on Buddhistic Millenarian Revolts in Northeastern Siam," *Journal of Southeast Asian Studies* 6 (1975): 121-126.

Had the Spanish abandoned the Philippines in the heyday of the tobacco monopoly or the Dutch left Java during the Cultivation System, something recognizably like the precolonial orders might have reemerged for, no matter how much local social structures had been buffeted or local leaders suborned, they had not been destroyed and nothing had emerged to take their place. By the time Spanish rule did collapse at the end of the nineteenth century, the situation was quite different, however: a new elite had arisen in areas of intense colonial development which, though it preserved many of the older claims to leadership, functioned and saw its role in a quite different way. In Madiun, soon after the Brotodiningrat affair, a new association began claiming popular loyalties—the Sarekat Islam, first of the modern Indonesian mass organizations and vanguard of an emerging nationalist political elite.

To appreciate the significance of these new sources of leadership, we must turn back to consider again the difference between the high period of colonial development and that preceding. We have mentioned that from the viewpoint of effect on local society, this was a matter of mass rather than quality. Nonetheless, the greatly increased weight of the colonial presence had certain consequences which themselves produced a qualitative change. The rapid expansion of administrative and economic infrastructure required far more trained manpower than could be supplied by European sources. On the economic side this gap tended to be filled by immigrant Asians, creating the three-tier society typical of late colonial Southeast Asia, but in administration recourse was generally had to indigenous talent. This meant providing a degree of Western-style education not simply for the scions of the traditional elite, who were increasingly expected to function as modern bureaucrats, but to people from wealthier village families and the fringes of the old ruling class, who might fill clerkly positions in the expanding technical services.

Looking at the ultimate result of this in terms of creating nationalist leaderships which eventually seized power, we might say that the colonialists succeeded in fulfilling the Trengganu ruler's ambition of defeating imperialism with its own weapon. It did not, however, succeed wholly in overcoming the contradictions which this effort experienced. In particular, the problem of ideological identification remained, but it was now transformed into the difficulty of establishing the self-image of a nationalist elite. Western education and ideas had undermined indigenous ones, and in any event leaders who did not have traditional claims to rule were not interested in restoring the old ideological system. Yet some means of separating one's self from the Western model was essential if the bond of psychological domination was to be broken. The struggle to define a national alternative characterized independence movements both before and after coming to power, and we can see some of the difficulties it presented both in terms of self-identification and the rallying of mass support in the essays on Pampanga and the Burmese delta.

The problem of self-identification gave a certain ideological hollowness to the efforts of the nationalists, which became critical directly formal independence was won. Nonetheless, they did appear united on certain decisive questions, which reflected their position in the emerging political and economic structure of Southeast Asia. For one thing, they were ideologically committed to modernity as a goal and Western-style (including Marxist) education and economic development as the means. Second, they were oriented about the idea of a national state, which was a derivative of the colonial state and not of previous political entities. Not only did the new national leaders in the capital determine that their interests lay in maintaining the former colonial unit, but leading groups at lesser levels seem to have sufficiently shared the belief that this was their natural political arena and goal as to make it possible for the Southeast Asian nation-states to survive in spite of divergent internal cultural and economic interests and the precipitous loss of central power which followed the end of colonial rule.

For the most part the new ruling elites were political and administrative in origin and orientation, agricultural or trading connections being downplayed in the desire to identify with traditional bureaucratic prestige and the new channel for upward mobility. There were exceptions, however: in particular, leaders emerging from populations which did not have a strong aristocratic-bureaucratic tradition or which had maintained relative economic independence and prosperity in the colonial period. On a national scale, the major exception is the Philippines, for reasons we have already discussed. We can see the emergence of one segment of this new elite in the study of the literary renaissance in Pampanga. Here local landowners were of sufficient substance and degree of involvement in a market economy to make it possible for them to support and share interests with an emerging independent bourgeoisie in market towns. These new leading groups developed a self-consciousness and confidence that led, among other things, to their sponsorship of a new art form.

It is interesting to look at the Capampangan zarzuela as an ideological expression, for it provides a useful comment on the problem of national self-identification introduced above. Neither its ideological connection nor its style was indigenous: the zarzuela had been a favorite art form of Spanish radicals of the nineteenth century, who had seen in its popular and national character an expression of the revolutionary liberalism which they espoused. The Pampangans took this over, translated into their own language and setting. As well as being fashionable in the metropolis, it suited their basic ideological leanings in its criticism of the established order and its stress on the individual liberty dear to an emergent independent bourgeoise. In a parallel development some decades later, nationalists in other Southeast Asian colonies were to find in socialist ideas a way of establishing an identity that was modern and yet distinct from the colonialists', and which was moreover compatible with their statist cultural heritage and bureaucratic interests.

Little attention has been paid so far to the emergence of new artistic and religious forms in colonial Southeast Asia, and yet these bring us closest to the perceptions of people undergoing major ideological change. They are worth looking at not simply to find evidence of emerging nationalist ideology but to see the ways in which the different groups became conscious of themselves and the paths which in some cases were entered but later abandoned. Not only successes are instructive, and not only developments that clearly feed into a mainstream are significant. In the Pampangan case, the zarzuela flourished as a local celebration of the revolution; very soon, however, it was eclipsed by the American cultural model and the movies, and from the expression of a self-confident local leadership it became the consolation of a poverty-stricken peasantry. Elsewhere in Southeast Asia we find analogous outpourings of emergent social groups, particularly before modern means of mass entertainment reached the local level. One can think, for example, of the *komedi stambul* theater of the Eurasian bourgeois culture which flourished in Indonesia early in this century; or the later, more proletarian Javanese forms such as *ketoprak* and *ludruk,* among the few which have been investigated for their social significance.[16] Why some groups should give rise to new artistic and religious forms and why some older arts should survive more or less successfully against modern mass entertainment are unstudied questions of considerable importance for comprehending Southeast Asian social change.

At the opposite pole from the early flowering of the modern Pampangan elite was the situation of leadership in the Burmese delta with the collapse of British rule. In a way the ideal of colonial domination had been reached there, for so thorough had been the transformation of the local economy and the division of the population into functionally and culturally competing parts that nothing united the society save the British presence itself. Once that linchpin was removed the whole structure collapsed, leaving groups desperately searching for leadership and for a sense of self that would both ward off the claims of others and provide a new basis for the whole. Not only was it impossible to overcome suspicions between cultural groups, but within any one group neither traditional nor revolutionary appeals could arouse massive support. The old ideologies and social ties had been lost or transmogrified; the creation of a new identity via revolution was the work of leaders far away in Rangoon or marginal men who established themselves as leaders of bands and whose activities often appeared less revolutionary than predatory. The ultimate solution—at least in the time compass considered here—was the imposition of order from the outside, by the Rangoon-based leaders and the Japanese. The question which remained was whether the peace that resulted provided space

16. The most ambitious study along this line, James Peacock's *The Rites of Modernization: Symbolic and Social Aspects of Indonesian Proletarian Drama* (Chicago and London: University of Chicago Press, 1968), is seriously flawed by its teleological assumptions concerning modernization and its insistence on Western sociological categories to the exclusion of indigenous cultural ones. In contrast an important study, Renaldo C. Illeto, "Pasión and the Interpretation of Change in Tagalog Society" (Ph.D. diss., Cornell University, 1975), illuminates a peasant mythology of protest brilliantly from its ideological interior. Ileto's work indicates an area of research as yet insufficiently explored for Southeast Asia: that of using traditional myths and art forms to reveal the social relations of their times. See also Alfonso P. Santos, ed., *Rizal Miracle Tales* (Manila: National Book Store, 1973); and Marcelino Foronda, *Cults Honoring Rizal* (Manila: n.p., 1961).

for a new order to emerge locally, in the national image now provided by the center, or whether the local social cracks were simply papered over by the new dispensation, to consolidate and harden underneath.

The Lower Burma experience was extreme but not unique: we find something like it occurring sporadically elsewhere in the local social revolutions that followed the collapse of European or Japanese rule. These, too, are phenomena that by and large have not been studied, partly for presumed want of material but mostly because they have been viewed as somewhat anomalous incidents in a larger national revolution. They do, however, afford us rare glimpses into the dynamics and inner tensions of rural and small-town society. Moreover, the question remains whether the postcolonial national hegemonies have actually rooted themselves deeply in society or whether they have simply—as proved to be the case in the Burmese delta—temporarily papered over yawning social gaps.

The Burmese experience becomes still more pertinent when we consider the direction which postcolonial regimes in the non-Communist states have taken to maintain their power. They possessed in the first instance far less might than the colonial regimes had wielded, for the collapse of Western colonialism in World War II had brought a radical deflation of central power—psychologically, adminstratively, and economically. From the viewpoint of the nationalists, the Japanese played a vital role in providing a source of central energy while giving an opportunity for the new elite to gain a greater hold. Even so, those nationalist forces that came to power faced a decline in disposable strength, resulting partly from the effects of war and partly from the withdrawal of outside backing. Moreover, while they dreamed of replacing the colonial administrators in function and living standard, they also believed their rule should provide more benefits for the population than the colonial regimes had thought necessary or possible. Here the ideas of socialism and radical democracy, which had been so useful in offering nationalists a way around the problem of identifying with modernity while rejecting the metropolis, produced their own dilemma, for they committed leaders psychologically and politically to a course which they could not pursue.

The problem of defining postcolonial goals was compounded by the emergence of effective lower-level claimants for a share in power. The nationalists had appealed for popular support against colonial rulers in their bids for power, and this meant concessions to popular opinion and local men of influence. It required, on the one hand, appeals to inherited ideas and interests and on the other calls for the overturn of the established order. The common method of dealing with these claims initially was to adopt some sort of parliamentary democracy. This was what Western-educated leaders felt was legitimate, it helped restore foreign confidence and support, and it provided an arena in which the purposes of national leadership could be defined and local demands mediated. Sooner or later, however, it appeared that the system did not serve to mobilize support for the center or to strengthen its unity. To the contrary, it made local interests more self-conscious and demanding, provided an alternative source of support for leaders who did not see their ambitions or ideals being fulfilled in the capital, and encouraged ambivalence among decision-makers reluctant to place all their political eggs in one basket.

The response to this was not the devolution of authority, abandoning responsibility to reflect the dispersal of power, but rather the withdrawal of all political resources to the top. Statist tradition, bureaucratic interests, the determination of ruling groups to preserve their position, the pressure of powerful outside economies, states, and ideas all encouraged the inclination to reduce strain on the system by shutting out lesser claimants to power. The degree but not the direction has varied, from the reduction to marginalities of the permitted area of political discourse through the symbolic concentration of power and popular will in a charismatic leader, to a bare reliance on command from above.

In the process of restricting access to power, the military has tended to assume ever greater importance. Aside from structural reasons for the army's prominence in postcolonial states, we should note that from the viewpoint of ruling elites it provides a cheap alternative to sharing power and resources with those below.[17] It is expensive to

17. As Samuel Huntington has pointed out, the reason why armies come to power in "new" states has less to do with their peculiar qualifications than with the absence of any countervailing institutions; *Political Order In Changing Society* (New Haven and London: Yale University Press, 1968), pp. 192–195. The local role and internal dynamics of the Southeast Asian military is a subject in need of further investigation, especially for those countries whose armies emerged from revolution. A seminal study is John Smail, "The Military Politics of North

support a military machine in the style to which it aspires—though outside aid for this has usually been easy to come by in Southeast Asia, while business and marriage alliances return the benefits to civilians—but it is less costly and risky than a devolution of power, with all its possible consequences for political disintegration or social revolution in states whose linkage between elite and mass is highly uncertain.

Reliance on armed force and bureaucratic control produces a mode of rule curiously similar to that of the colonial state. Thus Suharto's Indonesia, with its emphasis on administration, expertise, and order and its vision of the rural populace as a "floating mass" unsullied by political mobilization, is spiritual kin to the prewar Indies *Beamtenstaat*.[18] Moves in this direction involve a narrowing of rulers' perceptions as well as citizens' possibilities for dissent, so that in the end only what happens in the center counts. The protest of students in the capital can thus occasion the greatest consternation, for students, though clearly representing a feeble group, are visible and connected with the elite; at the same time, a high level of disaffection and even disorder may be tolerated in the countryside in spite of generalized concern at the danger of social unrest.

Regimes of this sort are in large part conceived as holding operations; insofar as their leaders have envisioned the future they have looked to filling the gap between elite and mass through education and economic growth, arguing that as the populace becomes ready for constructive participation it will be allowed a greater voice in the running of its affairs. Again, the argument is similar to that of colonial reform, and we may ask whether it does not present some of the same prob-

---

Sumatra, December 1956–October 1957," *Indonesia,* no. 6 (1968), pp. 128–187; and see David Charles Anderson, "The Military Aspects of the Madiun Affair," *Indonesia,* no. 21 (1976), pp. 1–63. Dorothy Guyot's "The Burma Independence Army: A Political Movement in Military Garb," in Josef Silverstein, ed., *Southeast Asia in World Warr II: Four Essays,* Yale University Southeast Asia Studies Monograph Series no. 7 (New Haven, 1966), deals with the BIA as a national entity but provides important insights into its local recruitment and social role. See also Smail, *Bandung in the Early Revolution;* and Anderson, *Java in a Time of Revolution.*

18. The *Beamtenstaat* character of the Netherlands Indies is discussed in Benda, "The Pattern of Administrative Reforms in the Closing Years of Dutch Rule in Indonesia."

lems. In principle, of course, the establishment of an effective circulation of values and personnel should be easier under indigenous than under foreign rule, but this may be true only for members of the politically dominant ethnic group. Moreover, although both countryside and city experience Westernizing cultural change through modernization, the pace of change is far swifter in the urban centers, so that the cultural gap which opened in the colonial era between urban elite and rural mass persists and may grow wider. Finally, if a society does not maintain a high rate of economic and institutional growth there is a good chance that the boundaries of the ruling class may become fixed, through the elite's reservation of positions and resources to itself.

This freezing of membership in the ruling elite is the more likely when, as has been common in recent Southeast Asian history, the principal source of pressure on and backing for national leaderships has come not from below but from outside, so that, like the coopted elites of colonial days, they have little immediate reason to yield power and benefits downward. In such cases, upwardly mobile people denied a share in privilege are likely to look, when feasible, to local and lower-class backing rather than to continue waiting for favor from above. The problem is compounded by the fact that most major Southeast Asian cultures identify elite membership with government service, so that it is difficult for a ruling group to suggest alternative routes upward or to otherwise deflect from itself blame for noninclusion. Indeed, the arguments of social justice by which the postcolonial leaderships justified their own struggle toward rule may now be used against them, and realization of this strengthens their opponents and saps their own belief in themselves.

Inevitably, given Southeast Asia's geographic position, the ideological past of most of its nationalist movements, and its recent history, the search for a solution on the part of both ruling elites and their challengers has come to center on the applicability of the Communist experience. In itself, Marxist-Leninist ideology appears to provide a recipe for an elite seeking to balance mobilization and control in the centralization of power, for this has been one of the Communists' crucial concerns; and we accordingly find non-Communist rulers of various stripe adopting aspects of Marxist-Leninist practice which they believe may rejuvenate their regimes. Indeed, with its greater central control over material and human resources, its bureaucratism, its assumption that state leadership has a monopoly on truth and a responsibility for the prosperity and morals of the realm, the Communist system is in important ways more "natural" to the precolonial traditions of most major Southeast Asia polities than the parliamentary systems earlier adopted. However, one reason for the greater discipline and vitality of Communist movements in the region is that they have not attracted as wide a social range of participants and their cadres are less likely to have ascriptive as well as organizational sources of support; moreover, effective outside patronage has thus far been much less available to them than to non-Communist aspirants to rule. Their accession to power is therefore more improbable, but their energy once in command seems more certain. Conversely, attempts by established national leaders to endow their regimes with "Leninist" attributes have merely added new ritual to their rule.

Insofar as Marxist-Leninist regimes may emerge from national liberation struggles or social revolutions, they are likely to provide much greater scope for popular participation and upward mobility than whatever went before. In the case of Vietnam, the paramount Communist example in the region, the long revolutionary war provided a common focus for both elite and mass, a pressing reason for leaders to stress positive mobilization of popular sympathies as well as control, and a continuing—indeed, unparalleled—destruction of any viable alternative centers of loyalty. However, because the Communist regimes of the area did arise through armed struggles and have not long been in power, there is a tendency for observers to assume that the correlation is automatic, that there is something in Marxism-Leninism which guarantees a coincidence between elite will and mass desire, a fusing of the interests of center and periphery. This is not necessarily so. Indeed, the overcoming of tension between peasant perceptions and party aims, the restructuring of local situations into centrally conceived scenarios, has been a major concern of Chinese and Vietnamese Communists in the consolidation of their regimes. Although there is an obvious problem of access and the bias of available literature, it is a subject that deserves greater attention from scholars of Southeast Asia.[19]

19. The Democratic (now Socialist) Republic of Vietnam has sponsored the collection of histories of the course of the revolution, agrarian reform, and

Perhaps the final irony lies in the future, for if Communist movements in Southeast Asia have thus far shown the greatest ability to engage the common people, Communist regimes in general enhance the concentration of power at the top–through their organization for mass mobilization and control, their emphasis on state-run industrialism, and the hierarchy-reinforcing practices of democratic centralism. Thus in spite of efforts at revolutionary revitalization, they show a fatal tropism toward bureaucratic rule. In the end, the movement which has done most to arouse popular rejection of domination from above also provides the most powerful instrument for its insurance. The overwhelming central power claimed by traditional rulers, which was made materially achievable through colonialism, may thus be realized by the functionaries of "people's" regimes, which with different slogans but for familiar ends restrict the voice of their subjects to proclaiming the glories of the realm and the just and prosperous dispensation of its rulers.

History, however, is not constructed of inevitabilities; nor is there a point at which it stops. The possibilities of the future are far richer and more terrible than those that can be imagined by contemplating one thread in the tapestry of Southeast Asia's past. To appreciate this, turn to the essays below, in which the complex weaving of motives, forces, and cultures will yield more subtle and vivid panoramas of change.

---

resistance to U.S. bombings; some of these have been made available in English, notably in the series *Vietnamese Studies*. Western works on Southeast Asian Communist movements and leftist insurrections have concentrated on the national and international level. An important early exception was Schrieke's study, mentioned in footnote 15. Lucian Pye's *Guerrilla Communism in Malaya* (Princeton: Princeton University Press, 1956) made a start toward looking at such movements "from the bottom up" by considering the motivation of their participants. More recent studies have moved further toward placing them in their social context, relating them to rural economic change and relations between political center and social periphery; see especially Jeffrey Race, *War Comes to Long An* (Cambridge: Harvard University Press, 1972); Robert Sansom, *The Economics of Insurgency in the Mekong Delta of Vietnam* (Cambridge and London: M.I.T. Press, 1970); and Benedict Kerkvliet, "Peasant Rebellion in the Philippines: Origins and Growth of the HMB" (Ph.D. diss., University of Wisconsin, 1972).

The Taming of the Trengganu Elite

HEATHER SUTHERLAND

Of government there was practically none. The Sultan, having alienated most of his powers and prerogatives to his relatives, passed his life in religious seclusion. The revenues were devoured by his relatives. . . . There were no written laws, no courts and no police. All manner of crime was rampant, the peasantry was mercilessly downtrodden, but the land was full of holy men and the cries of the miserable were drowned in the noise of ostentatious prayer. In fine, Trengganu presented in the beginning of the year 1909 the type of untrammeled Malay rule which

This essay is based on material held by the Arkib Negara, Malaysia; the Public Record Office, London; Rhodes House Library, Oxford; and the Perpustakaan Universiti Malaya. I am grateful for permission to use these institutions, to their staffs for their helpfulness, and also to the Universiti Malaya for welcome financial assistance. Among the many people who contributed to my understanding of Trengganu society and history and facilitated my research were: Encik Abdullah Ngah, Dr. Khoo Kay Kim, Datuk Tan Sri Haji Mubin Sheppard, and Tan Sri Mohamed Suffian b. Hashim in Kuala Lumpur; my students in the Jabatan Sejarah Universiti Malaya from 1972 to 1974; Cikgu Mamat Adam b. Taib, Encik Baharuddin Ismail, Engku Embong b. Abdul Kadir and his brother Engku Chik, Datuk Chik Embong, Encik Mohammed b. Endut, Encik Mohammed Anuar b. Omar, and Haji Omar b. Haji Arshad; Haji Taib b. Haji Yusuf, the Mufti, Legal Adviser, and Chief Kathi in Trengganu; and particularly Tungku Jaya Pekerma Wira, Datuk Purba di-Raja, and Tuan Haji Mohd. Salleh b. Haji Awang, who shared their extensive knowledge of Trengganu history with me. Professor W. R. Roff and Dr. Barbara Andaya made useful comments on an earlier draft of this essay, and Christopher S. Gray, in addition to his detailed examination of several drafts, graciously spent hours discussing Malay history, from which conversations many ideas emerged. In late 1977, Leslie Robert submitted a doctoral dissertation on "Malay Ruling Class and British Empire: The Case of Trengganu, 1881–1941" to the History Department, Monash University, Melbourne; unfortunately I have been unable to consult this thesis.

had fortunately disappeared from every other state in the peninsula.[1]

Thus a British view of Trengganu on the eve of its subjection to the blessings of imperial rule. It expressed the contempt of a world power for a sultanate that seemed backward compared even to its Malay neighbors; yet it was not just disdain that is voiced here but fundamental misunderstanding. The British observer, like most modern Westerners, thought of a state as a clearly bounded territorial unit, focused on a single center, managed by an extensive and specialized administration, and defined internationally by legal agreements and treaties; and by these standards Trengganu was woefully lacking. Its internal government was easily characterized as grossly inadequate, its foreign policy myopic to a degree. But formal institutions and avowedly political activity were not as all-important to Trengganu as to a Western state. Its world was defined by personal, religious, and cultural ties as well, and in many ways these were more important. It played a power game, but to rules the British did not recognize.

In reality, Trengganu was a stable and relatively prosperous state, supporting over a hundred thousand Malays by the turn of the century. The industry and productivity of its artisans, traders, farmers, and fishermen formed the basis for a lively export trade, but such activity did not depend on efficient governance.[2] As with other traditional

1. W. A. Graham, section on Trengganu, in *Encyclopaedia Britannica,* 11th ed., s.v. "Malay States."

2. J. de Vere Allen, "The Ancien Regime in Trengganu, 1909–1919," *Journal of the Malayan Branch of the Royal Asiatic Society* (hereafter cited as *JMBRAS*) 41, no. 1 (July 1968): 23–53, 25, notes population estimates for 1905 of 115,000 and 1912 of 154,000. In 1895 Hugh Clifford described the Trengganu Malays of the time as "quite the most ingenious, and among the most industrious Malays on the Peninsula" and viewed their economic activities with some admiration ("Report of Mr. Clifford, Acting British Resident of Pahang, on the Expedition Recently Led into Trengganu and Kelantan on the East Coast of the Malay Peninsula," *JMBRAS* 24, no. 11 [May 1961]: 88–98.) In "Reminiscences of the Cambridge University Expedition to the North Eastern Malay States, 1899–1900: Personal accounts of the late W. W. Skeat and Dr. F. F. Laidlaw," *JMBRAS* 26, no. 4 (December 1953): 122, the town of Kuala Trengganu is described as a "hive of industry." The annual reports of the British agents give useful information on trade, industry, and agriculture; see e.g., *The Annual Report of the British Agent, Trengganu* for 1910, 1911, 1912 (by W. D. Scott) and 1913 (by E. A. Dickson).

Malay states, Trengganu's administration was not constructed of bureaucratic hierarchies. Rather, the state was a collection of revenue-producing regions, which its ruler allocated to individual members of the elite, who were linked to each other by personal ties and derived their status from royal recognition. There was no effective distinction between official and personal revenue and little managerial effort by government. Authority was not specific, functional, and institutionalized, but personal and generalized. There were no recognizable officials at the village level, no functionaries who drew salaries and sent in taxes to an impersonal treasury. Instead, there were the personal agents or followers of individual chiefs, who delivered fluctuating and often apparently arbitrary dues to their patrons.

To European eyes such a system might seem disorganized and amorphous, but this is because the boundaries between state and society were not as clear as in the modern West. Society was structured and integrated through series of vertical relationships, which could be specific or general but were always personal. Religious prestige, economic rights, and political power might be concentrated in one individual whose influence encompassed all the inhabitants of a given area, but it was also possible—particularly in areas close to the capital, where there was more competition among members of the elite—that peasant families or individuals participated in several networks. They might be linked simultaneously to various royal appanage holders, to Arab religious leaders, to Chinese moneylenders, and to the sultan. In such a polycentric system, specific personal ties connected clients with patrons in diverse but defined arenas. The political link was only one of several, and the scope of political demands was limited not only by custom and the availability of power and administrative resources but also by the space demanded by other patrons. This was not the simplistic "feudal" pyramid of king, nobles, and peasants so often asserted by colonial observers as the basis of traditional Southeast Asian states like Trengganu; the formal pattern of social stratification

---

These reports, to which frequent reference will be made, were published by the Singapore Government Printing Office until 1911, then by the FMS Government Printing Office, Kuala Lumpur, and from 1923 again in Singapore: 1923 to 1935 by the Government Printing Office, 1936 to 1937 by Lithographs Ltd., and from 1938 by G. H. Keat & Co.

might appear to follow this model, but the distribution of power was much more complex.[3]

Formal relationships are equally deceptive as a guide to Trengganu's position in the world. Every three years since the late eighteenth century it had sent to the court of Siam its token of fealty, the Gold and Silver Flower, *Bunga Mas dan Perak.* This appeared to European eyes to be a clear acknowledgment of Thai suzerainty, so that when the British assumed control of Trengganu they did so by forcing a treaty of cession from Siam. But sending the tributary token was much vaguer than anything comprehended by European legal categories; it might mean anything from friendship to total subordination, and one of the central characteristics of Southeast Asian state relationships was the constant reinterpretation of such ties, reflecting the waxing and waning of relative power. Indeed, the very difference beween intrastate and interstate was far from distinct in premodern Southeast Asia. In the more highly organized states local powerholders might have the aspect of governors, but this was usually no more than an aspect which faded into insignificance with distance from the capital; otherwise the autonomy of local chiefs was nearly complete, and whether the effective boundaries of a major state encompassed a certain area depended on ties of blood and marriage, calculations of alliance, and force of arms—the same things that determined relations between sovereign powers.

That a Malay Muslim sultanate could be linked to a Thai Buddhist kingdom was not anomalous under a system in which effective integration meant only the reliable supplying of tribute and troops. It was not until late in the nineteenth century, when Siam itself began to adopt Western concepts of administration and the nation-state, that the relationship became problematical for Malay rulers on grounds other than those of maintaining room for maneuver against all claimants. Even this Trengganu was spared, for as the most distant of all

---

3. The analogy between the systems of the Southeast Asian states and of "feudal" Europe was common, and there were indeed some political parallels—in the personal and religiously buttressed relationships between local and central rulers, in the appanage system—but the absence of a manorial economy and a comparable legal tradition in Southeast Asia ensured that the parallel obscured as much as it clarified.

Siam's Malay tributaries, it never felt Thai domination as more than an intermittent threat.[4]

Yet we will be very mistaken if we conclude on this basis that Trengganu existed in isolation. It was very much part of the Malayo-Muslim world, a community which stretched from the Malayan peninsula across the Indonesian archipelago and which was defined by religion and culture as much as by political ties.[5] It had no single capital, no fixed boundaries, and no encompassing administrative network, but it was much more than simply an arena for interstate action. It did not satisfy the Western definition of a state, yet it had greater political meaning than many of the states within it. The European powers ignored it, and with the nineteenth-century division of island and peninsular Southeast Asia between British, Dutch, and later Siamese they carved it into three arbitrary and by local understanding meaningless segments.

When our story opens, Trengganu was beginning to feel the consequences of this. It was still completely free from any significant outside domination, preserving the "untrammeled Malay rule" which was its rulers' pride and the Englishman's despair. Indeed, Trengganu's geographic isolation and its rulers' defense of independence and the old ways made it the last guardian of Malay greatness, the remaining bastion of a political and cultural tradition which stretched back through the historical centers of Riau/Johor, Aceh, and Malacca to ancient Srivijaya.[6]

The Trengganu sultans were connected by blood and marriage to other leading dynasties of the Malayo-Muslim world, notably those of Riau, Singapore, and Johor. These ties were not severed by the division of this community into Netherlands and British spheres of

4. L. A. Mills, "British Malaya 1824–67," *JMBRAS* 33, no. 3 (1960): 195–201, discusses Trengganu's relationship with Siam.

5. William R. Roff, *The Origins of Malay Nationalism* (New Haven: Yale University Press, 1967), and William R. Roff, ed., *Kelantan: Religion, Society and Politics in a Malay State* (Kuala Lumpur: Oxford University Press, 1974), illuminate aspects of Malayo-Muslim interaction and identity.

6. On changes in the Malay world, see Leonard Y. Andaya, *The Kingdom of Johor, 1641–1728* (Kuala Lumpur: Oxford University Press, 1975); Mills, "British Malaya," pp. 9–424. On Trengganu before the nineteenth century, see Barbara W. Andaya, "An Examination of the Sources Concerning the Reign of Sultan Mansur Shah of Trengganu, 1741–1795," *JMBRAS* 49, no. 2 (1976): 80–106.

influence via the Anglo-Dutch treaty of 1824. Instead, they continued to be reinforced through frequent and protracted visits by members of Trengganu's royal family, so that at the turn of the century some chiefs were described by the British as "resident in Singapore and Trengganu," and the heir apparent and many other notables maintained their own Singapore establishments as well as making regular trips to Riau.[7] Trengganu was thus in touch with the vigorous religious and political revival which was both stimulated and aborted by European intervention in the Malay communities of Singapore and the Riau capital of Daik.

Trengganu's great days came with the reign of Baginda Omar, sultan from 1839 to 1876. The state had not seen a ruler of such stamp since Sultan Mansur had made himself the focus of Malay resistance to Buginese invasion a century before.[8] Responding vigorously to new ideas circulating in the Malayo-Muslim and wider Islamic world, Baginda Omar encouraged religious activity and reform, appointing Trengganu's first *mufti* (religious jurisconsult) and bringing Islamic teachers from Riau.[9] Moreover, he was able to achieve a degree of political centralization remarkable for a Malay state. Through his personal force and astuteness he appears to have succeeded in over-riding the territorial headmen and drawing all revenues directly into his own hands. Since revenue was power, and the proof and purpose

7. Many relatives of the deposed Sultan Ali of Singapore settled in Trengganu permanently or regularly spent part of the year there. When Sultan Zainal Abidin visited Singapore he stayed with his retinue (which could exceed 150 people) in the family's house at Sultan's Gate, Kampung Glam. Tg. Abdullah b. Sultan Ali "of Trengganu and Singapore" married one of Zainal Abidin's daughters, while another daughter married Tg. Kazakir b. Tg. Abu Bakar, another relative of Sultan Ali, whose father lived in Trengganu and drew revenues from the Duyung River. The Singapore line also intermarried with Riau. Trengganu sultans married several times with Daik, while both the heir apparent's consecutive wives were from that family. After his deposition in 1911, ex-Sultan Abdul Rahman of Riau spent much time in Singapore and Trengganu. On earlier ties, see Virginia Matheson, "Mahmud, Sultan of Riau and Lingga (1823–1864)," *Indonesia* 13 April 1972): 119–146.

8. Barbara Andaya, "Sources concerning the Reign of Sultan Mansur Shah," pp. 99–103.

9. Clifford, "Report," pp. 69, 91, 99; on the appointment of the first mufti, interview with Datuk Purba di-Raja (Haji Wan Abdul Rahim bin Long), retired chief kathi, Kuala Trengganu, 27 April 1974.

of political authority was the collection of dues, this economic by-
passing of the hereditary local chiefs signaled their defeat, and they
were either reduced to the level of commoners or absorbed into the
central elite that formed the ruler's entourage.

Trengganu was known in this time as a center of religious devotion,
and wandering Arab, Indonesian, and Malay scholars found a welcome
at the palace and the houses of the elite. Pious Trengganu Malays also
traveled the peninsula to visit shrines and to seek religious knowledge,
many journeying north to study in the great schools of Patani. This
religious communication brought with it a steady stream of political
information concerning events in the Middle East and India; Ottoman
Turkey, as seat of the caliphate and the world's major Muslim power,
was a particular focus of the Trengganu elite's concern.[10]

Yet all this took place against a vanishing background. The Malayo-
Muslim world which was so essential to Trengganu's sense of place
was dissolving, its perspectives gradually narrowing, its formerly dynamic centers robbed of power. Trengganu's chief families could not
ignore the change, for the dethroned sultans and exiled princes who
were their relatives sought refuge with them. Nor could it be hoped
that this pressure was somehow local and therefore temporary, for
the news brought from Trengganu's more distant religious contacts
reported analogous trends elsewhere in Asia. The economic conse-

10. Interviews, Kuala Trengganu, with Tuan Haji Mohamed Salleh b. Haji
Awang and Mohamed b. Endut, 23 and 28 August 1973; Baharuddin Ismail, 26
August 1973; Tungku Jaya Pekerma Wira (Tungku Chik Abubakar b. Mustaffa)
and Datuk Purba, 1 May 1974. Allen, "Ancien Regime," p. 43, summarizes
Journal references to the Sultan's interest in international affairs. Sultan Zainal
Abidin's visit to Egypt in 1913-14 while performing the Mecca pilgrimage greatly
impressed the ruler with Islamic potential (Maxwell, "Extracts from the Journal
of the British Agent, Trengganu, Sept. 9, 1914," CO273/412 Desp. 518, p.
318). Agents' journals are hereafter cited by name of agent, Journal, date of
entry, Public Record Office reference, and, where relevant, page of the file.

In his conclusion to his March Journal, 1914, Dickson noted that many of
the outstation Malays believed that the Sultan's destination "was not Mecca but
Stamboul (Constantinople) where he was going to get a flag from the Sultan of
Turkey" (CO273/410 Desp. 195, p. 363). We shall see the symbol of the Bendera
Stambul (Turkish flag) recurring during the rebellion of 1928. For Turkish
influence in Muslim Southeast Asia, see Anthony Reid, "Nineteenth Century
Pan-Islam in Indonesia and Malaysia," Journal of Asian Studies 26, no. 2
(February 1967): 267-283.

quences were also felt, for Trengganu was a maritime state whose people engaged not only in fishing and small coastal traffic but in sending great trading prahus as far as Cochin China, Manila, and Borneo; and as the century wore on European competition and state regulations impinged ever more on their freedom to operate. They were also affected by the broader organizational and technological transformations which accompanied the growing influence of the industrial West. Small Chinese steamers began to ply the prahus' accustomed waters, and because their activity was on roughly the same scale but better organized, capitalized, and equipped than the Malays' they presented a more immediate threat to Trengganu shipping than did the Europeans' grander vessels. Chinese coolies came to work the mines which Chinese merchants acquired in concession. And indeed nearly all the revenue farms in the state were given into the hands of the Chinese. Though the immigrant presence was very small compared to that in other Malay states, it represented powerful interests—for both Chinese and European merchants in Singapore pressed for the opening up of Trengganu to their enterprise—and it also reflected a broader economic change which the Malays could ignore only at the cost of being pushed to the margins of an emerging modern world.[11]

In this essay we shall see how the Trengganu leaders attempted to deal with this diminishing of their sphere and with the challenge of a growing British presence which rested on a completely different political and intellectual system. Eventually, the British were to tame the Trengganu elite—not in the sense of making its members completely docile, for to the end they obstructed British rule, but in the sense of training them to an administrative behavior pattern completely different from that of their natural state. They were to fit Trengganu's leaders into roles in a monocentric, bureaucratic, constitutional kingdom which was in many ways the antithesis of what the Malay state

11. On the Trengganu-built schooners, see Humphreys, *Annual Report*, 1919, pp. 16–17; the Foreign Office's "Report on the Unfederated Malay State of Trengganu," 31 August 1923 (FO 371/9224), pp. 243, 250, notes that in 1923 there were still about 200 of these ships in Trengganu, capable of carrying between 50 and 200 tons of cargo. I am grateful to Baharuddin Ismail for discussing these ships and their importance with me. For the Chinese control of revenue farms, see note 27 below.

had been. The old relationships did not die and in many respects retained more power than the official new ones, but the traditional system grew ever more shadowy, constricted in scope and nostalgic in sentiment.

At the beginning of this century the overriding fact in Trengganu society was the gulf between those with power—members of the elite and their followers—and those without, the common people or *ra'ayat*. Although the ra'ayat, particularly in the more accessible areas, was linked to this elite by a variety of economic and social ties, nonetheless the distinction between ruler and ruled was usually the decisive factor in any confrontation. There was, of course, considerable differentiation within both village and elite society, but since in this essay attention will be focused upon the latter we shall consider here only the main features of the dominant group.

We have already sketched the wider contacts of Trengganu's elite in the Malayo-Muslim world; let us now turn to its local context, the area over which it ruled. Unlike most Malay states, Trengganu was not centered upon a single stream which provided the main focus of settlement and transportation. It consisted of a series of north-south ecological belts running parallel to the east coast of the Malay peninsula, cut across by over a dozen significant rivers debouching into the South China Sea. Such an arrangement, preventing the monopolization of riverine access to the sea by a single center, might have encouraged regionalism; but in fact population was concentrated on the fertile plain which extended twenty miles up from the mouth of the Trengganu river. This region of intense cultivation was the principal area of Kuala Trengganu's direct control. Beyond this, population clustered in scattered villages along the coast and on river mouths, with a very few farming and mining communities inland.[12] This meant that the people of Trengganu were, on the whole, within easy boat communication of the center, except when monsoon rains rendered all transport

12. Allen, "Ancien Regime," pp. 26–31, discussed this problem. On population distribution, see *Annual Report*, 1910, p. 12; and Conlay, Journal, 14 August 1909, CO273/351 Desp. 303, p. 212. See also Clifford, "Report," pp. 51–57; and *Annual Report*, 1936, p. 7.

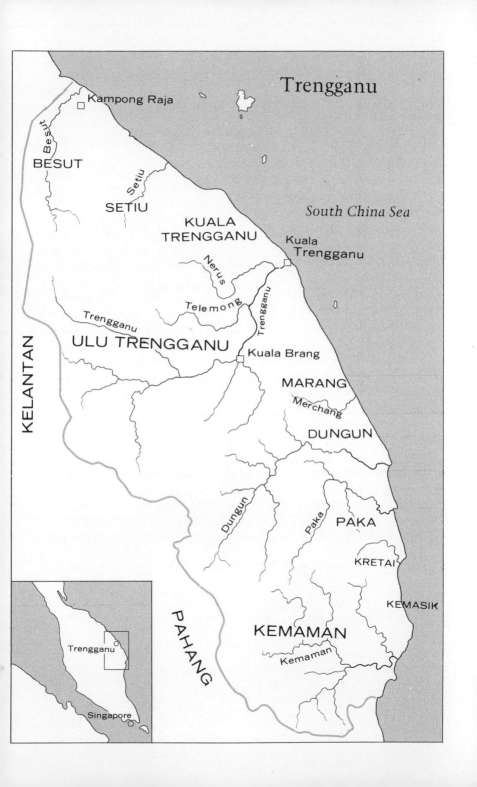

helpless; and they were thus subject to central control. The chiefs and officials who drew their income from these districts constituted their formal government, although, as we have seen, these persons lived in Kuala Trengganu itself and made their presence felt locally through agents.

There were, however, three more distant regions which had a degree of autonomy from the capital, their relationship to it ranging, according to circumstances, from clear dependency to a vagueness reminiscent of Trengganu's own relations with Siam. As they will be of importance later in our story, we should describe them here. The valleys of the Besut River in the north and the Kemaman in the south were under locally resident chiefs, who acknowledged the suzerainty of the sultan by the irregular remission of dues but who resisted all attempts at reducing their factual independence. In Besut, authority lay with the hereditary chiefs of the Tungku Long family, who had ruled the troublesome border area near Kelantan for several generations and who maintained family ties with both Trengganu and Kelantan sultans. Kemaman was under Che Drahman (Abdul Rahman bin Ishak, Datuk Seri Lela di-Raja), in theory an official sent out from the center but in practice an autonomous chief who sent revenue only when pressed.[13]

The third region where the power of the central elite was limited was the upstream (*ulu*) area of the Trengganu River itself. Cut off by rapids, peopled in many places by immigrants, the remote Ulu Trengganu region seems to have eluded effective outside control. As far as we can tell from the sparse references to it, government was restricted to efforts to profit from the occasional tax or levy, and in the far interior the scattered population sometimes avoided contact with the agents of the capital by using *orang asli* (Sakai) bearers to carry jungle produce over the mountains and into the western part of the peninsula.

13. Humphreys, Journal, 9 March 1916, CO273/445 Desp. 117, p. 196; Conlay, Journal, 5 October 1909, CO273/351 Desp. 345, p. 388. For Kemaman, see Sulong bin Zainal, "Dato Lela: Viceroy of Kemaman," *Malaysia in History* 12, no. 1 (October 1968): 16–19; Conlay, Journal, 19 August 1909, CO273/351 Desp. 303, p. 214; and the outline history of Kemaman in J. W. Simmons, *Annual Report,* 1925, pp. 16–17. Insight into Che Drahman's traditional administrative style can be gained by reading *Report of the Commission Appointed by His Excellency the High Commissioner to Enquire into Certain Matters Relating to the State of Trengganu,* 1918 (hereafter cited as Bucknill Commission, *Report*), (Singapore: Government Printing Office, 1918); this includes a 1917 report by Humphreys on Kemaman administration, pp. 145–152.

In the central plain, the elite had its focus and usual residence in Kuala Trengganu, a town lying on the seacoast at the mouth of the Trengganu River which is still the capital. There political power was monopolized by a complex of related families; access to wealth and influence depended upon status within this group, and ultimately this status derived from connection with the sultan. It was the ruler's relatives, confidants, advisers, and religious and military experts who formed the nucleus of the elite, and as generation followed generation a certain hereditary specialization was established. From the latter part of the nineteenth century until at least World War II, Trengganu was dominated by four extended families, each of which controlled a particular sphere.

The central family was, of course, that of the sultan. His kin, bearing the title *tungku,* held power as their birthright. From the ranks of this clan the ruler selected those who because of the closeness of their relationship, as well as their experience, loyalty, character, and abilities, were regarded as qualified for the highest offices. Since many Trengganu tungkus lived in the same cluster of family compounds, Kampung Dalem (also known as Kampung Aur), this particular urban village and royal enclave was recognized as a natural focus of authority and political intrigue.

There was no legal limit to the power of the sultan, and royal rhetoric proclaimed the utter subjection of all to him; therefore the British wrongly concluded that his rule was absolute. The ruler was limited by custom, a far more flexible container than that of law or institutions, and because of this plasticity the sultan's personality played a great role in determining where the practical limits of his power lay. Baginda Omar had brought it far, but though he was attuned to the need for change he had increased central control in the usual manner—through a tour de force of personal appeal and astute maneuvering—which provided no permanent basis for the concentration of power. Baginda Omar's successor, Sultan Ahmad II (ruled 1876-1881), had little time to make an impression on the state. Zainal Abidin (ruled 1881-1918), whose reign was to witness Trengganu's transition to colonial rule, had neither the ruthlessness nor the taste for intrigue that would have enabled him to continue such a degree of control. A young man of nineteen at his succession, he grew to be a humane and learned man, of some note as an Islamic scholar, and much of his attention was devoted to religious and intellectual activity. As we shall see, he eventually began to accept the need for a modern administration, but these efforts by no means substituted for Baginda Omar's great personal power as a means of maintaining control.

Soon after the succession Zainal Abidin began to relinquish some of his predecessor's gains. In the early 1880s he parceled out major rivers and tributaries, following the traditional prerogative for allocating income to royal relatives, officials, chiefs, and clients. Those thus favored, almost all resident in Kuala Trengganu, were then responsible for revenue collection and the maintenance of order via their own agents (*wakil*). British advisers (and some historians) were to view this as a forfeiture of the ruler's sovereign rights that threatened the hegemony of the central elite and implied the fragmentation of the state.[14] But in Trengganu sovereignty was not seen in that way, nor did such allocation set a precedent or confirm a right. The parceling out of authority was both normal and temporary, its extent depending on how much direct responsibility a ruler felt he could hold in his own hands in a system with only a rudimentary bureaucracy, and how many members of the elite he felt constrained to supply with a living.

Relations between members of the royal family were less clearcut than in a Western state. The sultan headed the clan of course, but there was no fixed mode of succession, and with most of the royal relatives resident in the capital they were a constant source of intrigue and demands. In traditional Malay states royal sons were usually the most troublesome of all, for rivalry and ambition combined with a desire for income which the sultan's purse and their usefulness hardly justified; often, the solution was to take their followers roving against merchant ships or more distant and prosperous shores.[15] If a particular son was chosen or obvious as heir he might be given a direct voice in the affairs of state, being declared Yang di-Pertuan Muda (or less

14. Allen, "Ancien Regime," gives a detailed account of Zainal Abidin's reign; a somewhat popularized version appeared as "Sultan Zainal Abidin III," *Malaysia in History* 12, no. 1 (October 1968): 2–14. On courts and laws under Zainal Abidin, see the letter of W. D. Scott to the Secretary of the High Commissioner, 30 November 1912, Public Record Office reference CO273/388 Desp. 696, p. 310; Conlay, Journal, 2 and 5 August 1909, CO273/351 Desp. 303, pp. 206, 209; and idem, Journal, 2 October 1909, CO273/351 Desp. 345, p. 391.

15. For a discussion of the problem of accommodating the ruler's sons (*anak raja*) in the Malay system, see Barbara Andaya, "Perak, the Abode of Grace: A Study of an Eighteenth Century Malay State" (Ph.D. diss., Cornell University, 1975), pp. 51–58.

formally Yam Tuan Muda), the Young Ruler; and, if so, a struggle for supremacy between the embryo lord and the old might occur, or a gradual effacement of the old ruler by the young. This last is what took place in the latter years of Zainal Abidin's reign, when the proud and impatient Yam Tuan Muda Mohamed assumed an increasingly powerful role.

One of the ways in which the ruling clan maintained its dominance was by staffing the major offices of the state with royal relatives.[16] However, the royal family did not have exclusive control over Trengganu's governance, for a second of the state's four important clans was also specialized in this occupation. This was the family of Kampung Kling, which was centered in a neighborhood (*kampung*) close to the palace. The family provided so many high officials who were awarded the title *datuk* that the settlement became known as Kampung Datuk. Like most families which enjoyed power and privilege over several generations, this second major line had intermarried with sultans and tungkus and could claim distinguished descent in its own right. The ultimate forebears of the Kampung Kling line included the ancient Megat rulers of Trengganu, and so reached back to migrant princes from "Batak Minangkabau" in Sumatra and settlers from the once-powerful political and religious centers of Patani and Aceh; more immediately, the line stemmed from Johor and had been in close service of the sultans since the first came to Trengganu from that state. During the twentieth century almost all nonroyal high officials who were close to the throne came from Kampung Kling.[17]

16. Among the royal advisers and relatives the senior ministers were Tungku Mahmud b. Tungku Mohamed (Tungku Bentara Delam) and two sons-in-law of Zainal Abidin, Tungku Ngah Omar b. Abdul Rahim (Tungku Seri Utama di-Raja) and Tungku Embong Musa b. Suleiman. Other prominent officials of high birth were Tungku Omar b. Osman (Tg. Seri Setia di-Raja), the state secretary; Tungku Ali b. Mustuffa (Tg. Nara di-Raja), treasurer; and Tungku Chik Ahmad b. Abdul Rahman (Tg. Seri Bijaya di-Raja), commissioner of lands. These men, who will appear again in the course of this essay, held high rank for many years. (In giving names of Trengganu leaders, the names by which they were usually known will be used; their formal names, where different, and their court names will be given parenthetically.) Unless otherwise specified, biographies and titles were pieced together from scattered references in the agents' journals and annual reports.

17. Interview, Che Awang Kastam (Mohamed Anuar b. Omar), Kuala Trengganu, 28 April 1974, and genealogy held by him. Apart from Datuk Amar/Haji Ngah, for whose role see below, the most important representatives of Kampung

The third leading Trengganu family derived its high status from the royal recognition won by religious expertise. This was the Duyung line, which provided all the mufti and many of the *hakim* (judges) and magistrates in Trengganu down to World War II. They were related to Baginda Omar's original mufti, Sheikh Abdul Kadir, who had come from the Hadramaut but was ultimately of Patani descent. He had been succeeded by a close relative, Haji Abdullah bin Mohammed Amin, who was brought to Trengganu from Patani as a baby when his family fled Siam's reassertion of control there. Haji Abdullah became the leader of a pious community of traders and fishermen on the island of Duyung two miles up the Trengganu River; hence he was known as To' Sheikh Duyung and his family as the Duyung line. He was one of the earliest Trengganu Malays to study in Mecca, and this established a family tradition of Middle Eastern education followed by high office in Trengganu. His son, Haji Mohamed, taught Sultan Zainal Abidin and was appointed mufti in his turn. The Duyung family would continue to dominate that post until the early 1940s, when a new—and by some Malays resented—tradition began of importing Arab mufti direct from the Middle East. Duyung was thus the source of Trengganu's religious establishment for over a century and, although there were other esteemed teachers and families with a tradition of religious learning, none were as close to government as the Duyung line.[18]

The people of Trengganu were recognized as the most zealous Muslims in the Malay peninsula, and it has been said that their devotion

---

Kling in elite circles were two brothers, Che Mat (Mohamed) and Mohamed Ali b. Abdul Rahim (Datuk Nara Wangsa). In the early days the former was joint treasurer with Tungku Embong, while the latter as Datuk Mata Mata was in charge of state security. A son of Datuk Mata Mata, Che Da Omar b. Mohamed Ali (Datuk Seri Andika di-Raja) became one of the leading officials after the establishment of British influence; together with his cousin Che Da Omar b. Mahmud (Datuk Jaya Perkasa), he was one of the few Malay administrators to be regularly praised by the European advisers. See "'Dato Mata-Mata': A Note Compiled from Information Provided by Y. T. M. Tengku Ahmad ibni Almarhom Sultan Zainal Abidin," *Malaysia in History* 12, no. 1 (October 1968): 33; and Abdullah Zakaria bin Ghazali, "Haji Ngah Mohamed bin Yusof: Datuk Seri Amar Di Raja Trengganu," *Jernal Sejarah* 14 (1976/1977): 13.

18. Interviews with Datuk Purba di-Raja, from the Duyung family, Kuala Trengganu, 27 April and 1 May 1974, and genealogy in his possession.

stemmed from three sources: Patani, via Duyung; Baghdad, whence came the revered eighteenth-century sheik whose grave at Pulau Manis is one of the state's most sacred places; and the Hadramaut, via the al-Idrus line.[19] This last, the fourth family of the Trengganu central elite, was part of the long established and much respected Arab community. The colony included many *syed* (descendants of the Prophet), among whom the most influential were the al-Idrus, whose ancestor arrived from Java in the eighteenth century. The son of this first settler became a famous religious teacher, as did his grandson Abdul Rahman bin Mohammed al-Idrus, the famous *keramat* (holy man) known as To' Ku Paloh (Datuk Engku, of the village of Paloh). The charisma of these saintly men intensified the respect the al-Idrus already enjoyed as syeds, and the family became a powerful line with close ties to the sultans but with their own, religiously based source of authority. Zainal Abidin included representatives of the al-Idrus in the inner councils of state, and all the twentieth-century sultans seem to have had syeds in their personal retinues.[20]

The head of the al-Idrus family might be titled Sheikh-ul-Islam, recognizing him as the most prominent religious teacher in the state, or Sheikh-ul-Ulama, leader of the religious scholars, or Sheikh-ul-Sa'adah, head of the syeds and thus of the whole Arab community. But these titles reflected status rather than function, and officials who dealt with matters of religion and Islamic law tended to be drawn from the Duyung rather than the al-Idrus line.[21]

19. Datuk Purba di-Raja, interviews, Kuala Trengganu, 27 April and 1 May 1974.

20. "A Conqueror's Correspondence a Century Ago: Related by Unku Pengiren Anum (Ungku Syed Abdul Kadir of Kuala Trengganu)," *Malaya in History* 6, no. 2 (April 1961): 9–19, discusses Ungku Said Zain, chief minister of Baginda Omar; his son, Abdullah, married Sharifah Fatimah, daughter of Baginda Omar's sister and Said Hassan Asagof of Riau (interview, Engku Embong b. Abdul Kadir al-Idrus, Cabang Tiga, Trengganu, 27 April 1974). Engku Chik b. Abdul Kadir al-Idrus, younger brother of Engku Embong, holds the al-Idrus genealogy, a document essential to the family's syed status as it traces their descent from the Prophet.

21. Even after the creation ca. 1919 of a Religious Affairs Department, the authority of the then Sheikh-ul-Islam, Tuan Embong (Syed Abu Bakar b. Syed Abdul Rahman al-Idrus), was recognized by linking him to the department, although it was under the general administrative supervision of Tungku Ngah Omar b. Abdul Rahim, Minister of Religion and Justice. Khoo Kay Kim, "Malay

The al-Idrus' position epitomized the fact that there was no inevitable correlation between high status and administrative position in the Trengganu elite. Status in Trengganu's leading circles depended upon recognition by the sultan, and in return members of the elite were at the ruler's service. However, not all might be called to serve in specific functions and some, like the al-Idrus, served by embellishing the ruler with the prestige of their name. Those called to active service might perform routine administrative work, but a chief assigned such minor tasks was not thereby reduced in honor. His prestige, authority, and frequently erratic income derived primarily from his rank, not his function. Naturally, the highest posts usually went to the most trusted and/or able members of the elite, but official position tended to follow status rather than the reverse.

In spite of the importance of status in precolonial Trengganu there was some recruitment of leaders on grounds of functional expertise. Influential chiefs and officials might be drawn into the central elite from other families and social strata or from outside the state. Thus, the various *panglima* who commanded the fighting forces raised in time of crisis could come from either high or humble families, as the main criteria in their selection were their military talents and courage.[22] Recruitment and absorption of "foreign Malays" was not uncommon, although the newcomers were often not as alien as they seemed, for their acceptance frequently reflected ancestral ties with Trengganu. On the whole, however, the affairs of state rested in the four families' hands. Let us now see what happened to them when British power began to assert itself.

By the turn of this century, Trengganu's accustomed mode of governance was becoming an anomaly. The British, at Siamese expense, were

Society, 1874–1920s," *Journal of Southeast Asian Studies* 5, no. 2 (September 1974): 185, note 16, notes the uncertainty concerning the Sheikh-ul-Islam's role in Malay society.

22. Interview, Tuan Haji Muhamed Salleh b. Haji Awang, Kuala Trengganu, 29 April 1974. Under the Pax Brittanica there was little for such warriors to do, so they tended to be relegated to police work, where they attracted British criticism and contempt. See Journal references, passim, to Tungku Panglima

consolidating their hold on the Malay peninsula; by 1906 all the unfederated states except Trengganu would accept Advisers of British
nationality whose recommendations had to be followed on all matters
but religion and custom. In Singapore and Penang, British officials
and both European and Chinese merchants argued that Trengganu
should be incorporated into the new order, and that the inefficient,
exploitative, unproductive rule of its native elite should make way for
a rational government alive to the benefits of British institutions and
British investment. The handwriting on the wall, the Trengganu elite
began to consider change.

Sultan Zainal Abidin and his circle of advisers took much of the
initiative on reform. By 1902 Trengganu had, in contrast to the claims
of our initial quotation, courts, police, and even written laws, and it
maintained by means of *wakaf* (charitable settlement) a network of
paths, bridges, and resthouses which were a boon to local communications.[23] Yet he and other members of the Trengganu elite had grave
doubts about the consequences of change. They recognized that some
adoption of Western-style institutions would be necessary to fend off
waxing European power; but they were also reluctant to follow infidel
ways, as this involved the risk of religious contamination and cultural
decline. Moreover, the elite did not want to introduce a meritocracy,
for any general opening of the way to talent would weaken their own
grip on the state. Elite interest also militated against administrative
reform: tight financial control and the depersonalization of authority
would inevitably curtail the notables' perquisites and license. The
transitional period that occupied the first two decades of the century
was shaped by this tension between the desire for political restructuring
as a means to survival and the disinclination to abandon Malayo-
Muslim models or to endanger the hegemony of the central elite.

One sign of the increasing interest in institutional development was
the immigration of a growing number of Malays who had acquired
modern skills in the more Westernized states and the Straits Settlements and who saw an opportunity to use them in Trengganu. The

---

Besar (Abdullah Othman, also known as Tengku Long b. Tengku Woh), the
"Police Chief," and Datuk Panglima Prang (Che Yusuf b. Musa).

23. For more on the courts, see Conlay, Journal, 2 October 1909, CO273/351
Desp. 345, p. 391; on *wakaf*, Humphreys, *Annual Report*, 1915, p. 15.

earliest such immigrant specialists tended to be Malay "lawyers" (licensed pleaders with no formal professional training, called variously *wakil, peguam,* or *loyar*) and school teachers, who were highly respected in local society although not admitted to the aristocratic elite. Then, in about 1908, the first secular school was founded at Kampung Kling. The teacher was Ungku Abu Bakar bin Long (Ungku Seri Wangsa di-Raja), a man of Trengganu parentage who had been born in Johor, to whose ruling house he seems to have been related. There he had become a teacher and later joined the Johor Military Forces. Emigrating to Trengganu, he set up a school where he taught reading and writing (including romanized script) together with a little history in a fairly systematic four-year program.

Ungku Bakar may have taken his history materials from old Malay sources, but he was a "modern" man who wore Western dress and introduced his pupils to quite new ways of thought. It is interesting, therefore, to note that most of his thirty to forty students were sons of chiefs, who wanted their children to acquire modern skills alongside their traditional religious education. For, by this time, a younger generation of Trengganu chiefs had emerged whose contact with Singapore, Riau, and Johor had oriented them toward modernization. Many of Ungku Bakar's students went on to become leading officials; he himself seems to have tutored the yam tuan muda and was to hold high office when his pupil succeeded to the throne.[24]

Changes were taking place in the economy as well. Very gradually, Trengganu began to feel the effects of the plantation and mining development that was growing apace elsewhere in the peninsula: new interest was shown by outsiders in obtaining the concession of exploitation rights, and Chinese settlement increased. Around the turn of the century, with non-Malays applying for concession rights in growing

24. For Ungku Bakar's instruction of the Yam Tuan Muda, see Conlay, Journal, 2 October 1909, CO273/351 Desp. 345, p. 388. An article, "Penkhabaran Trengganu," *al Imam* 2 (3 May 1908), reported the opening of the first school in Trengganu; I am indebted to Encik Abdul Aziz b. Mat Ton for this reference. Conlay describes the school in his Journal entry for 27 August 1909: "There is only one school in the State, a small one at Kuala Trengganu accommodating 30 to 40 boys, sons of chiefs principally. . . . The one schoolmaster is a very capable Johor Malay and teaches Romanized Malay very well" (CO273/351 Desp. 303, p. 221). For the group of progressive young chiefs, see Conlay, Journal, 5 October 1909, CO273/351 Desp. 345, p. 388.

numbers, the Trengganu government abandoned its practice of making land grants via a simple letter with the sultan's seal and began to issue more formal documents specifying the length, terms, and purpose of the contract. A few years later, and particularly between 1908 and 1910, there was a sudden rush of concession-granting to members of the royal family and entrepreneurs.[25] While the leasing of rights to Chinese, Arabs, or Europeans was no doubt a simple matter of profit, the granting of documented control over large areas of land to tungkus was a move to strengthen their hands in dealing with the foreign businessmen who were sure to stream into Trengganu in the wake of expanding British influence. In this way, European form could be used to ensure that the traditional elite received its due share of the benefits. Since the royal concession-holders had neither the capital nor the expertise to exploit their lands, the documents were intended to enable them to sell or lease their rights as profitably as possible: they would, in short, continue their old practices of collecting dues from territories allotted for their exploitation under a new, "modern" guise.

Around the turn of the century, Trengganu began to adopt some of the trappings of a bureaucratic state. A civil service was established on paper, though in fact it seems simply to have meant that certain chiefs were designated departmental heads. A formal system of courts based on a written enactment was realized, and judges learned in Islamic law

25. Conlay, Journal, 1 and 2 August 1909, CO273/351 Desp. 303, pp. 205–271. Of the thirty-four concessions listed in Scott, *Annual Report,* 1911, appendix I, pp. 9–13, ten were granted in 1908, one in 1909, twelve in 1910, and five in 1911. Of the fourteen concessions granted to tungkus, one was given in 1906, five in 1908, and eight in 1910; at least six of these were granted to chiefs who drew revenue from different areas of the state, while in other cases the concessions coincided geographically with appanage territories; compare Scott's list with that in Conlay, Journal, 19 August 1909, CO273/351 Desp. 303, pp. 214–218. The only significant European-owned concessions were those of the Danish East Asiatic Company (plantations at Kretai) and Guthrie's three mines in Kemaman (*Annual Report,* 1911 and 1912). Humphreys, *Annual Report,* 1918, pp. 9–10, gives details of eleven ruling house concessions; only one (in Kretai) was located outside mining areas. A typical concession gave the land as a royal gift in perpetuity; no premium or land-rent was paid, the only revenue to the state being export duties of 2.5 to 5 percent ad valorem on agricultural exports and 10 percent on minerals. Import duties were charged, most importantly, on opium used by the Chinese miners. Boundaries of the concessions were usually vague; their size ranged from 20,000 to 200,000 acres. See especially the *Annual Report* for 1915, 1918, and 1923.

replaced the small panel of major chiefs which had previously heard cases in the state hall. Nonetheless, the character of Trengganu government in 1909 was still determined by the personal inclinations and interests of members of the elite. Zainal Abidin and the yam tuan muda held power, assisted by the sultan's secretary, Haji Ngah. This last, Muhammed bin Yusuf Seri Amar di-Raja, known in later life as Datuk Amar, was of the nonroyal governing clan of Kampung Kling. Born in Manir, Trengganu, in 1878, he was thirty years old at the time of the British takeover. In spite of his youth he was to be promoted not long after to deputy chief minister over a royal relative who had claims to the post, and from 1924 to 1941 he would hold the highest nonroyal position of chief minister (*menteri besar*). The most durable and perhaps the most significant personality in Trengganu politics of this century, he appears to have been a man of canniness and considerable executive ability. Moreover, he was an *alim,* a religious scholar; he had spent three years studying in Mecca and spoke Arabic fluently, always seeking out Arab visitors to Trengganu to discuss religion and the affairs of the Islamic world.[26] Not one to turn his back on reality or to yield power unnecessarily, he shared the Trengganu rulers' desire to proceed with change, but cautiously.

These three most powerful leaders were advised by an informal and aristocratic council. For the rest, there was a rudimentary administration. Kuala Trengganu, the capital, was managed by a Datuk Panglima Dalam, who maintained a token police force, while the port and customs came under a Datuk Bandar (Shahbandar). The Chinese com-

26. For an early description of Haji Ngah, see Conlay, Journal, 19 August 1909, CO273/351 Desp. 303/219. For Haji Ngah's discourse with Arab visitors, interview, Tuan Haji Muda Salleh b. Haji Awang, Kuala Trengganu, 23 August 1973. The Foreign Office's "Report on the Unfederated Malay State of Trengganu," 31 August 1923 (FO371/9224), pp. 243, 250, noted his interest in events in India and Egypt. His appointment as deputy chief minister instead of the royal relative Tungku Chik Ahmad was based on his long experience in government and his reputation as a man of religious learning; see the file from the Setia Usaha Kerajaan, Trengganu (hereafter cited as SUK), in Arkib Negara, Malaysia, SUK/90/1335. Abdullah Zakaria, "Haji Ngah," pp. 13–14, gives details of Datuk Amar's religious career. The breadth of Trengganu's contacts in the Islamic world is reflected in the fact that, of his nine religious teachers, four were Arabs resident in Trengganu but born in the Middle East and two were from other Malay states (Negri Sembilan and Kelantan). Of the three Trengganu-born teachers, two were from the al Idrus and one from the Pulau Manis family.

munity was under its own "Kapitan China," who was responsible for the preservation of internal order and compliance with royal decrees. A state treasury collected a fluctuating and rather small income from farms, monopolies, customs, and pepper plantations but, since it supplied the personal incomes of the royal household and assorted client chiefs as well as administrative funds, it was in fact simply the royal purse.[27] Trengganu had changed, but it had not changed very greatly.

In March 1909 the signing of the Anglo-Siamese treaty completed the division of the Malayo-Muslim world between Britain, the Netherlands, and Siam. Henceforth, Patani was to be part of Siam while Kelantan, Kedah, and Trengganu came into the British sphere. In July

27. Clifford, "Report," pp. 72–80; Allen, Ancien Regime," p. 27. Conlay, Journal, 18 August 1909, CO273/351 Desp. 303, p. 213, notes that the royal revenues of approximately M$100,000 were derived from nine major revenue farms, all then in Chinese hands: opium imports, Chinese gambling, pawnshops, spirit imports, purchase of produce for export, export duties, Kuala Trengganu pork farm, kerosene imports, and boat licensing. Scott, *Annual Report*, 1910, noted the yearly income of various farms: Kuala Trengganu gambling, $7,500; Kuala Trengganu pawnshop, $800, Kuala Trengganu region import farm, $24,000, kerosene imports, $15,000. The pig slaughter (pork) farm, which was abolished in 1911, paid no rent but the farmer was obliged to light and scavenge the town.
In 1912 both the opium and the Kuala Trengganu export and import farms were obtained by Towkay Ang Siah Im of the Chap Hap Teck Seng of Singapore. The opium farm, which covered all the state except Kemaman and Paka, gave him the right to import opium at $120 a chest, for a payment of $10,000 down and $1,800 a month. Six years' import-export rights for the coastal stretch from Kuala Marang to Bukit Baru cost him $184,000 (Scott, Journal, January 1912, CO273/384 Desp. 70, p. 412). It was quite common for the sultan to borrow heavily from the farmers, thereby forgoing revenue (*Annual Report,* 1915/1916, p. 2).
Various monopolies also contributed to the incomes of Trengganu leaders. For example, a daughter of the sultan had the right to compulsory purchase of all pandanus in Paka against an artificially low price, so that she made a handsome profit on the resale (*Annual Report,* 1915, p. 8). The Marang farmer had a monopoly on gambier purchase at 30 percent less than market price; he made huge profits, but over half the gambier gardens went out of production (Humphreys, Journal, 31 December 1918, CO273/486 Desp. 17, p. 75).

a British official arrived in Kuala Trengganu accompanied by a Siamese commissioner; they informed the sultan that the state was now officially under British influence and that the Englishman would stay on as Britain's agent. This announcement that Trengganu's long-husbanded independence was at an end seems to have come as a shock to the sultan; he had great difficulty in concealing his emotion and requested time to think. Months of negotiation ensued, during which the Trengganu government sought a relationship similar to that enjoyed by Johor, whereby the British agent sent up from Singapore was simply a consul with no power to enforce obedience. Meanwhile, Trengganu's leaders kept close watch on events in Kedah and Kelantan, wondering if they would accept the transfer to British rule or resist by force. But eventually, on 22 April 1910, a treaty was signed between "the independent Malayo-Muslim State of Trengganu" (*Karajaan Trengganu yang Islamiatu'l Melayuiah yang berkarajaan sendiri*) and His Majesty's Government. It was agreed that Trengganu would not enter into contracts with outside powers, or intervene in the affairs of other Malay states, or cede extensive tracts of land to non-Trengganu subjects without the permission of the High Commissioner in Singapore. In return the British promised to protect the state from external threat and were granted the right to post an Agent (*wakil*) in Kuala Trengganu to act as consul.[28]

Reading the treaty, it does not seem that the agent's presence would be a very disturbing element in Trengganu life: his only functions were to represent British subjects and to act as liaison between British and local economic interests. Nevertheless, the entry of the agent inaugurated a difficult period for the Trengganu elite, not only because it brought the chiefs into direct and formal contact with increasingly impatient businessmen and officials from Singapore, but also because the agent's very existence threatened their social and political position. His arrival broke their monopoly of authority; he was outside the closed, mutually supportive circle which exploited the state, and since in a crisis he could call on the power of Singapore he was not suscepti-

28. For the treaty, see CO273/361 Desp. 160, p. 182; and on the context, High Commissioner's Office Record (hereafter cited as HCO) 401/1910. Detailed descriptions of the lengthy discussions between Conlay and the Sultan appear in Conlay, Journal, July 1909–May 1910, passim. For the Sultan's distress over the manner of the transfer to the British sphere, see HCO 920/1909.

ble to intimidation. The agent did not share the values or interests of the elite, and so he could not be coopted, while the treaty prevented his expulsion. Hence he was an uncontrollable factor in any situation; the only way his disruptive potential could be checked was by excluding him from as much of Trengganu life as possible. Since he was an outsider with no real power, this was not so difficult. But the agent did have two points of access into the local establishment: on the one hand he had a formal position as judge of the Joint Court set up following the treaty (about which more later) and on the other he had inevitable personal contacts with members of the elite, some of whom became his friends and informants.

In considering how to develop their personal relationships with the agent, individual members of the elite had to balance their general inclination to keep him out of Trengganu affairs with their specific desire to be on good terms with a man who might well have control over their future. W. L. Conlay, the first agent, recorded the elite's unsurprising suspicion that his appointment was "the thin end of a wedge intended to lead to complete British contol." He also noted that the nonroyal chiefs and officials felt themselves to have special grounds for concern, for they believed on the basis of what they had seen happening in other states that British policy always favored sultans and rajas over the lesser chiefs. On the whole, however, Conlay found the Trengganu leaders quite prepared to be friendly; he ascribed this to their recognition that their fates lay ultimately in his hands, as full British control was inevitable.[29]

The agents themselves shared general European assumptions about the nature and purpose of the state, believing that there must be an effective separation between legislature, judiciary, and executive and that the ultimate function of government was to develop a prosperous citizenry which would provide the necessary revenue for administration. Within the context of British Malaya, this meant that the colonial officers favored the nominal supremacy of a docile, aristocratic Malay elite which devoted its energies to sport rather than politics, and a watchful European supervision of legal and financial institutions. Within this framework, economic development should proceed to the

29. Conlay, Journal, 26 July 1909, CO273/351 Desp. 303, p. 203; and December 1909, CO273/360 Desp. 37, p. 170.

benefit of all—or at least to the profit of state treasuries, foreign capitalists, and local elites.

But these assumptions were not shared by those who ran Trengganu society. The notion of "separation of powers" was alien to the Malayo-Muslim idea of the state, and the elite was not prepared to tolerate any curbing of its authority. Not only did Islamic doctrine emphasize the indivisible nature of the polity, but the chiefs themselves were accustomed to using the institutions and resources of the society as they wished, so long as their position was sanctioned by the sultan. Hence, tungkus and datuks intervened in court cases whenever these touched on their interests and viewed the economy as existing for their benefit. It is not surprising, then, that the early agents were strongly critical of the "incompetence and corruption" they saw in Trengganu, and that their struggles with the existing system centered on the judiciary and the economy.

In 1910 a Joint Court was constituted to enable the agent to act as cojudge in cases involving British subjects. It was not a Western-style court, for it derived its authority from the sultan, applied "Muhammedan Law and the Law of the State," and was, in many ways, simply a special sitting of the traditional Mahkamah Balai. The agent held his seat on the bench by virtue of a letter of authority (*kuasa*) from the sultan, so that his influence in the court depended very much on his personal relationship with the Malay judge and on his own force of character.[30] Nonetheless, the court brought Conlay and his successors into working contact with Trengganu institutions, and it also provided for the first time a source of authority outside the Trengganu elite's control, with the result that thwarted litigants and malcontents sought to bring their cases before it and both court and agent became the foci of complaints and politicking. The agents, for their part, regarded the courts and the law they applied as unjust, and they deplored the financial and political use of the legal system by the chiefs; they tended to see what their presence did not change rather than what it did, and they felt themselves profoundly frustrated.

The agents also felt thwarted in their economic efforts, most notably through the system of royal concessions. We have seen how the

30. *Annual Report,* 1915, p. 31; Humphreys, Journal, 25 May 1916, CO273/445 Desp. 186, p. 417; 30 March 1916, CO273/445 Desp. 117, p. 196, on the organization of the court.

granting of documented control over large areas of land increased greatly in the first decade of this century, as Trengganu's elite sought to bolster their position legally and economically against the expansion of foreign enterprise. The royal grants gave them a strong bargaining position and, if leased out, a lump sum down and an income. But if they made sense to Trengganu's traditional exploiters they did not to the new ones, for in British eyes they locked up large areas of valuable agricultural and mining land and hampered the entry of foreign capital. In combination with the system of revenue farms, they prevented any real economic growth and so hindered administrative development as there were no funds for salaries and equipment. The agents found it exasperating that the government should "pawn the economic future of the state" for such paltry sums when abolition of the farms and concessions would allow systematic exploitation of customs, land, and opium revenues. Limitation of the sultan's freedom to grant concessions had been one of the immediate aims of British intervention and was a major clause in the 1910 treaty;[31] nonetheless, as consular officers the agents had no power to impose their ideas of reform and, the Trengganu elite having no interest in adopting their recommendations, they achieved very little. Seven years later, the then Agent Humphreys had to report that, much as he would like to recommend investment in Trengganu, he still could not do so given the prevailing insecurity and corruption.[32]

The usual method by which the Trengganu chiefs dealt with the importunate Europeans was to delay decisions, agreeing in principle but doing nothing, and to refer all questions endlessly to each other. Their response to any proposal originating from the agent or Singapore was one of "suspicious inaction" as they fought their long rear-guard battle against the British forward movement.[33] But the more far-sighted of them were aware that mere obstructionism would not be enough. The threat of a forcibly renegotiated treaty was ever present:

31. CO273/362 Confidential (dated 2 July 1910), p. 51; CO273/360 Confidential (dated 4 January 1910), p. 2.
32. Humphreys, Journal, 4 June 1917, CO273/460 Desp. 208, p. 338; 14 March 1918, CO273/472 Desp. 115, p. 24.
33. For some agents' expressions of exasperation on the problem, see Maxwell, Journal, 10 December 1914, CO273/425 Desp. 22, p. 130; Humphreys, Journal, 20 May 1916, CO273/445 Desp. 186, p. 417; and 27 January 1917, CO273/459 Desp. 36, p. 207.

the other Malay states had agents with real power, and Trengganu
might easily be made to join them.

Chief among the more stubborn opponents of the protectorate was
the yam tuan muda, Mohamed, Sultan Zainal Abidin's son and heir.
A fiercely proud man, he knew from his Riau connections and his
frequent travels what the British presence was costing Malay chiefs in
terms of honor and power. He determined to meet the foreign threat
by a judicious modernization that would keep all real power out of
British hands. Though only twenty-four at the time of the British
take-over, he was already a powerful personality, and later in 1909
the sultan granted him day-to-day control of Trengganu's administration, assisted by a special junior council of young chiefs. Conlay, the
British agent, saw this early move to give an active role to the heir as
an indication that Trengganu would embark on a "purely Native"
course of reform. He was not too pleased; the scholarly sultan would,
he felt, acquiesce to Trengganu's evolution along the lines of the
Federated Malay States, but the yam tuan muda would be a force-
ful opponent.[34]

34. Maxwell found the Sultan interested in modeling Trengganu "on the exact
lines of the FMS" but too "indolent" to do anything about it (Journal, 3 February 1915, CO273/425 Desp. 131, p. 522; also 8 June 1915, CO273/427 Desp.
336, p. 376). For other agents' comments on Zainal Abidin's interest in the FMS
model, see Scott, Journal, 7 August 1911, CO273/375 Desp. 435, p. 225;
Humphreys, Journal, 18 November 1915, CO273/444 Desp. 7, p. 262.

A photograph of Mohamed taken about 1907 shows an almost crew-cut young
man in a stiff-collared European suit, holding a book: the modernizing young
aristocrat, probably photographed during a visit to Singapore; *Malaysia in History*
12, no. 1 (October 1968): 9. The British, however, generally preferred to see him
as a profligate Malay princeling; Conlay described him as boorish and probably
epileptic (Journal, 20 October 1909, CO273/351 Desp. 345, p. 391) and also
noted (2 October 1909) that he was "almost illiterate" and (4 October 1909)
resembled his father "in neither indolence nor piety." Scott was also critical of his
"incivility" and "lack of manners" (Journal, 15 January 1911, CO273/372
Desp. 105, p. 368). This called forth a minute from a Colonial Office official
which is a nice example of the imperial self-image of Britain defending sturdy
native commoners against a decadent and tyrannical elite: "I fancy that the Yam
Tuan Muda is half-witted like many of the East Coast Rajahs. In striking contrast
to the handsome and vigorous peasantry, the Rajahs all present the appearance of
degenerate or criminal lunatics. I am not sure whether it is this gentleman or the
Rajah Muda of Kelantan who is reported to display no interest in anything but
pederasty" (HCO368/191).

Led by the yam tuan muda, Trengganu's more farsighted leaders moved to reinforce their independence on two fronts: by formally reasserting the state's sovereignty in the face of the alien threat and by initiating a series of reforms designed to neutralize and outflank their opponent. They secured the promulgation, in 1911, of a "Constitution of the Way of Illustrious Sovereignty," the drafting of which was initiated by the yam tuan muda and guided by Ungku Bakar. Though it drew on Arabic models, this fundamental law was immediately influenced by the Johor Constitution of 1886, reflecting both Ungku Bakar's Johor experience and the regard which that state enjoyed for its relatively successful containment of British pressure. The proclamation of so important a formal document required general elite acceptance, given Trengganu's dispersed power and reliance on custom; it was therefore signed by a variety of royal relatives, religious leaders, and officials, whose participation reflected the continuing importance of ascriptive status and the diffuseness of administrative function in Trengganu's governance.[35]

The constitution endorsed administrative reform as well as obliging Trengganu's rulers to preserve sovereignty; with this encouragement the yam tuan muda moved during 1912 and 1913 to reorganize government structure along Johor lines. A cabinet was installed, as prescribed by the constitution, and a state council, which was in effect a formalization of the existing regular consultation between the sultan and his chiefs, officials, and relatives. Most important, the yam tuan muda acted decisively to restructure central adminstration, tighten fiscal control, and to place capital-region relationships on an entirely new footing. He decreed that departments under ministers, staffed by clerks, should take over functions previously held by individuals. Thus, for example, land matters passed from Haji Ngah, holder of the sultan's seal, to a formally constituted Land Office. Though much of the

35. After the sultan and the yam tuan muda are listed Tungku Ngah Omar and Tungku Embong Musa, "close kin and Minister" (Kerabat yang Akrab, Wazir dan Menteri). They are followed by two al-Idrus syeds, including To' 'Ku Paloh; then come six "general relatives" (Kerabat yang Am), four of whom are described as ministers while the remaining two were members of the State Council. Next is listed the legal establishment of the mufti and two hakim, followed by three non-noble officials and council members (Datuk, Pegawai dan Ahli Meshurat). The last signatories are Haji Ngah as the sultan's secretary, a deputy judge, and a few more minor officials.

bureaucratic hierarchy that was thus created existed in form rather than content, the change did represent a major step away from the principle of personal administration.

Such moves were aimed not only at preempting British pressures for rationalization but also at strengthening the hand of Trengganu's chief administrator, the yam tuan muda. This dual concern was also evident in the yam tuan muda's efforts to assume direct control of all territory in the state, canceling all appanage and what the British termed "feudal" rights. He intended to establish a network of out-stations under district officers subject to the central administration in Kuala Trengganu. But the state did not have the resources to control outlying regions in this fashion: there were no trained officials, not enough cash available for salaries, and virtually no roads outside the capital. Moreover, the chiefs who had previously maintained agents in the districts from which they drew their income were thus deprived of any interest in or responsibility for their territories, and so they tended to withdraw from local government. The existing system was destroyed, but the central administration could provide nothing to replace it, no links which could bring security to the districts and revenue to the center. Moreover, the wealthy territories of Besut and Kemaman, which remained under their established chiefs, became more rather than less independent of central control in the confusion which ensued.[36]

This predicament reflected a fundamental dilemma in modernizing a state of Trengganu's type. The old system had provided a low level of economic and political control to the central power, but it had also demanded very little from it in the way of expertise, funds, and infrastructure. A modern "bureaucratic-rational" polity would provide much greater yields—but where would the ruler get the resources necessary to bring this about? Few even among Trengganu's central elite would be willing to go far against custom, self-interest, and proud

36. The first reference in the Journals to the ending of appanage rights is by Dickson, 19 March 1913, CO273/399 Desp. 284, p. 300; "I hear the Yam Tuan Muda on behalf of the Government is taking over all the rivers from the feudal chiefs to whom compensation will be paid at a later date." Compensation was in fact not paid for years, and details of the problems resulting and the attitude of the yam tuan muda are given in Dickson's Journal, 10 June 1914, CO273/411 Desp. 370, p. 278. For the position of Besut and Kemaman, see the *Annual Report* for 1913, pp. 9ff.; 1915, pp. 1–10; 1919, p. 19.

independence to support a major effort at internal mobilization and self-discipline, and the more peripheral chiefs had a clear interest against strengthening central rule. Furthermore, the British agent, while a symbol of the immediate foreign menace, was also a focus of power to which the ruler's opponents could look, and he endeavored to ensure that efforts to improve central control did not stay the course of British penetration. The internal generation of resources was therefore most difficult. The British were the obvious and indeed only apparent outside source and they were happy to help—at a price. Thus the efforts undertaken to strengthen the state against foreign penetration by self-generated modernization were to become a principal means of achieving foreign control.

The yam tuan muda's first reaction to the critical shortage of resources attendant on his assumption of direct control of the districts was to tighten his grip on central government funds. Whereas before chiefs had always drawn on the treasury as they required, Mohamed decreed in June 1913 that all withdrawals required his signature. He also borrowed a copy of the Kelantan Estimates from the agent, with the intention of creating a formal Trengganu budget.[37] But already it was too late: salaries were months in arrears, the police were threatening mass resignation, and the agent was visited alternately by creditors seeking his aid in debt collection and by representatives of the Trengganu government soliciting a loan from the British.[38] In July 1914, after considerable negotiation, the Straits Settlements government granted Trengganu a loan, on the condition that most of it be used for fiscal reforms regarded as essential by the British. Singapore and the Colonial Office seem to have decided to be patient on the assumption that Trengganu's economic and administrative position would deteriorate to a point where further extension of British con-

37. Dickson, Journal, 27 June 1913, CO273/399 Desp. 353, p. 641.
38. See Dickson, Journal, August 1913 to February 1914, especially CO273/400 Desp. 467, p. 271; CO273/400 Desp. 577, p. 611; CO273/401 Desp. 628, p. 213; CO273/409 Desp. 53, p. 307; CO273/409 Desp. 76, p. 390; CO273/410 Desp. 147, p. 159. By February 1914 there was only $400 left in the Treasury. For the agent's appreciation of the political opportunities afforded by the situation, see especially Maxwell, Journal, entries for July 1914 to October 1915. At the Colonial Office an official minuted on 19 January 1914: "The Trengganu Government seems to be very short of cash and possibly there might be an opportunity here to advance a stage with the country" (CO273/401 Desp. 628, p. 213).

trol would provoke little opposition in either England or Malaya.
They could also hope that the crisis would bring the sultan to push
the yam tuan muda to one side, for the agents continued to believe
that Zainal Abidin was unhappy with his heir's policies and would
be more amenable to development along lines desired by the British.[39]

Relations between the British and the yam tuan muda became further
strained when a new agent, John Lissiter Humphreys, began to assert
a role beyond that originally acknowledged for his office. When
Mohamed attempted to snub the agent, Humphreys sent a special
report on the yam tuan muda's character and attitudes to Arthur
Young, the High Commissioner. The result, in September 1916, was
a personal invitation from Young to Mohamed, asking him to Singapore so that he could enjoy the benefit of the commissioner's "personal
advice." After this visit the yam tuan muda apologized to Humphreys
for delays in reform and began to consult him frequently.[40] Nonetheless, he persisted in his effort to preempt Singapore's intervention by
proving that his state could advance under its own steam, and during
1917 Trengganu witnessed a further burst of reform. Though Mohamed
re-let some of the revenue farms as their terms lapsed—much to Humphreys' annoyance—he replaced the opium farm with a government
monopoly and charged district officers with customs collection on

39. These British hopes seemed to move toward realization when in September
1915 the sultan traveled to Singapore to request both another loan and the
secondment of a Malayan Civil Service officer to his administration. The officer
was to be attached to the Trengganu Civil Service and would be president of the
State Council, in which capacity he would lead a reform program. This proposal
was eminently acceptable to His Majesty's Government; but since in fact the
officer was without effective power and all initiative lay with the yam tuan
muda and the tight circle of governing chiefs, it soon appeared that Trengganu
had gained financially without losing any real control and that victory in this
instance lay with the Malays. See Maxwell, Journal, January–September 1915;
HCO2577/1915; CO273/428 Confidential, p. 414; Annual Report, 1915, p. 11.

40. For Humphreys' redefinition of the agent's position, see his Journal, 15
November 1915, CO273/444 Desp. 7, p. 262; 10 May 1916, CO273/445 Desp.
186, p. 417; 9 July 1916, CO273/446 Desp. 275, p. 230. For his difficulties
with the yam tuan muda, see his Journal, March–May 1916, especially CO273/
445 Desp. 117, p. 196, and Desp. 186, p. 417. For the pressure brought to
bear on Mohamed, see the Journal, August–November 1916, CO273/446
Desp. 275, p. 230; Desp. 308, p. 344; Desp. 329, p. 398; and CO273/459 Desp.
11, p. 20.

some rivers. Opium and customs dues became the mainstay of Trengganu's revenue, and at last the more serious financial inhibitions upon institutional reform were removed.[41] It soon became evident, however, that this was not enough: leading members of the elite remained in opposition to changes which threatened their status or challenged their values, and no major restructuring was possible so long as they monopolized effective power. Recognizing this, the British prepared to move.

During 1918 the agent began to complain repeatedly of matters which had previously been ignored or tolerated, an indication that British forbearance was at an end. Hastening its curtailment was the fact that Trengganu had rich wolfram (tungsten) mines, important in munitions manufacture—and His Majesty's Government was fighting World War I. The mining interests through which the British sought to obtain the mineral had been finding Trengganu difficult to deal with, and it seemed imperative to take corrective action.[42] The

41. The *Annual Report,* 1918, p. 1, summarizes the development of Trengganu revenue as follows:

Source	1333AH (1914/15)	1334AH (1915/16)	1335AH (1916/17)	1336AH (1917/18)	+1336AH	-1336AH
Land	14,717	11,517	19,774	26,543	6,771	–
Courts	7,052	16,101	13,045	18,777	5,732	–
Farms	95,272	88,939	97,739	64,596	–	33,145
Mineral export	38,179	56,761	63,953	118,016	54,063	–
Customs and harbor	7,978	40,809	103,466	115,039	11,573	–
Opium sales	–	–	117,874	265,085	147,211	–
Postoffice	7,089	7,805	5,073	12,780	7,707	–
Other depts.	13,306	13,124	7,451	3,605	–	3,846
Misc.	130	1,742	1,820	2,392	572	–
Total	183,723	236,798	430,195	626,195	233,629	36,989

42. Since 1915 all wolfram had been purchased by His Majesty's Government direct from the able Chinese who mined it, but the latter had problems obtaining permission from the Trengganu government to expand his operations (see CO273/ 471 Desp. 57; CO717/459 Desp. 109; CO717/460 Desp. 134). During 1917 and

sultan, visiting Singapore in July 1918, was informed that the High
Commissioner had decided to appoint a Commission of Enquiry into
Trengganu to examine the administration of the rich mining district
of Kemaman, the rate of prison mortality, and the conduct of Trengganu's police and courts during their investigation of a particularly
unpleasant rape. Led by the Honorable Sir John Alexander Strachey
Bucknill, K.C., of Singapore, its members came to Kuala Trengganu in
September and heard evidence concerning the personal and arbitrary
administration of Che Drahman in Kemaman, the gray existence of
Trengganu prisoners, and the subservience of police and courts to
people of power. Their report, published before the end of the year,
predictably concluded that conditions could only improve if British
control were extended. Trengganu needed to be reduced to the same
obedience as the other Malay states, and that meant a new treaty.[43]

But the ruler with whom the British had to negotiate was no longer
the mild and scholarly Zainal Abidin. After a brief illness, the fifty-five-
year-old sultan had died in late November and, in accordance with
Trengganu custom, the yam tuan muda had been installed as sultan
before his father was buried. Mohamed and his chief advisers, Datuk
Amar (Haji Ngah) and Tungku Chik Ahmad, were in no way inclined
to submit meekly to the advice of Humphreys, who came to explain
the terms and implications of the commission's report.[44] In April 1919
Humphreys went again to Singapore and returned with another
"invitation" from Young. This was refused on the grounds of Mohamed's "indisposition"—a deliberate ambiguity. His Excellency wrote

1918 the important mining interests of Guthrie's were in conflict with the Trengganu government over their mine at Sungei Sendok, and the Colonial Office was
unhappy at the failure of the agent and high commissioner to support Guthrie's
effectively against the Sultan and his ministers (CO273/461 Desp. 298; CO273/
473 Desp. 282; and CO273/374 Desp. 348, p. 466).

43. Bucknill Commission, *Report*, passim; *Annual Report*, 1919, p. 35. To add
insult to injury the British government tried for two years to make Trengganu
pay for the costs of the commission—which Trengganu had never invited and
certainly did not welcome.

44. C. A. de C. de Moubray, "Trengganu under the British," p. 5; Rhodes
House (Oxford) Mss. Ind. Ocn. S 159 (2); Humphreys, Journal, January–May
1919, CO273/486 Desp. 46, p. 373, CO273/486 Desp. 81, p. 530; CO273/487
Desp. 122, p. 57, and also CO273/486 Telegram dated 26 March 1919, p. 666;
CO273/487 Confidential dated 4 June 1919, p. 272; interview, Datuk Chik
Embong b. Datuk Jaya, Kuala Trengganu, 3 May 1974.

from Singapore, expressing his surprise at this reply and requesting an immediate response. It was clear that there was no more room for maneuver; the sultan, Datuk Amar, and other leading chiefs sailed for Singapore. Once there, they tried yet again to escape the trap closing around them, by producing several alternative drafts of the treaty; all were rejected out of hand. Finally, on 24 May 1919, the new treaty was signed, and by its terms the British Agent was replaced by an Adviser whose opinion must be asked and acted upon in all matters "excepting those touching the Mohamedan religion." And so Trengganu, after nine years' evasion, was finally forced into the British fold.

The pride of the sultan and the irritation of the agent turned the last act of Trengganu absolutism into a farce. One of Humphreys' first actions in his new role as adviser was to slash the sultan's allowance, whereupon the latter, declaring he would shoot anyone who prevented his entering the Treasury, set off with his gun toward that building. On hearing of the sultan's response Humphreys, unarmed and half-dressed, hurried to the Treasury and physically blocked the door. Eventually, during what was reported to be an extremely heated argument, Mohamed stated that he could not accept the constraints laid upon him by the new treaty; either he was to be given special liberty and higher status than other Malay rulers or he would take the unprecedented step of abdication. After considerable confusion, he was replaced by his younger brother, Suleiman, who was installed in 1920 with very subdued ceremonial.[45]

Suleiman was to rule until 1942. A self-effacing man, he had little inclination to lead resistance to the British or to impose his authority

45. For Humphreys' attack on the Sultan's purse, see *Annual Report*, 1920, p. 2; and interview, Datuk Chik Embong, Kuala Trengganu, 5 May 1974. The circumstances of Mohamed's resignation are based on interviews, Kuala Trengganu, May 1974. For Suleiman's installation, see *Annual Report*, 1920, p. 11; HCO129/1921 SUK Trengganu 524/AH1338 (1919–1920). Interview sources suggest the palace was in turmoil; Suleiman refused to succeed and fled south to Kuala Ibar. Mohamed meanwhile tried to withdraw his resignation but was refused by the British. Finally Datuk Amar and Datuk Nara Wangsa persuaded Suleiman to return to the capital and become sultan. Mohamed was offered financial inducements to leave the state and to take up residence in Singapore, where he remained until the Japanese occupation. Official documents ascribe Mohamed's abdication to "ill-health." Colonial Office accounts suggest that Mohamed, in his rejection of the British, had adopted an extreme version of the traditional Malay raja style; CO537/797.

on the local elite, so that from this point the formal ruler ceased to be an active leader of Trengganu politics. It fell to the chiefs, and particularly to Datuk Amar, on whom Suleiman relied heavily, to lead Trengganu's remaining efforts to contain British influence.

Though the key members of the governing elite on whom power now devolved had grown up with the values of the nineteenth-century Malayo-Muslim world, they recognized the futility of pressing Trengganu's claims to complete sovereignty and were prepared to compromise. Moreover, they had worked personally with Humphreys for over four years, and their relationship with him had been a key source of stability during Mohamed's reign and in the confusion surrounding his abdication. Humphreys himself was a man who favored a genuine partnership between Malays and British, and his career as agent had given him a sound knowledge of local affairs; Datuk Amar was a personal friend of his. These individual qualities aside, there were certain benefits Trengganu's established elite could derive from a situation which, although fundamentally undesirable, seemed unavoidable. The crucial fact was that the old elite completely controlled the embryonic bureaucracy. The British imposition of a more rigid governmental framework limited that elite's freedom, but it offered security to those who were already at the apex of political life, for their positions were no longer held at the sultan's will. New departments and offices continued to be regarded as elite perquisites, and so the central members of Trengganu's establishment, while they were by no means pro-British, bent with the imperial wind.

But there were also leaders who were outside the circle of those who dealt directly with the adviser, people who had had access to power, prestige, or wealth in the more open Trengganu society before 1919 but who now saw centralization and the stabilization of office leaving them without prospects. Such people were less likely to compromise; their distance from the center of power made them less appreciative of British strength, they lost much and gained little from the new regime, and they had religious and cultural reasons to hate the aliens. Those most affected were the more peripheral members of the extended royal family who lost aristocratic privilege and license, the more aware or uncompromising religious leaders who gained no place in the developing Islamic establishment, and the chiefs of the more distant and autonomous territories. Gradually, they were to become the focus of a new resistance.

In the new dispensation, the primary concern of the British adviser was to improve administration, to create a climate in which investment could flourish, revenues increase, and progress take place. But in order to achieve this, many of the old ways had to go. The established value system rested heavily upon two mutually supporting convictions— the centrality of religion and the unquestionable supremacy of elite interests—and these now came under attack.

British pressure was wholly negative in its effects on Islam. This was not part of a conscious campaign to weaken the faith but rather an inevitable side effect of efforts at rationalization and of the modern Western tendency to relegate religion to limited areas of personal belief and social ethics. Since Islam was traditionally the basis and animating principle of law and education in Trengganu, the introduction of British forms of jurisdiction and secular education inevitably weakened indigenous Islamic institutions.

Before 1920 nonreligious education in Trengganu had been very limited. Apart from Ungku Bakar's school there were only two other secular schools in the state, at Banggol (Kuala Trengganu) and Kemasik, both of which seem to have opened around the time of World War I. In 1920, however, an education department was created under the supervision of a committee headed by Ungku Bakar. During the next year two new schools were opened, and four more followed in 1922. Most teachers were Malays from other states (notably Johor, but also Pahang), the Straits Settlements, and elsewhere. In spite of Ungku Bakar's leadership, Malay staffing, and the interest of members of the ruling elite in modern schooling, this extension of secular education was a far from neutral matter. It was widely believed that Western-style schools encouraged Christianity, or at best introduced dangerous and unnecessary ways of thought. There was widespread opposition from Malay parents, especially in the villages, which only began to weaken during the late 1920s.

European observers generally ascribed this hostility to local ignorance

and fanaticism, for the very breadth of the point at issue—the maintenance of religious and cultural values—helped to prevent its easy
identification. Much the same blindness to implications was evident in
the British reform of the law. In 1921, after months of insistent re-
minders, Humphreys forced the Trengganu government to pass a New
Courts Enactment creating a formal hierarchy of courts with specific
powers similar to those in other Malay states under British protection.
No doubt the adviser felt he had carefully considered Muslim sensi-
bilities in his reorganization, but the establishment of *kathi* (religious
judge) courts separate from those trying general civil and criminal cases
sharply limited the role of Islamic law. Moreover, the very act of drawing rigid lines according to bureaucratic criteria seemed to go against
the divine origin and holistic spirit of the Shari'a. Finally, though the
courts continued to apply Islamic law, they did so only when they were
not overridden by new, more specific enactments. It became clear to
Trengganu's Muslims that not only had law become subject to the will
of man but it was also subject to revision by a government under strong
infidel influence.

The adviser's immediate aim was to create an effective central
administration. This meant the appointment of British officers to key
departments, but since the abrupt displacement of Malay officials was
unacceptable a rather uneasy period of dual control began. Four
departments—public works, police, lands, and post office—were regarded as particularly important by Humphreys, as their efficient
functioning was prerequisite for economic development and increased
revenue. The council and sultan attempted as best they could to stem
the tide, stressing that Europeans should serve "as long as it is considered desirable or until a suitable native officer can be appointed to
the post."

The British, acquiescing with reluctance, comforted themselves that
"after all, this is the thin end of the wedge," for "once you get the
right man in the saddle it will not be easy for them to dislodge him."[46]
In 1920 the first three Europeans were appointed, two of whom—in

46. Comment of Sherwood, secretary to the High Commissioner, HCO130/
1921. See also *Annual Report*, 1920, p. 5; Chan Su-ming, "Kelantan and
Trengganu 1909-1939," *JMBRAS* 38, no. 1 (July 1965): 159-198; and M. C.
Sheppard, "A Short History of Trengganu," *JMBRAS* 22, no. 3 (June 1949):
1-74.

police and public works—functioned alongside Malay departmental heads. Indeed, within a few years headship of the four key departments had passed entirely out of Malay hands; they remained under non-Malay control until the Japanese occupation, as did such specialized services as the medical, legal, survey, and forestry offices, which were created in the late 1920s and 1930s.

These changes bit deeply into the power of Trengganu's ruling elite; nevertheless, as we have seen, there were personal and general reasons why its leading members tended to acquiesce. There were broader effects, however, which encouraged a differentiation of the elite between those who could accept the new dispensation and those who could not. The increased institutionalization attendant on the intensification of British influence made for a division between a central establishment of chiefs with formal power bases in government offices and a wider aristocratic-religious elite. The central establishment was a direct continuation of the old inner circle, but whereas previously all high status derived from ties with the ruler, which *might* result in government office, bureaucratic identification now played an increasingly direct role. This became more important as the adviser regularized state finances, which involved both higher salaries for government employees and a major reduction in the loose money available for the support of peripheral ruling house members. More specifically, British determination to abolish the royal concessions and centralize revenues cut right across the elite's view that the whole state was the patrimony of its ruling house, and it directly hurt the pockets of a number of tungkus.

Since the reforms initiated in 1917, Trengganu's revenues had increased rapidly, but the usual main source of funds for a predominantly agricultural state, land, remained relatively insignificant. For this the British blamed staff inefficiency, poor communications, and the locking up of large areas in royal concessions. Humphreys himself was determined to break the concessions, which covered three-quarters of the state's known mining land and were concentrated in the proven ore-rich area of Kemaman. But in order to do this it would be necessary to buy off concerned members of the Trengganu elite whose hostility it would be unwise to incur—that is, the sultan and his relatives—and it was obvious that this would be a very expensive business. So in 1923 a loan was arranged, Trengganu borrowing a million dollars from

Singapore to be used for public works, the resumption of concessions, land surveys, and town improvements. During the same year eight of the twelve royal concessions were repurchased against cash payments and annuities; this took a considerable slice of the loan, but Humphreys was pleased, for he expected to see a steady growth in land revenues.[47]

The question of land revenues was not a simple one for, as we have seen in connection with the yam tuan muda's efforts, the right to exploit the land was, under the old regime, accompanied by a general responsibility for maintaining some sort of order; both income and duties were personally received and personally delegated, and any attempt at changing one aspect of the system brought the others into jeopardy. The British attitude was entirely different, for they distinguished sharply between government and landownership, between a professional salaried administration and individual property rights. Land, to them, was to be the basis for economic development; private capital was to exploit commercial agriculture and mining, while a sturdy peasantry should have clear title to the soil it tilled. The state would provide both entrepreneurs and peasants with stability and the essential infrastructure, while they in turn would contribute land rent, customs dues, and assorted license fees to the Treasury. Having the funds, the force, and the expertise to impose such a vision, they proceeded to do so, moving both to establish a European landownership system and to reorganize completely the administration of the districts.

In thus reshaping Trengganu, the British were aided by the fact that most of the important regional centers were now under control. The central plain had always been supervised fairly closely by Kuala Trengganu, while in Besut the traditional chief, Tungku Long bin Tungku Ngah (Tungku Seri Indera Segara) had been acknowledged as district officer in 1912 and served to the satisfaction of both Malays and British until his death in 1934. Che Drahman had been forced out of Kemaman in the wake of the Bucknill investigation and 1919 treaty revision; his territory was taken over by Datuk Jaya Perkasa, an unusually able official from Kampung Kling. In 1924 Kemaman and the southern districts were united into a single division under Datuk

47. *Annual Report,* 1923, p. 12; 1924, p. 13; 1926, pp. 7–8, 14. For Humphreys' earlier efforts to increase land revenue, see the *Annual Report,* passim, but particularly that for 1918, pp. 9–10. The Estimates are to be found in CO717/30.

Jaya and a European assistant adviser, and here, too, there was little
cause for political concern. The problem area was Ulu Trengganu, the
upper reaches of the Trengganu river, the most isolated and least
organized region in the state.

Partly because of its isolation, the British had very little information
on Ulu Trengganu; the advisers complained in their annual reports
that there was no machinery for government there, no link connecting
the state and the people. It is true that above the rapids of the Trengganu River the capital's uncertain control decreased dramatically. The
elite of the central plain held the Ulu to be theirs because it was drained
by the river whose lower course they dominated and because no other
power was able to contest it. But this was little reason for the population of the high valley of the interior to endorse their authority. Many
of them were immigrants from other states, and they had little use for
claimants who could impose their will only fitfully. Nonetheless, there
was a form of central influence in the Ulu Trengganu, and one reason
the British were unable to discern it was their tendency to ignore the
temporal role of the al-Idrus, the religious line of Trengganu's leading
families. They had generally overlooked the syeds, for they could not
categorize them easily as "chiefs" or "officials," the two groupings
they found proper to the Trengganu elite. The other religiously
specialized lineage, the Duyung, did not pose this problem, for their
role was linked to officialdom. The al-Idrus' titles did not reflect
bureaucratic function but only acknowledged preexisting status, and
one of the results of the general British effort to make status follow
official position had been to cut out that clan. The colonial authorities
were relatively successful in incorporating the royal, Kampung Kling,
and Duyung lines into a bureaucratic hierarchy, but the syeds found
themselves relegated to the periphery of the formal system.

This neglect was a mistake, for the al-Idrus had been powerful, and
they continued to have great influence, on occasion defying both
the British agents and, subtly, the sultan himself when these suggested
courses that threatened their interests.[48] Nor was Islamic leadership
a factor to be lightly ignored when trying to ensure popular docility.
Finally, the authority of the al-Idrus, though seemingly limited to

48. See e.g. Scott, Journal, July and August 1911, CO273/375 Desp. 423,
p. 151, and Desp. 435, p. 225; Maxwell, Journal, January and February 1915,
CO273/425 Desp. 100, p. 383, and CO273/425 Desp. 131, p. 522.

religious affairs, had in fact extended more widely. The distinction
between "secular" and "religious" was foreign to Islam, and the
boundaries of competence were never clearcut in a traditional Malay
state; and one of the areas over which the al-Idrus exercised authority
appears to have been Ulu Trengganu.

In 1909, we know, the upper reaches of the Trengganu River were
held by Tuan Embong of the al-Idrus, with the exception of the Telemong territory, which was allocated to Tungku Ngah Omar bin Tungku
Abdul Rahim, who later served as Minister of Religion and Justice and
had close ties to the al-Idrus. As of 1923 there existed an authority
known as the *ketua mukim*, who supervised the work of all the penghu-
lus in the Trengganu river area; he was Zain bin Abdul Rahman (Engku Syed Sheikhu'l Sa'adah), whose title suggests he was head of
the al-Idrus clan and recognized leader of Trengganu's community
of syeds. Significantly, the ketua mukim was based not in the capital
but at Iliran in the Cabang Tiga area, the central settlement of Trengganu Arabs and the long-established home of the al-Idrus. Since by
this time various experiments in extending government control to the
Ulu Trengganu had failed and both magistrate's and penghulu's courts
had been disbanded, it seems highly probable that the Ulu was then in
effect governed by syeds, whose authority was strengthened by—and
quite possibly based directly on—their al-Idrus descent and religious
prestige. The British, however, appear to have ignored the role of the
ketua mukim and of the al-Idrus generally when, in 1923, they formed
a new district of Ulu Trengganu with its capital at Kuala Brang.[49]

This reorganization brought with it the extension to Ulu Trengganu
of the roads, police, district officers, schools, land regulations, permits,
and passes that were being brought from Kuala Trengganu into the
rural areas as part of the British-sponsored reforms. But while to the
Europeans they represented progress, to many Malays they meant new
financial burdens, nagging interference, and a threat to their religion.
In other regions, coopted members of the traditional elite could

49. *Annual Report*, 1921, p. 6; Mohamed b. Endut, "1928—Penderhakaan di
Trengganu," academic exercise, Universiti Malaya, History Department, 1970,
pp. 37–38. For comments on headmen in Ulu Trengganu, see Clifford, "Report,"
pp. 68–70. For indications of the role of the al-Idrus, see Conlay, Journal, 19
August 1909, CO273/351 Desp. 303, pp. 216–218. The ketua mukim is mentioned in *Annual Report*, 1923, p. 15.

mediate acceptance of these changes, but in Ulu Trengganu, with leadership absent, or unrecognized and hostile, there was no such mitigating force. Moreover, the government had imposed a new land regulation in 1921 which, when applied in Ulu Trengganu, hit its poverty-stricken peasantry particularly hard. In the interest of checking the "indiscriminate" clearing of forest land to plant hill rice, the authorities insisted on permits for the temporary occupation of land. Inasmuch as the Ulu Trengganu farmers depended on hill rice for their subsistence, any curtailment of planting was a heavy burden on their very slender resources. By July 1922 the British became aware that there was widespread refusal by people of the Telemong river area to take out permits, and they concluded that this refusal was being encouraged by a religious teacher, Haji Drahman Limbong (Haji Abdul Rahman bin Abdul Hamid).

Haji Drahman was a native of Kuala Trengganu and had studied Islamic law and mysticism from, among others, the To' 'Ku Paloh, Syed Abdul Rahman al-Idrus. He was this great teacher's favorite pupil and was widely regarded as heir to his religious learning and charisma. Like many pious Muslims he was also a trader, traveling regularly to Kelantan, Pahang, Kedah, Patani, Siam, Sarawak, Sambas, Brunei, and Riau. He was revered throughout Trengganu, but the main center of his authority—which embraced secular as well as religious affairs, for neither he nor other Malays made such distinctions—was Ulu Trengganu, and particularly the Telemong river area.[50]

Humphreys described Haji Drahman as preaching "a Tolstoyan doctrine of prayer and agriculture, the leading tenets of which are that the land belongs to the people, that Government claims are contrary to Mohammedan law, and that Government itself is a superfluous vanity."[51] Elsewhere, he was referred to as "an extremely good man

50. Mohamed b. Endut, "1928," pp. 29–33, gives a biography of Haji Drahman based on interviews in Trengganu.

51. Humphreys, "Report on Certain Matters Connected with One Haji Drahman of Trengganu," dated 24 November 1922, CO717/61, p. 12. On p. 19 of this report he wrote, "Haji Drahman is a small, dark, ascetic-looking Malay of about 60 years. He has a great reputation for sanctity and good works, and great influence—secular as well as religious—among the people of the middle of the Trengganu river. Unlike most Trengganu 'Saints' he is extremely charitable and does not use his influence for his personal profit; he devotes himself to religious teaching, agriculture, and devotional exercises." Humphreys also gives (p. 7) examples of current stories concerning Haji Drahman's supernatural powers.

of the Gandhi type," a protector of the people against the exactions of the palace.[52] Datuk Amar complained that he was always setting up religious sanctions against the government, opposing the collection of rents, vaccination, and so on, and asking of every step its justification in Shari'a law. To many of the men who followed him or listened to hearsay accounts of his teaching, Haji Drahman's message was a call to action: government regulations were *peraturan kafir*—infidel rules— and anyone who took out a government permit followed the religion of the kafir. Government servants were *orang neraka,* people of hell, and those who obeyed the government were infamous in the eyes of all true Muslims.

The offense of clearing land without a permit was punishable by fines of up to one hundred dollars (astronomical to a peasant), and the land office, standing by its regulations, summoned three Telemong Malays for trial. Haji Drahman, as an expert in Islamic law, took out a license as pleader and assumed the defense of the accused. This caused great excitement in both the Ulu and the capital, and Humphreys observed that it was clearly seen as "a test cast of some importance." During the trial Haji Drahman overwhelmed the magistrate—one of his own ex-pupils—with quotations from the Koran, showing that the earth belonged to God and not the state; and finally the judge dismissed the case for lack of evidence. The land office immediately appealed, and the agitation in Trengganu grew; when the appeal was heard, Haji Drahman again conquered the magistrate, who postponed his decision and thus left all glory with the haji.

By this time a very large crowd "of uncertain temper" was following the case closely, and the atmosphere of religious excitation was felt by the authorities to be quite dangerous; Haji Drahman spent his time out of court in religious teaching and exercises, attended by hundreds of followers; he also enjoyed the support of Tungku Ngah Omar, Minister of Religion and Justice, whose appanage rights over the Telemong the British had thus far ignored.[53] The Haji refused to attend a

---

52. C. A. de C. de Moubray, Commissioner of Lands, evidence given before the enquiry of H. W. Thompson, Resident of Perak, into the rebellion of 1928; in "Enquiry into Recent Affairs in Trengganu," CO717/61, p. 62.

53. Thus, during the trial described above, Haji Drahman lived in the compound of Tungku Ngah Omar (Humphreys, "Report," pp. 4 and 9). Humphreys' comments that Tg. Ngah Omar "claims to possess hereditary rights over the Telemong

police enquiry into his influence over men found to be armed in the courtroom, precipitating a confrontation between himself and Police Commissioner E. Cheers in which Haji Drahman, threatened with arrest, "commenced the sword dancing and fencing attitudes rehearsed overnight and defied Mr. Cheers to lay hands on him: in a few moments he was posturing and shouting in the state of fanatical excitement known as *majzup*—the religious frenzy of the fighting Mohammedan inviting martyrdom."[54] When Cheers stepped forward anyway to arrest the haji, he was seized by his own policemen and forced away, as they felt he would be killed there and then if he insisted. Humphreys decided something must be done, but indirectly, using the cooperative leaders of the established elite. He persuaded Tuan Embong, the Sheikh-ul-Islam of the Religious Affairs Department, to call Haji Drahman before the State Council. There he was gradually calmed down by Datuk Amar and Tuan Embong. Humphreys used his best diplomacy to set aside the confrontation with the police and, in an effort to avoid further clashes, employed the council and Tuan Embong to persuade Haji Drahman to accept cancellation of his pleader's license.

The trouble seemed at first to be over. The British had ensured the backing of the central figures in the elite and subsequently—perhaps following the compensation paid to appanage holders in 1924—they succeeded in detaching Tungku Ngah Omar from Haji Drahman's cause. But the underlying religious and economic resentments had not been removed, and in 1925 another constellation of events precipitated a crisis, again centered on the Telemong area. Humphreys was about to leave Trengganu, and his replacement, an untried man named Simmons, was already in charge. The land office had recently alienated to some Chinese land on the Telemong claimed by Tungku Nik, sister of ex-Sultan Mohamed, thus exciting both traditional loyalties and ethnic-religious animosities. On 3 May, the night before

---

and consistently opposes Government control of the river" (p. 19). For Datuk Amar's comments on Haji Drahman, see his evidence before the Thompson "Enquiry," pp. 3–5; and further, evidence of Datuk Jaya, "Enquiry," pp. 99–101; evidence of Wan Mahmud b. Wan Muhammed, "Enquiry," pp. 53–55; H. W. Thompson, "Report on the Recent Disturbances in Trengganu," CO717/61, part II.

54. Humphreys, "Report," p. 10.

Humphreys departed, several hundred Malays assembled at Kuala Telemong, summoned by letters said to have been sent by Tungku Nik and using the name of Haji Drahman to ensure obedience. They had been called up ostensibly for corvée labor (*kerah*), clearing the land in furtherance of Tengku Nik's claim. Though the gathering was eventually dispersed peaceably there are indications that more had been intended.

One man reported that some of the assembled believed they had been called in order to march on Kuala Trengganu "to fight a Holy War against the State Council and the British Authority." There were also suggestions that the ultimate aim was to drive out the British "and restore ex-Sultan Mohamed who is a brother of Tungku Nik and install Haji Drahman as Chief Minister."[55] Prevalent rumors of the coming of the Mahdi (the Muslim messiah), the restoration of the former sultan, and a war against kafir rule testify to the uneasiness in Ulu Trengganu. In the year of his arrival, Simmons visited the well-known Telemong religious recluse To' Janggut (Khatib Abdul Rahman), who spat upon him and forecast the end of Christianity. He asked Simmons if he knew how long it would be before the Mahdi's coming; the adviser confessed his ignorance, and To' Janggut told him it would be only two years. Simmons retired, discomfited, and concluded his report on the incident with the note that the religious leader had "strange wild eyes; might easily be dangerous."

It is interesting to note that protest against the British encroachment does not seem to have been limited at this stage to generalized peasant resentment and the personal stance of popular religious leaders. Rather, there appears to have existed about this time a secret movement known as the Sharikat-ul-Islam.[56] A list was later found of Sharikat members dating from 1925, some eight hundred people from villages scattered

55. "Statement of Evidence of Penghulu Adam of Kuala Telemong," appended to J. W. Simmons; "Report on Further Activities of Haji Abdulrachman of Bladau," 10 July 1925, CO717/61; and the statement of Che Man Pendekar, appended to the same report.

56. Simmons, report of 23 August 1925, CO717/61, p. 108. On the Sarekat Islam in Indonesia see Deliar Noer, *The Modernist Muslim Movement in Indonesia, 1900–1942* (Kuala Lumpur: Oxford University Press, 1973), pp. 101–152. For rural peasant movements with parallels to the Trengganu disturbance, see Sartono Kartodirdjo, *Protest Movements in Rural Java* (Singapore: Oxford University Press, 1973), especially pp. 38–45.

the length of the Trengganu river. Since the Sharikat was said to extend along the coast in Pahang from Beserah to Kemaman, in addition to its strength in Trengganu, it seems to have been quite widespread. The British tended to assume it had connections with the Indonesian Sarekat Islam, which may have been the case. According to Datuk Amar, the Sharikat was first brought to Trengganu by a Syed Abdulrahman of Balok, and then a Syed Mohamed of Johor came seeking members; after being rebuffed by the menteri besar, the syed went to the house of Haji Drahman. Though we know very little about its activities, the Sharikat seems to have played a key role in the uprising of 1928. It is the first indication of some more or less politically oriented organization in Trengganu which seems to have had an anti-establishment as well as anti-British cast.[57]

As administrative pressures increased and British influence on the central establishment became more obvious, the popular sense of betrayal and anger increased particularly among the Ulu people. Islam was the focus and framework for their anger, and they found expression through their religious leaders, not only Haji Drahman but also Syed Saggaf bin Syed Abdul Rahman al-Idrus and Haji Musa Minangkabau. Syed Saggaf was a son of To' 'Ku Paloh and so vested with tremendous prestige, especially in Ulu Trengganu. Like his father, he was regarded as *keramat* and many people brought offerings to his home in Cabang Tiga. He seems to have been less saintly in fact than Haji Drahman, for he was said to have made a fortune trading on his reputation, selling talismans; he was also a moneylender of substance. Haji Musa Minangkabau (probably Haji Musa bin Abdul Rahim of Kampung Duyung) was the most political of the three leaders, and it may be that some of the more extreme antigovernment statements attributed to Haji Drahman originated in fact with him, for as a trader from the very radical and devout Minangkabau region of West Sumatra he was probably in touch with the Islamic anticolonial movement in the Dutch East Indies. He traveled regularly to the Ulu and was highly regarded in the upriver settlements.[58]

57. S. Caine, minute dated 20 August 1928, CO717/61, p. 68.
58. For Syed Saggaf's background and role, see Mohamed b. Endut, "1928," pp. 28, 31–34; Datuk Jaya, evidence in "Enquiry," pp. 99–101. Details of Syed Saggaf's finances are to be found in SUK Trengganu 1261/AH1347 (1928/1929). For Haji Musa Minangkabau, see Mohamed b. Endut, "1928," pp. 33–35; Haji

Undeterred by signs of resentment, the British moved apace to extend the legislation controlling land use. The introduction of the 1926 Land Enactment into Ulu Trengganu brought extra burdens to the upriver people: they had to buy permits for clearing land; they could no longer freely gather firewood, leaves to wrap sweetmeats, or palm for thatching; their buffalos could not graze at will; and they could not grow rice where they chose. For some local Malay officials, the regulations afforded scope for extortion and petty tyranny, thus exacerbating the strains between rulers and ruled. The final straw came in December 1926 when the still-remembered Bah Besar (Great Flood) devastated villages and destroyed crops and livestock. The classic causes of peasant disorder were all there: poverty and sharp economic blows, alienation from government, religious unrest, and charismatic leaders who gave voice to popular grievances.

During 1927 there was uneasy calm in Trengganu, but in early 1928 there were again signs of trouble. The Ulu peasants were refusing to take out permits; there were rumors of impending Holy War and small incidents began to assume disproportional importance.[59] By April the mood was so threatening that rumors of *jihad* were taken seriously by Malay as well as British officials, and at the beginning of May it was felt necessary to take unprecedented steps. The sultan himself, accompanied by Datuk Amar and other high-ranking Malays, went upriver to Kuala Brang to address the people. Over three thousand gathered to hear him promise pardons to those who had broken the pass law and to join in a great feast. This, together with the deferment of payment

---

Musa b. Abdul Rahman, evidence in "Enquiry," p. 95. On the role of Minang-kabau in Indonesian Islamic anticolonialism, see Noer, *Modernist Muslim Movement,* pp. 31–55.

59. A British ship arrived in Trengganu; the Sultan was too ill to repay the captain's courtesy call and deputized the Sheikh-ul-Islam instead. Arriving on the quarterdeck, the sheikh spat, an act which was viewed with great concern by the British officers. In February, the Malay staff of the Survey Office assaulted its European head; no reason is given in the reports, but it was regarded as a religious matter. When the collector of land revenue made a trip to Kuala Brang and the neighboring Tersat tributary of the Trengganu to enquire into the conflict over permits, he felt very unwelcome, "an absolute outsider," H. P. Bryson, evidence in "Enquiry," pp. 49–51; see also the evidence of Mills (p. 16) and Millington (p. 14).

for permits, was hoped to defuse the situation, but two weeks later upriver Malays gathered at Kuala Brang to raise the Bendera Stambul, the red flag of war, and to march on Kuala Trengganu. The crowd occupied the police station at Kuala Brang and then began to advance downriver. On 21 May the procession encountered a relief police party coming up from the capital under the command of Datuk Seri Lela di-Raja (the Che Drahman of Kemaman, now safely on the government side) and the state treasurer, Tungku Nara. The crowd was led by To' Janggut, who advanced under a yellow umbrella, traditional sign of a ruler; they bore the Bendera Stambul and were chanting prayers. Many believed themselves to be invulnerable, having gained esoteric knowledge from Syed Saggaf. The police called out that they were all brother Muslims, under a Muslim ruler, but the crowd kept advancing. The police opened fire, and eleven men were killed, including To' Janggut.[60]

The 1928 "disturbance" was the culmination of tension which had accumulated over six or seven years; it was the only such outburst in Trengganu. It seems clear that its main aim was to alleviate the pressures on the Ulu peasantry and to restore Trengganu by removing the kafir advisers and, possibly, the sultan himself. Letters were found which called men together from all over the state; some of these, purporting to be from Haji Drahman and Syed Saggaf, were addressed to members of the Sharikat-ul-Islam, instructing them to gather at Kuala Brang, while syeds and hajis were to meet at the shrine of Pulau Manis. One suggested the replacement of kafir government in the state by the tripartite rule of Raja (ex-Sultan Mohamed), Syed (Syed Saggaf), and Fakih (Islamic legal experts; Haji Drahman).[61]

Suggestions that the former sultan had morally or financially backed the revolt had no hard evidence to support them, though it was noted that Haji Drahman had been a friend of Mohamed's, and some participants claimed to have been given arms by the ex-sultan's men. Since

60. Dato Seri Lela di-Raja, "The Ulu Trengganu Disturbances of May 1928" (tr. Datuk Haji Mubin Sheppard), *Malaysia in History* 12, no. 1 (October 1968): 21–26. For detailed accounts, see Thompson, "Report" and "Enquiry." On the significance of the Bendera Stambul, see note 14 above.

61. Haji Musa b. Abdul Rahim, evidence in "Enquiry," p. 95; Datuk Jaya, evidence in "Enquiry," pp. 101–104; De Moubray, "Trengganu under the British," p. 10. A *fakih* is an expert on Islamic law.

everyone pleaded ignorance and little could be proved, it was decided to imprison a few people and to lay the general guilt at the door of Haji Drahman. It is questionable whether he had in fact played a role. He had been in Patani at the time of the affair; returning to Trengganu he had made no effort to avoid capture, but rather came to the palace and expressed great concern over the events. He was, however, too powerful, and his uncompromising criticism made him a dangerous nuisance; and so he was banished from the state and sent to Mecca.[62]

The British concluded from the 1928 affair that the fault lay with the slow pace of colonial assertion, which had allowed the sultan and the "palace group" to get out of hand. They tended, in other words, still to see themselves as defending the interests of progress and the population against the exactions of a tyrannical and backward local elite. The Colonial Office therefore decided that the adviser's behavior must be less conciliatory in future, and the rationalization of land administration must be speeded up. A Land Court was created, European collectors of land revenue were appointed, and the pace of survey work in the Ulu was increased. In order to improve the atmosphere in Kuala Brang the existing Trengganu Malay district officer was replaced by a Perak man, an outsider evidently being regarded as more neutral than one of Trengganu's own elite.[63]

The British, however, did not achieve much by way of reform, either in this or in subsequent attempts to modernize Trengganu's governance.[64] For in their own way they had become as much entangled

62. High Commissioner, Hayes Marriot, to Amery, Colonial Office, 20 September 1928, CO717/61, p. 64; Millington, evidence in "Enquiry," pp. 10–11. Dato Seri Lela di-Raja, "The Ulu Trengganu Disturbances," p. 26, records Haji Drahman's death in Mecca, 16 November 1929.

63. For an example of the British view, see High Commissioner to Passfield, 24 July 1929, CO717/68.

64. During the Depression the Advisers concentrated on economizing and had little energy to spare for political maneuverings, but after 1934 a renewed drive began to restructure Trengganu into a less Islamic, more "British Malay" state. The crucial events in this process were the financial and legal reforms of 1934, the reorganization of the civil service—including efforts to diminish some palace and religious posts—and an attempt to redefine the competence of the religious

with the Trengganu system as Trengganu's elite was with theirs. The modus vivendi that had been forged between Humphreys and the central elite, enabling a smooth transfer of power during the crises of 1919 and 1920, had established a pattern which subsequent advisers found almost impossible to break. In other regions the extension of colonial influence had disrupted the established order, providing an opportunity for social mobility and flexibility; in Trengganu the central elite had succeeded in maintaining its dominant position. As long as Datuk Amar and what the British termed the "old gang" of chiefs remained in office—and Datuk Amar did not die until 1940—no real change took place. To replace the incumbents would have gone against the principles of diplomacy and stability worked out earlier, and there was no compelling reason to do so, for the pace of economic development and social change on Malaya's East Coast between the World Wars remained slow, and neither internal nor external pressures warranted a major restructuring. The British therefore continued to endorse the elite whose social relevance their presence undermined.

Nonetheless, the Trengganu elite could not rest easy, for the 1928 affair had made all too clear how much its position had been compromised in popular eyes. The crowd had expressed hostility to the sultan and the government as a whole, and special animus had been shown to the state council and Datuk Amar. Perhaps influenced by British prompting, Sultan Suleiman concluded that he must strengthen the bonds between ruler and people. The High Commissioner observed His Highness' new interest and activity with satisfaction, regarding it as the happiest result of the incident. But we should note that Suleiman's efforts to regain popular affection were based less on the actions expected of a traditional Malay ruler than on an English model: the first of Suleiman's annual tours of the outer districts, in 1929, was patterned after a British royal tour, complete with triumphal arches and speeches. He began to play the part of a constitutional monarch, his major functions ceremonial and socially pacifying.[65] Thus, even

---

affairs department in 1936-1937. No clear victor emerged from the conflicts surrounding these measures, which were strongly opposed by powerful older-generation Malay leaders.

65. *Annual Report*, 1927/1929, pp. 13-14. High Commissioner to Lord Passfield of the Colonial Office, 24 July 1929, CO717/68, records the High Commissioner's satisfaction with the Sultan's new attitudes.

the ritual behavior of Trengganu's leaders became suffused with elements from an alien model.

The main figures in Trengganu's attempt to stave off colonial dominion had made their efforts and suffered defeat in ways which had their counterparts elsewhere in Southeast Asia. The gentle Zainal Abidin's retreat into spiritual affairs—varied, in his last years, by a young new wife—presented no threat to the British, who supported nonpolitical diversions for a coopted traditional elite. The Yam Tuan Muda Mohamed would not retreat, but he found that his effort to strengthen central control against the British provided the very means for colonial entry. As with leaders elsewhere who sought to reinforce their position by adopting European institutions, he ensured the victory of the institutions but not of himself. His final protest was furious but solitary: he no longer had the confidence or probably the leverage to call on his people in the role of their chief. The last person to appear, if inadvertently, as head of a following was the saintly Haji Drahman, whose charisma sprang largely from his religious quality. This too followed a more widespread pattern, for religion was something which most colonial authorities in Southeast Asia found difficult to accommodate, and it was the thing which provided the first focus for a popular sense of common cause after the collapse of traditional rule.

Though during the Ulu disturbances there were calls for Mohamed's reinstatement, neither he nor any other central official gave the movement discernible support. Certain notables appear to have hoped the protest would result in their advantage, but they were too impressed by British power, too comforted by colonial security and preference, and too unsure of their hold on their old followings to respond openly to invitations for revolt. They continued instead to endorse the new order, which they served first as legitimation, later as embellishment, and finally as an impatiently tolerated anomaly.

The epitome of this adjustment was Datuk Amar, once the innovative and vigorous *alim* Haji Ngah. His *Realpolitik* ensured his own survival and a minimum disruption of Trengganu's social order, but the victory was truly hollow. He held the reins of state while Zainal Abidin's grasp loosened; he deflected Mohamed's impotent wrath; and he assumed the leadership which the ineffectual Suleiman could not command. He had lost the confidence of the Ulu peasants but was still able to help neutralize their charismatic focus. Whereas in some states the

British takeover provided a shock which loosened the social structure, Datuk Amar smoothed Trengganu's transition, helping to maintain the power of the old elite without forcing it to creative effort. In the course of all this he made himself disliked—first by those people who saw him in 1928 as their betrayer to colonial oppression, and later by the British, who found him an obstacle on the road to modernity. He ended as the spokesman for Trengganu's traditional order—an order whose irrelevance the success of his policy had done so much to ensure.

Three of Trengganu's four leading families managed to weather the restructuring of their state and to consolidate their position on the colonial basis. While the sultan and tungkus became the monarch and the royal family, Duyung moved into the role of clergy, and Kampung Kling provided the civil servants. Only the al-Idrus remained outside, too alien to British concepts and perhaps too unwilling to be recast in an acceptable Western mold. The other families' acquiescence in the relegation of nonofficial Islam to the fringe of the political system showed how much they had come to emphasize their links with colonial central authority rather than with traditional values. We have seen one consequence of this: it was to nonofficial Islam and the al-Idrus that the ra'ayat looked when, despairing of their ruler's ability to fend off colonial demands, they rose in protest. Yet the syeds were unable to provide a coherent and permanent source of opposition; they had not the skills nor the strength to challenge the British successfully, and they had the alternative of relying on their traditional prestige and their informal connections to ensure them a continuing place in the elite. Al-Idrus influence remained, but in shadow; the common people looked to the syeds with respect but not, after 1928, for political salvation.

The rest of the Trengganu elite had moved too close to British power and interests. They could not speak directly to popular grievances; lacking confidence, unnerved by the erosion of popular loyalty, their response was to rely on the outmoded old order to block the encroachments of the alien new, and on the new order to provide support and protection against the possible assertion of claims from below. Members of the older generation remained attached to the ideas which had originally guaranteed their position and fought against moves which would lessen proximity to the ruler, Islamic expertise, and multiplicity of functions as bases of power. They also took care to dominate the efforts of a younger generation in the mid-1930s to develop political activity and a press. These initiatives centered on graduates of Sultan Idris Training College and Trengganu's cautiously modernist Madrasah al-Sultan Zainal Abidin, but patronage and support came from Datuk Amar, Datuk Bentara Luar, Datuk Andika, State Secretary Tungku Setia, and other members of the established elite.

Not surprisingly, this embryo political movement did not attack Trengganu's establishment but restricted itself to stressing Malay solidarity and a cautious anticolonialism. It had no visible connection with the populace, no ancestry in the shadowy protopolitical organization of the Sharikat-ul-Islam. The movement was not radical enough, and the population not disaffected and detraditionalized enough, to find a new elite role as vanguard of a modern movement of salvation. Even more than the "old gang" the members of the younger generation had adjusted to the British system; the colonial advisers found them more congenial and looked forward to the day when they would take office. The Trengganu elite was tamed; and yet, because the new role it had learned was not the one in which the ra'ayat had recognized its authority, the ultimate consequence of the adjustments it made to survive the Malayo-Muslim world's decline was that it too was condemned to irrelevance beyond a constantly diminishing context.

By 1940 the formal framework of public life in Trengganu was close to that of a European state, with apparently separate niches for royalty, law, religion, legislature, and executive. At second glance, the persistence of the old central elite, the close personal ties between its members, and the continuing influence of the holistic spirit of Islam made it seem there was no real break with the past. In reality, there had been a great change, more significant and less tangible than these appearances. It left the feeling that somehow Trengganu had lost energy and creativity, a capacity for original development. As long as its rulers could respond to the imperial challenge by attempting an independent Malayo-Muslim modernization, they were able to act creatively; but once a British model was substituted for the Malayo-Muslim one the taproot which nourished the state's political and intellectual life was severed. Trengganu became what it had not been in the eighteenth or nineteenth centuries, a backwater. The old Malayo-Muslim world had been pushed aside by the European-Chinese cities of Singapore and the peninsular West Coast; Trengganu had no close ties with them, only a peripheral touch of their Westernized economy and culture. Its remaining spiritual possessions were a sense of past Malay and Islamic greatness, a desire to preserve these treasures against innovation that would inevitably mean decline, a need to shut itself off from British Malaya and the changing world around it.

The Tobacco Monopoly in the Cagayan Valley, 1786–1881

EDILBERTO C. DE JESÚS

> We have pushed our researches into the minutest details
> of Rizal's life to almost incredible lengths; but so decisive
> a development in our economic and social history as the
> Tobacco Monopoly remains, as far as our understanding of
> it is concerned, where the last Spanish publicists of the
> nineteenth century left it.[1]

Since Horacio de la Costa, S.J., deplored this disproportion over ten
years ago, the already embarrassing wealth of Rizaliana has continued
to grow. The Tobacco Monopoly, in the meantime, remains virtually
untrodden territory.

Perhaps the very factors which make reserarch into the monopoly
a compelling need—the sheer scope of its operations and its remarkable
longevity—have also inhibited its investigation. The monopoly ran
between 1782 and 1882 and, before its abolition, had come to embrace
all the provinces of Luzon, while not leaving the Visayan islands un-
touched. In the Philippine National Archives alone rests a collection
of over 250 bundles marked *Tabacos*.[2] An immediate problem is fixing
a handle on an enterprise of these dimensions.

Local history may present a way of scaling the subject down to more
manageable size. Studying the monopoly's impact on a limited area
may shed light, not only on the social and economic development of
one geographical unit, but also on the nature of the system itself. Indeed, to go beyond the administrative structure and bureaucratic
history of the monopoly requires taking account of the different ways

---

1. Horacio de la Costa, S.J., *The Background of Nationalism and Other Essays*
(Manila: Solidaridad Publishing House, 1965), p. 23.

2. E. de Jesús, Jr., "Tobacco Monopoly and the Philippine National Archives,"
Archiviniana 2, no. 1 (May 1971): 6.

in which it affected different areas. Because tobacco occupied such a pivotal place in the life of the region, the Cagayan Valley offers a logical starting point for the study of the monopoly.[3] The government's policies toward tobacco cultivation in the Cagayan Valley provide the clearest clue to the basic intent of the institution and the way that this changed over time.

The monopoly involved government control over the cultivation of tobacco, its manufacture into cigars, cigarettes, and snuff, and the sale of these products. As promulgated in 1781, the ban on tobacco cultivation and trade covered Manila and the central Luzon provinces of Tondo, Cavite, Batangas, Tayabas, Laguna de Bay, Pampanga, Bataan, and Bulacan.[4] Over the next five years, the government imposed the monopoly on the rest of Luzon, completing the process in September 1786 with the establishment of the monopoly in the province of Cagayan.[5] Tobacco could be grown on the island of Luzon only for the use of the government and only by those contracted for the

3. Until well into the nineteenth century, the province of Cagayan extended over the entire valley watered by the Rio Grande de Cagayan and its tributaries on the northeastern end of Luzon. Bounded on the north by the China Sea and by the mountain ranges of the Cordillera on the west, the Caraballos on the south, and the Sierra Madre on the east, the Cagayan Valley comprised a well-defined area of some 5,500 square miles. In 1839 and in 1856, the Spanish colonial government redefined the valley's administrative boundaries, so that the region, after 1856, included the three provinces of Cagayan, Isabela, and Nueva Vizcaya. For a description of the geographical features of the valley, see Frederick Wernstedt and Joseph Spencer, *The Philippine Island World: A Physical, Cultural, and Regional Geography* (Berkeley: University of California Press, 1967), pp. 17, 314-317. For a discussion of population movements between the valley and the surrounding highlands, see Felix Keesing, *The Ethnohistory of Northern Luzon* (1962), pp. 168-343.

4. Don Joseph Basco y Bargas Balderrama, y Ribera, Cavallero del Orden de Santiago, etc., "El importante fin de atender a las precisas cargas del estado...," Manila, 13 December 1781, Philippine National Archives, "Tobacco Monopoly." The materials from the PNA used in this study came from twenty-six bundles of documents originally marked simply "Tabacos." Since the contents of the bundles had not been catalogued, the director, Dr. Domingo Abella, graciously gave the writer permission to gather the documents pertaining to the monopoly in a separate file, in preparation for their inclusion in the archives' card catalogue. All PNA materials cited, therefore, will be found under the category "Tobacco Monopoly."

5. Carvajal González to José Gálvez, No. 16, Manila, 16 June 1785, Archivo General de Indias (Seville), Ultramar 638 (hereafter cited as AGI).

purpose by the monopoly's administration. A government factory in Binondo handled the processing of the leaves, and a network of government tobacco shops or *estanquillos* sold the finished articles to the public at officially prescribed rates.[6]

Land and people had proven particularly receptive to the plant. Introduced by the Spaniards to the Philippines in the last quarter of the sixteenth century, tobacco had spread all over the islands with remarkable ease, penetrating even those areas under Muslim or pagan control where neither missionaries nor soldiers could gain a foothold. In Cagayan, as in the rest of Luzon, tobacco had become a product of general use, regarded almost as a necessary antidote to the baneful influence of a humid, tropical climate. Interference with the use of an article second in importance only to rice was enough in itself to arouse popular opposition to the monopoly.[7]

But the people of Cagayan, Spanish and Indio alike, had further reason to resent the new system;[8] the ban on tobacco cultivation deprived the province of its most valuable commercial product and virtually its only source of cash. Pagan tribes came down from the surrounding highlands to barter beeswax and gold for Cagayan tobacco. Sales to the Ilocos, Pangasinan, Zambales, and Manila paid for imports of Ilocano cotton cloth and also enabled the Cagayanes to settle their tribute obligations.[9] The prohibition of tobacco cultivation in Cagayan disrupted traditional trade patterns, provoked the flight of able-

6. For a more detailed discussion of the monopoly's organization and operations, see the writer's "The Tobacco Monopoly in the Philippines, 1782–1882" (Ph.D. diss., Yale University, 1973), pp. 40–71.

7. Diego de Gardoqui, in José Basco y Vargas to Gálvez, No. 1019, Manila, 17 June 1787, AGI, Ultramar 636.

8. The Spaniards perpetuated Columbus' error in thinking that he had reached India by labeling the indigenous population of their overseas possessions *Indios*. The Malay lowland peoples of the Philippines, like the indigenous peoples of the Americas, were Indios to the Spaniards. The term Filipino, now used to identify the ethnic or national origins of the people of the Philippines, referred during the Spanish period to pure-blooded Spaniards born in the colony. See Domingo Abella, "From *Indio* to Filipino," *Philippine Historical Review* 4 (1971): 1–34.

9. Joaquín de la Cuesta, Ilocos, 16 July 1785, in González to Gálvez, No. 48, Manila, 10 November 1785, AGI, Ultramar 638. The tribute was a head tax imposed by the government on the colony's non-Spanish population. Rates varied according to ethnic classification. Indio householders paid ten reales a year, Chinese mestizos twenty reales, and full-blooded Chinese forty-eight reales.

bodied workers out of the valley, and cast the province into a deep depression.[10]

The decline in the people's cash income showed in the monopoly's inability to dispose of its tobacco stocks in the province. Returns from Cagayan's estanquillos were not even sufficient to cover the salaries of the supervisor and the ten guards assigned to the province, and the monopoly's commissioner in Ilocos had to subsidize the Cagayan operations.[11] A more unequivocal proof, since smuggling greatly affected monopoly sales, was the difficulty in collecting tribute dues from the people. It became necessary in 1789 to threaten floggings and imprisonment before the people would pay the tax, and many simply fled to the hills. The following year, the government had to suspend tribute collection altogether to save the people from total ruin. Frequent typhoons in 1789 and 1790 and plagues of rats and locusts had brought famine to the province.[12] People were slaughtering even their work animals for food, their own livestock and their neighbors'.[13] Others were subsisting on forest leaves and roots. Along with famine came an epidemic which ravaged the province. From deaths and desertion, the government lost an estimated one thousand tribute payers.[14] Missionaries and provincial governors (alcaldes) alike blamed the monopoly for the miseries of the province and pleaded that tobacco cultivation in Cagayan be permitted.[15]

Unmarried adults paid half the amount collected from the head of a household. A law of 13 November 1783 stipulated payment of the tribute in cash.

10. "Informe sobre la Provincia de Cagayan, y decadencia de ella desde que se proivió el plantío del tabaco, y estanco de este," Archivo de la Provincia del Santísimo Rosario (Quezon City), Mss. Cagayan, 1:10, fols. 404–404v (hereafter cited as APSR).

11. Antonio Feixas, O.P., to Provincial, Lallo, 22 August 1788, APSR, Mss. Cagayan, 1:4, fol. 80v; Soto to Gardoqui, No. 64, Manila, 15 November 1793, AGI, Filipinas 887.

12. "Certifico de Fray Manuel de Mora, vicario y ministro de doctrina de Santa Rosa de Gamu y visita de San Martin de Furao," in "Testimonio del expediente sobre poner siembras de tabaco en la Provincia de Cagayan," AGI, Ultramar 638.

13. "Certifico de Fray Thomas Figuerola, Pueblo de San Fernando de Ylagan, 10 April 1790," ibid.

14. "Certifico de Fray Joaquín Sancho, Lallo, 7 May 1791," ibid.

15. The alcalde or provincial governor enforced the directives emanating from the central government in Manila. Though not called upon to formulate policies,

Appeals by provincial governors and parish priests for the relief of Cagayan failed to move the central government. Neither did Cagayan's capacity for producing bumper crops of top-grade tobacco merit consideration. The government's objective was to exploit, through the monopoly, the domestic demand for tobacco products in order to generate revenue for the colony. Since practically every province in Luzon could grow some tobacco, securing an adequate supply of the leaves was a minor organizational problem. The key to the profitability of the monopoly was not so much an abundant stock of tobacco as a secure lock on what supplies were available. A bumper crop, in fact, threatened to depress profits. The monopoly had to spend more on the purchase of leaves from the farmers, and smugglers had a better chance to obtain tobacco to sell outside the estanquillos.[16] The government could not allow the rescue of Cagayan to jeopardize what had become the single biggest contribution to the colonial treasury.[17]

Two developments paved the way for Cagayan's recovery. In the Bulacan *colección*, the group of towns assigned to grow tobacco for

---

he was expected to do practically everything else. He served as the chief political, administrative, judicial, fiscal, and military officer of the province. In general, however, the alcalde confined himself to the provincial capital and effective power at the municipal level resided in the parish priests. In the majority of cases, the priest was the only Spaniard to come into direct contact with the Indios; he therefore served as the visible agent not only of the Catholic Church but also of the Spanish king. Recognizing the central role played by the priest at the local level, the government made him jointly responsible with the alcalde and the cabeza de barangay or town magistrate for maintaining the accuracy of the tribute lists.

16. Luis Urrejola to Secretary of State, Manila, 2 February 1823, AGI, Filipinas 888.

17. As a fiscal measure, the tobacco monopoly was an instant success. Between 1783 and 1795, the colonial government was able to remit directly to Spain nearly two million pesos drawn from monopoly profits (see Angel de la Fuente, Contaduría General, Manila, 6 July 1802, AGI, Ultramar 631). Before the end of the century, profits from the monopoly had become available to meet the ordinary costs of maintaining the colony. Access to these funds enabled the colony to balance its budget, thus relieving the empire of the burden of supporting it with a subsidy from Mexico. The subsidy, or *situado*, came to an end in 1804. See William Schurz, "The Philippine Situado," *Hispanic American Historical Review* 1 (1918): 461–464.

the monopoly, smuggling reached serious proportions. A government investigation in 1796 concluded that one-third to two-thirds of the Bulacan crop ended up in the hands of smugglers. The report estimated that over the period from 1791 to 1796, the loss to the government in Bulacan alone amounted to more than 200,000 pesos. Rather than attempt to plug the leaks in the Bulacan colección, Don Pedro de la Peña, the government investigator, recommended that the monopoly simply terminate the contract to purchase tobacco from the Bulacan farmers and transfer cultivation to a more easily controlled region. Cagayan, which was both less densely populated and, because of the surrounding mountain ranges, less accessible to outsiders, seemed to offer a promising alternative.[18] The government did not immediately implement de la Peña's proposal; Bulacan continued to grow tobacco for the monopoly until 1805.[19] But in May 1797 the government authorized cultivation in San Fernando de Illagan in Cagayan, assigning to the province a staff of three officials and forty-four guards. The 1797 decree became the wedge with which other towns in Cagayan gradually pried themselves loose from the ban on tobacco cultivation. The process took some years to complete, despite the discretionary power given to the Cagayan administrator in 1799 to open up suitable lands to tobacco. But further progress also came to Cagayan in the way of more favorable terms conceded to the farmers. Under continuing pressure from the parish priest, the monopoly awarded price increases in March 1800, January 1801, February 1812, and September 1821. In 1810, farmers also obtained exemption from the labor draft for provincial projects, though they remained subject to the call for personal service required by their own towns.[20]

18. De la Peña's reports, dated 22 August and 15 September 1796, are filed together with "Copia del oficio que pasó el Señor Superintendente General de estas Yslas al Factor General Don Pedro de la Peña, en 22 de agosto de 1796, y planos propuestos para extender las siembras de tabaco a la provincia de Cagayan e Isla de Marinduque," AGI, Ultramar 634.

19. Pedro de la Peña to King, Manila, 20 June 1821, AGI, Ultramar 634.

20. José Ferrer, "Expediente en que se trata de promover las siembras de Cagayan hasta el grado de perfección posible; formar un reglamento que fija las respectivas funciones de los empleados de aquella colección y medios que puedan ponerse en planta para evitar en lo sucesivo las vejaciones a que han expuestos los naturales de dicha provincia por varios de sus colectores. . . ." Pieza 1ª., 1831, PNA, Tobacco Monopoly, fols. 60–66. Pieza 2ª. or second

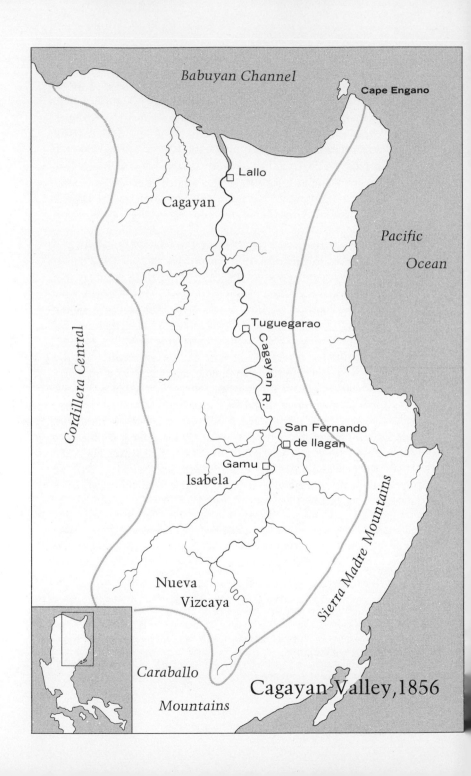

Babuyan Channel

Cape Engano

Lallo

Cagayan

Pacific

Ocean

Cordillera Central

Tuguegarao

Cagayan R.

San Fernando
de Ilagan

Gamu

Isabela

Sierra Madre Mountains

Nueva
Vizcaya

Caraballo

Mountains

Cagayan Valley, 1856

The second development favorable to Cagayan was the growing interest in the export potential of tobacco. As officials became convinced in the 1820s that an export market existed for Philippine tobacco products, the government began to show an active concern for expanding production in Cagayan. By 1830, the Cagayan colección included twenty-one towns with a total of over 9,500 tributes.[21] That year marked the first time that Cagayan delivered more tobacco than Gapan, hitherto the monopoly's prime source of leaves: 47,412 *fardos* or bales worth 80,392 pesos as against Gapan's 32,990 fardos worth 40,954 pesos.[22]

Success as a government colección brought to Cagayan problems of a somewhat different order from those caused by the ban on tobacco cultivation. The promise of instant wealth from tobacco was a temptation for both Spanish and Indio officials to exploit the common people or *cailianes*. The dispatch of Don José Ferrer to investigate alleged official abuses in Cagayan in 1831 provided the occasion for the drafting of a more comprehensive set of regulations for the management of the colección.

Ferrer arrived in Lallo, the provincial capital, on 23 March 1831 and held his commission for almost exactly a year. Though not immune from contemporary Spanish biases regarding Indio abilities, he was a sensible and perceptive observer, and his report provides some indication of how the monopoly had affected Cagayan. Ferrer immediately recognized the justice of farmers' complaints about having to transport their tobacco to the government warehouses at Lallo. Within a week of his arrival, he was receiving bids for contracts to handle the transport of tobacco from the towns where it was grown to the warehouses in the capital. The alternative to contracting the job was continued reliance on corvée labor, a practice Ferrer considered both unsatisfactory and unjust: unsatisfactory because the work interfered with preparations for the next planting season; unjust because the obligation

---

part, which is separately bound, consists of thirty-one folio pages, but only the first seventeen leaves have survived the insects. Hereafter cited as Ferrer, 1 and Ferrer, 2.

21. Ferrer, 1, fol. 49.

22. Gapan annual accounts to 1830 are in AGI, Filipinas 884; Cagayan annual accounts to 1830 are in AGI, Filipinas 885.

did not fall equally upon all. The Indio notables known as *principales* either enjoyed exemption from corvée labor because of service in the bureaucracy or had the money to buy their way out of the obliga- tion.[23] The burden therefore pressed most heavily on the people least able to support it.[24]

His sympathy for the commoners—the "gente pleveya" as Ferrer called them—did not preclude appreciation of the usefulness of the principales to the monopoly. The various arrangements for the super- vision of tobacco-growing in Cagayan which the monopoly had tried had always centered on the principales. Though these had not proven particularly effective, Ferrer tended to blame the failure on the system rather than the personnel. The working unit assigned to the *caudillo* or tobacco overseer had been either too small to be financially worth- while or too big to be effectively manageable. It was also true, however, that the *cabezas* and *gobernadorcillos,* the village chiefs and town magistrates, often lacked the requisite technical background. Only in recent years had they turned to tobacco cultivation, and many did not do the planting themselves but had the cailianes do it for them. Nevertheless, Ferrer considered the principales best fitted for the job of caudillo, and for the very reason others regarded them as unsuit- able—because they wielded an inordinate amount of influence over the people. The principales, especially the cabezas, were "pequeños tiranos," but these "petty tyrants" were necessary, because without them "it would not be possible to derive the slightest profit from the town."[25] What inclined Ferrer to this opinion was his view of the Cagayan Indio as a child to whom play was more important than profit, so that he needed to be alternately threatened and cajoled to persevere at hard work.[26]

The pattern of settlement in the valley added to the need for super- vision. Cagayan was the province, according to Ferrer, where the laws requiring Indios to live in communities within sound of the church

23. The principales were the leading citizens of the Indio community. Initially, entry into the ranks of the indigenous elite depended upon appointment as cabeza de barangay, but people of wealth later came to be counted among the principales.

24. Ferrer, 1, fols. 30–41.

25. Ibid., fols. 73–74.

26. Ibid., fol. 67.

bells were least observed. In the town of Tuguegarao, the province's biggest tobacco producer, hardly 500 of 2,826 tributes resided within the prescribed distance. Its villages, like those of other towns, did not really serve as population centers because the people preferred to keep their small huts in remote places, close to the fields they were cultivating.[27]

It was obvious to officials on the spot that the obstacle to progress in Cagayan was not shortage of land but lack of labor. Ferrer reported that private ownership of land was almost unknown in the province. With the exception of Tuguegarao, the greater part of which was already under the plow, the other towns had wide areas of fertile land available. Present occupation was the only title recognized. Any unoccupied land was for the Indio to cultivate, though in previous years someone else may have tilled it. The only transfer or sale of land Ferrer observed followed upon population growth. The Cagayan Indio preferred to have his field near his home. It happened, on occasion, that the area surrounding a farmer's original homesite filled up with other settlers, leaving him little room to expand his field as the needs of his household expanded. The farmer might then decide to turn over his holdings to a neighbor on condition that the other family, with their tools and carabaos, come to help him clear new land and build a new house. Sale of land for cash was extremely rare, and even in these cases no deed or instrument of transfer changed hands.[28]

An indication of changes introduced by the monopoly appeared in the instructions for the Cagayan colección published in 1849, a section of which recognized the possibility of disputes concerning landownership. The monopoly's principal concern was that such disputes did not interfere with the use of land for tobacco. Thus, it gave the alcalde the power to lease a piece of contested land to a person of his choice, who would pay a moderate rent based on the prevailing rates in the province. The money remained in the custody of the judge hearing the case until the court arrived at its decision. The alcalde received jurisdiction over privately owned land left uncultivated. Upon determining its suitability for tobacco, he set a deadline for the owner to plant the land to the crop. Should the owner fail to meet the deadline, the

27. Ibid., fol. 74.
28. Ibid., fol. 80.

alcalde turned over use of the land to the informer who had called his attention to its existence. The owner did not lose his title to the property, but could not regain its use, nor collect any kind of rent from the occupant, until after three years.[29]

The resumption of tobacco-growing under government auspices opened up new opportunities for the province. As usual, however, the immediate beneficiaries were the Spanish officials and the native principales. The provincial governor was also the monopoly's chief agent in the province. Commissions from cultivating tobacco made the post of *alcalde-colector* one of the most coveted in the colony. Though the office paid an annual salary of only 6,000 pesos, an incumbent could easily make over 20,000 pesos a year.[30] Cabezas and gobernadorcillos also secured an additional source of income from their new role as caudillos. Even tobacco-farming apparently became profitable enough for the principales themselves to engage in it. These were merely the legitimate ways of cashing in on the new dispensation; officials also resorted to more dubious means of raking in a fast profit at the expense of their subjects. The 1849 instructions warned the alcalde to watch for abuses still practiced by the caudillos in the requisitioning of provisions from their towns for the use of the monopoly. He was to make sure that the caudillos did not demand more than necessary from the people in order to have a surplus to sell and that they paid the proper prices for the goods they took.[31]

Extortion of the type condemned in the instructions had already drawn Ferrer's attention in 1831, and the caudillos were not the only offenders. Because the Cagayan Indios were then virtually self-sufficient as far as their staples were concerned—and therefore had no need for markets—officials could secure provisions only by requiring the people to sell them at the prices fixed by the government.

---

29. *Instrucción general para la dirección, administración e intervención de las rentas del estanco y sus colecciones, aprobada por S.M. en Real Orden del 10 de agosto de 1840* (Madrid: José María Alonso, 1849), art. 337, p. 75; art. 351, pp. 77–78.

30. "Memoria sobre los presupuestos de gastos e ingresos de las Islas Filipinas para 1839," AGI, Filipinas 903; Robert MacMicking, *Recollections of Manilla and the Philippines during 1848, 1849, and 1850* (London: R. Bentley, 1851), pp. 28–29.

31. *Instrucción general, 1840*, art. 404, p. 89.

At the time of Ferrer's visit, monopoly guards were cordially hated by the people because they brought along friends and relatives on their inspection tours, requisitioning provisions for the entire retinue and paying not even a third of the real value of the cows, carabaos, and chickens they demanded.[32] But the alcalde-colector was hardly the ideal watchdog to set against such abuses, as he himself participated in the business of manipulating the system for private profit. Another problem that Ferrer noted was the alcalde's involvement in commerce. In almost every town, the alcalde had an agent—usually a principal, sometimes the gobernadorcillo himself—who sold his merchandise to the people for tobacco. The tobacco thus cheaply obtained, the alcalde sold to the monopoly at a handsome profit. Ferrer realistically admitted that the practice was impossible to eliminate entirely.[33]

The parish priest provided some defense against alcalde oppression. The alcalde was too highly visible a personage to succeed for long in concealing large-scale graft from the missionaries; and although he sometimes secured the connivance of one or two priests, the rest usually formed a united front against him. Ferrer regretted the fact that his investigation occurred under what seemed to him abnormal conditions: the province was divided into two parties headed by the alcalde and the parish priests respectively.[34] But though the two parties were not necessarily at daggers drawn all the time, the balance of power they represented was probably a permanent condition in the province.[35] Cagayan's growth as a colección perhaps increased the tension between the two forces, as their interests did not always coincide.

The parish priests did not have as clear and immediate a stake in raising productivity as did the alcalde-colector, who received a commission from each bundle of tobacco he delivered. They complained, in

32. Ferrer, 1, fol. 93; Ferrer, 2, fol. 16v.
33. Ferrer, 1, fol. 69.
34. Ibid., fol. 94.
35. Missionary-alcalde rivalry was not peculiar to Cagayan. In every province, the priests and the alcalde did in fact constitute distinct sources of authority and both tended to assume a proprietary attitude toward their common Indio constituents. But the recurring theme of missionary-alcalde conflict emerges in perhaps somewhat sharper focus in Cagayan because distance from Manila left the contending forces to maneuver against each other with little intervention from the central government.

fact, that the alcalde's push for higher and higher yields interfered with missionary activities. The only way to increase deliveries was to open new lands to cultivation, but the best tobacco fields stretched out in narrow strips of land running along the Cagayan River and its tributaries. Expansion of cultivation, therefore, dispersed the population in small, littoral settlements, while the Christianizing and civilizing process, as well as the king's laws, required the concentration of the populace around the town's parish churches.[36]

And though they may have won the souls of the people, the missionaries evidently lost the battle for the bodies; the pattern of scattered settlements continued to prevail in the valley until the mid-twentieth century when immigration from Central Luzon and the Ilocos region began to swell Cagayan's population.[37]

Their limited number and the dispersal of the population made the missionaries less effective in curbing principales' abuse of the cailianes. Dependence on the cabezas and gobernadorcillos for manpower and provisions already inclined the missionaries to favor the principales, a tendency the latter sought to reinforce by judicious and generous gift-giving.[38] The natural reluctance of the cailianes to testify against their oppressors added a further protective screen behind which the principales could exercise arbitrary rule.

The ban on tobacco cultivation originally imposed by the monopoly had hurt the principales, because the flight from the province that it provoked reduced the number of their subjects. Those who remained

36. Tobacco culture, moreover, tended to favor dispersed holdings. The tobacco plant demanded intensive, individual care and thrived better when tended in small plots by householders than in large plantations worked by hired hands. In making tobacco cultivation compulsory in Cagayan, the government defined the nuclear family as the basic working unit. Each household was required to raise a minimum of 8,000 plants in a plot of land measuring around 5,000 square meters. "Comunicación del Superior Gobierno al Provincial sobre el expediente promovido por varios parrocos de la Isabela para que los habitantes se concentren y no vivan esparcidos, 27 de abril de 1865," APSR, Comunicaciones con las autoridades eclesiasticas y civiles, 1866 a 1888, Legajo No. 7, I:33, fols. 17–18.

37. Wernstedt and Spencer, *Philippine Island World*, p. 325.

38. "Conflictos sobre elecciones en Tuguegarao y en otras ocasiones," APSR, Mss. Cagayan, XIV:28, fols. 505–518. The document presents the grievances of the pleveyos against the principales, who enjoyed the support of the parish priest.

in the province tended to fall into heavier dependence on the principales, who were better situated to weather the depression. The most
oppressive burden on the peasants was the need to raise cash to pay
their taxes. Families left fatherless had little recourse but to borrow
money from the principales on terms that virtually reduced them to
a status of servitude.[39]

But the period of the ban was probably one time when the obligations of office outweighed the benefits. It was not too much of an
advantage to have even absolute power over people who had absolutely
nothing to give. The lifting of the ban on tobacco-farming halted the
drain of laborers and tribute-payers from the province. As people
began to earn money once again, debts once again became meaningful
because they could now be collected.

Cagayan's establishment as a colección did not alter the power
relationships in indigenous society. The principales were the dominant
elements in the Indio community before and after the province became
a colección. But the monopoly's intervention in Cagayan undoubtedly
strengthened the principalía—not so much because the principales
obtained additional formal powers, but because the cailianes became
less able to escape from them.

Faced with intolerable exploitation, the peasant had always had
the traditional option of running away. The threat of flight acquired
special substance in a situation where labor was already in short supply
in relation to the available land. The establishment of the colección
probably raised the Indio's tolerance level at the same time that it made
flight more difficult. A certain amount of alcalde and cabeza exploitation was bearable so long as the Indio retained enough to support his
family and so long as he could look forward to the next harvest. Having
just witnessed the Indio's willingness to leave the province, the officials
themselves would have been reluctant to push against the limit. But
the job security provided by the colección brought with it an unwelcome amount of bureaucratic attention. The meticulous record-keeping
required by the monopoly deprived the Indio of the protection that
obscurity provided. Caudillos kept track of where he lived, the number

39. Diego Martín, O.P., to Governor, Santa Barbara de Pangasinan, 26 May
1797, in Julián Malumbres, O.P., *Historia de Cagayan* (Manila: Santo Tomás,
1918), pp. 93–95.

of able workers in his household, the size and location of his fields, the number of seedlings he planted in a given season, the probable size and quality of his harvest. From this body of information, the principales so inclined could figure out the farmer's approximate income and thus determine what debts were collectible and what level of extortion was safe. Apart from keeping the census up to date, the caudillos also plotted the tobacco season for the farmers, setting the schedule for every phase of production, from the preparation of the seedbeds to the final delivery of the harvest.[40] The monopoly thus introduced Cagayan to the most direct, sustained, and intensive pressure ever applied by the colonial government on the Indio population.

Under the system of the colección, the farmers could not sell their tobacco to anyone but the government; in a sense, therefore, the colección—like any type of monopoly—involved a restriction of freedom. Compulsion in the cultivation of tobacco, introduced by a Cagayan alcalde in 1830 and maintained by the monopoly from then on, technically brought a system of forced labor to Cagayan. For the majority of the people, however, the legal obligation to plant tobacco was a matter more of form than of substance. The real compulsion came not from the rules in the books, but from the properties of the soil. With or without the colección, most of the people would plant tobacco, because this happened to be the only commercial crop that the province had developed. Critics of the monopoly tended to stress the amount of work required in growing tobacco.[41] Producing a top quality crop was indeed a painstaking process, as Spanish agricultural experts tried—without too much success—to impress upon the Indios.[42] But Cagayan had been growing tobacco long before the monopoly's establishment, and thanks to favorable soil and climatic

40. Ferrer, 2, fols. 3–4v.

41. J. Lannoy, *Iles Philippines* (Brussels: Delevingne et Callewaert, 1849), p. 63; Feodor Jagor, *Travels in the Philippines* (London: Chapman and Hall, 1875), p. 325; Frederic Sawyer, *The Inhabitants of the Philippines* (London: Sampson, Low, Marston and Co., 1900), pp. 131–132.

42. Spanish agricultural manuals bewailed the Indio's ignorance or disregard of the steps required to produce a superior grade of tobacco leaves: Felipe Govantes, *Estudios ó cartilla sobre el cultivo del tabaco filipino* (Binondo: El Oriente, 1869), pp. 4–5; Rafael Zaragoza, *Cartilla agraria para el cultivo y beneficio del tabaco en Filipinas* (Madrid, 1875), pp. 42–47, 49–50, 65–67, 91, 108–109, 122.

conditions Cagayan could harvest a passable crop without undue difficulty. The minimum quota imposed on each household—forty brazas by fifty brazas, or about 5,000 square meters, and 8,000 plants—took into account the people's need to grow their food crops. It was to the monopoly's advantage, Ferrer insisted, that the tobacco farmers did not have to leave their towns to obtain their food.[43] Prescribing both the size of the field and the number of plants was designed simply to prevent the farmers from packing the seedlings too closely together. From the 8,000 plants would come between 40,000 and 48,000 leaves. At the rate of 4,000 leaves to a fardo of tobacco, the quota amounted to only twelve fardos for each household. Between 1865 and 1874, each tobacco-growing household in the Cagayan Valley delivered an annual average of over thirty-two fardos.[44]

So long, therefore, as the monopoly paid promptly and in full for what it purchased, compulsory cultivation was not an onerous obligation. The quota was not unreasonable, and prices, despite recurrent complaints from the farmers, were generally fair and, because of the complaints, subject to periodic revision. After 1863, however, the government began to fall behind in the payments to tobacco farmers.[45] Instead of paying farmers in cash, the monopoly began issuing certificates of credit or *papeletas*. As it took the government two to three years to redeem the papeletas, the monopoly was in a state of permanent indebtedness to the tobacco farmers. In 1871, this debt amounted to 1,600,000 pesos for the 1869 and 1870 crops.[46] Delays

43. *Instrucción general, 1840*, art. 361, p. 80; art. 465, p. 101.

44. Estimated from figures given in Francisco Mosquera y García, *Memoria sobre el tabaco de Filipinas; su producción, elaboración, y distribución* (Madrid: A. J. Alaria, 1880), pp. 22–26.

45. "Minuta de la comunicación de 11 de enero de 1881 al Gobernador general participando el estado floreciente de la Hacienda y de haberse satisfecho en tabla y mano la cosecha de tabaco de 1880," PNA, Tobacco Monopoly. This note from the department of finance points out that the government had been behind in payments to tobacco farmers since 1863 and observes that this had been the most serious problem in the field of economic administration in the last twenty years.

46. José Jimeno Agius, *Memoria sobre el desestanco del tabaco en las Islas Filipinas* (Binondo: Bruno Gonzalez Moras, 1871), pp. 7–10; Malumbres, *Cagayan*, pp. 112–116; P. Guel, O.P., "Descripción de Malaueg, 1872," APSR, Mss. Cagayan, XV:1.

in tobacco payments offered attractive opportunities to speculators who could afford to hold on to the papeletas until their redemption by the government. To solve the immediate need for cash or goods, farmers were willing to sell their papeletas at 20 to 50 percent below their face value.[47]

For the Cagayan Valley, the introduction of the papeletas marked a swift and stunning reversal of fortune. Until their appearance, tobacco farmers did not have too much to complain about. They had an assured market for the only commercial crop they could grow, and because they could freely consume all the tobacco they wanted they were spared the worst excesses of the tobacco revenue police or *resguardo*. Payment in papeletas reduced them to a condition which Intendant José Jimeno Agius described as worse than that of Cuban slaves. Slaveowners at least maintained their chattel in good health. The farmers of the Cagayan Valley labored in the tobacco fields under the same compulsion as slaves, without assurance that they would receive from the government enough to meet at least their basic needs.[48] Cagayan's plight was no secret to foreigners, as shown by a dispatch filed by British Consul Oswald Coates in 1873:

> The natives of Cagayan at the North of Luzon have also great cause for complaint: Cagayan is the great Tobacco Field of the Philippines. The labour is forced, as every native is obliged to cultivate a certain amount of Tobacco land, the produce of which if equal to the standard size and quality is received and paid for in receipts made payable by the Philippine Government, whilst the remainder is either burnt or returned to the farmer who cannot sell it in that district, and is not permitted to send it to any other. The money to pay for the Tobacco Crop of 1871 left Manila for Cagayan in 1873 and in the meantime the natives have been driven by necessity to sell their receipts at absurd and ruinous discounts

47. Malumbres, *Cagayan*, p. 126; Alfred Marche, *Luzon and Palawan*, trans. Carmen Ojeda and Juanita Castro (Manila: Filipiniana Book Guild, 1970), pp. 119–120; Great Britain, *Parliamentary Papers* (House of Commons & Command), 1878–1879, vol. 70, "Report of Acting Consul MacKenzie on the Trade and Commerce of the Philippines for the Year 1878, Manila, 10 January 1879," p. 591. The commercial reports of the British consuls are in the series *Accounts and Papers*.

48. Jimeno Agius, *Memoria sobre el desestanco*, pp. 11–12.

to the Governor, Magistrate or some other Government Employee.
How can the Spanish Government expect that the natives are happy
with them or (although I suppose they are the most patient people
in the world) desirous of remaining under Spanish Rule, which so
far from being as they pretend a civilized and enlightened one,
renders the natives in some districts worse than slaves, in as much
as that slaves are always provided with the main necessities of life,
whilst on the other hand, the Philippine system at present in vogue
tends to deprive them of both money and food as well as liberty.[49]

When drought struck northern Luzon in 1877, the Dominicans, the
Augustinians, and the Recollects took the initiative in raising 50,000
pesos to lend the government so that it could avert famine in the
valley.[50] In 1879, just two years before the monopoly's abolition,
the government still owed about one million pesos to the tobacco
farmers.[51]

Concern over popular disaffection with the monopoly was one of
the factors which finally persuaded the government to abolish the
system in 1881.[52] But in the Cagayan Valley, the immediate effect of
abolition appeared to have been a drop in the earnings from tobacco.
As usual, the reflex response of some Spaniards was to blame this
decline in the valley's income on the indolence of the Indios. Opponents of abolition had predicted a drop in production because the
Indios allegedly would not work without compulsion.[53] And, perhaps,
the Indios did relax their efforts when the monopoly finally came to

49. Coates to Granville, Political No. 3, Manila, 18 October 1873, Public
Records Office (London), Foreign Office 72/1355. Also quoted in Nicholas
Cushner, S.J., *Spain in the Philippines: From Conquest to Revolution* (Quezon
City: Ateneo de Manila University Press, 1971), p. 203.

50. "Documentos y recibos del arroz que las Corporaciones Dominicos,
Agustinos y Recoletos adelantaron al Gobierno para socorrer a los pueblos de
Cagayan: Año de 1877," APSR, Mss. Cagayan, XII:10.

51. "Report by Acting-Consul MacKenzie on the Trade and Commerce of
the Philippines for the Year 1878, Manila, 10 January 1879," *Parliamentary
Papers, 1878-1879*, vol. 70, p. 591.

52. Primo de Rivera to José Ramon González, O.P., Manila, 23 September
1881, APSR, Comunicaciones Oficiales, Doc. 141, fols. 85-86.

53. *Guía oficial de Filipinas para el año 1886* (Manila: Ramírez y Giraudier,
1885), pp. 720, 763; Francisco Mosquera y García, *Apendice a la memoria sobre
el tabaco de Filipinas* (Madrid: A. J. Alaria, 1884), pp. 6-7.

a close. But forces other than the Spanish hobby-horse of indolence were at work. Regimentation under the monopoly had been strictest in the Cagayan Valley; it was not surprising that after fifty years of controls, the cultivators should need time to adjust to the new conditions of freedom. A former official of the monopoly insisted in 1884 that it was still too early to judge the response of the Indios to abolition:

> A country accustomed to any kind of economic system, in order to pass to another, not only has to break away from the conditions of the former, but also to prepare itself for the conditions of the new, especially when they are as diametrically opposed as those of monopoly and competition [*desestanco*]. The latter, like any system founded on the principle of freedom, requires special abilities and skills, abilities which cannot be improvised or acquired except through experience.[54]

It was also natural that with the loss of their assured market, the farmers should hold back on production until they had some indication of the likely demand for their crops. Finally, farmers had to learn the new rules introduced by private enterprise.

The end of government supervision of tobacco growing affected the quality more than the quantity of the crops produced. With the abolition of the monopoly, the farmers lost their right to obtain cash advances from the government or at least a postponement in the paying of tribute. The haste to get the tobacco to the market in time for the tax payments resulted in badly cured leaves and a further deterioration in the quality of their deliveries. Private enterprise, in the meantime, had also raised the standards for grading tobacco, adding a fifth class to the four which the monopoly had maintained in the last thirty years of operation. Thus, although private buyers offered higher prices for top-grade tobacco than the monopoly had paid, farmers failed to profit from the new rates because the decline in quality consigned most of their crop to the poorly paid fifth class. Fraud also played a part in reducing the returns to the cultivators. Appraisers for private companies were no more immune to the temptation to manipulate the process of grading tobacco for private profit than the government

54. Mosquera, *Apendice*, p. 24.

personnel before them. In some cases, tobacco which should have passed for third class ended up in fifth, and the farmers received for each bale of tobacco half a peso instead of the three pesos it was worth.[55] The Spanish historian Montero y Vidal cited a province whose alcalde erected a monument to commemorate the abolition of the monopoly. The people, however, considered abolition more a matter for regret than rejoicing, and the monument became known as the "monument of hunger."[56] If not apocryphal, the incident could easily have taken place in the former Cagayan Valley colecciones.

The abolition of the monopoly did not change the basic economy of the Cagayan Valley. The people continued to grow tobacco, though no longer compelled to do so by the government, because it was the region's most valuable crop. But the end of the monopoly did introduce new elements in the society of the Cagayan Valley. Agents of Tabacalera, the company which virtually took over the tobacco business from the government, composed one new element. The company maintained warehouses in all of the tobacco-growing towns in the valley. A variable number of foreigners floated in and out of the region. In 1885, the province of Cagayan had five German residents buying tobacco from German firms.[57] Of the new groups coming into the valley, the most important were the Chinese.

At the turn of the nineteenth century, the Chinese were conspicuously absent in the Cagayan Valley.[58] They had little reason to settle in the region. The place was remote and the people poor. The region had good agricultural potential, but government incentives designed to bring Chinese labor to the tobacco fields of Cagayan were notable only for their lack of success.[59] The Chinese sought business, not

55. Pedro Nolasco de Medio, O.P., "Noticias de Cagayan con motivo de la Exposición Hispano-Filipina de 1887," Malaueg, 16 December 1886, APSR, Mss. Cagayan, XVIIa, fols. 249v–250; Agustín Calvo, O.P., "Memoria de esta provincia de Cagayan en 1886," APSR, Mss. Cagayan, XIII: 9, fol. 210.

56. *Historia general de Filipinas,* 3 vols. (Madrid: M. Tello, 1887–95), 3: 296.

57. Refael Tejada, "Memoria de la provincia de Cagayan en la Ysla de Luzon," Tuguegarao, 1 May 1888, PNA, Cagayan, pp. 5–15, 27; Nolasco de Medio, "Noticias de Cagayan," fol. 225.

58. "Numero de almas de la provincia de Cagayan administrada por los religiosos del sagrado orden de Predicadores, 29 de diciembre de 1803," APSR, Mss. Cagayan, I: 11.

59. *Chinos: Sus reglamentos y sus contribuciones* (Manila: Estab. Tipo-lito-gráfico de Ramírez y Comp., 1893), pp. 6–8.

agricultural, opportunities, and the government, through the monopoly, controlled the only commercial crop in the valley. By the 1870s, however, the Chinese had begun to filter into Cagayan and Isabela, attracted by the business in discounting the government papeletas paid to farmers.[60] The end of the monopoly opened new opportunities for the Chinese. Their operations were on a much more modest scale than those of the European companies, but those who ventured into the tobacco trade managed to make a living by gathering the scrap tobacco which the bigger buyers declined to take. Going into the villages, they bought tobacco or bartered for it with merchandise that the farmers needed. As they handled the entire enterprise themselves—from grading to purchase to transport—they were able to cut costs and raise their profits.[61]

By 1885, the province of Cagayan alone had a resident Chinese population of over 400.[62] Three years later, the alcalde raised the estimate of the "ambulant Chinese colony" to around 700. This number was still fairly small, compared to an Indio population of over 125,000.[63] But it was big enough to cause some alarm among the missionaries. Apart from the danger that the heathens posed to the morality of the Indios, Fray Agustín Calvo complained that they were displacing the natives from virtually every branch of commerce.[64]

By the 1880s, the Chinese had a firm grip on the retailing of imported goods, especially textiles, to the natives, and only one or two towns in the province did not have its own Chinese store. Tuguegarao in 1886 had thirty-six Chinese shops and Gamu in Isabela had eighteen Chinese-owned *tiendas de sari-sari* or general merchandise stores. The alcalde also noted in 1888 that the Chinese lent money to the Indios but at very onerous terms.[65]

60. Bonifacio Corrujedo, O.P., Ilagan, 27 December 1878; Pedro García, O.P., Enrile, 8 February 1877; Juan Antonio Alonso, O.P., Tuao, 14 February 1877: all in APSR, Mss. Cagayan, "Respuesta de los padres de Cagayan e Isabela al cuestionario de 1877 y 1878."

61. Tejada, "Memoria de la provincia de Cagayan," pp. 27–28; Edgar Wickberg, *The Chinese in Philippine Life, 1850-1898* (New Haven: Yale University Press, 1965), pp. 98–101.

62. Nolasco de Medio, "Noticias de Cagayan," fols. 224v–225.

63. Tejada, "Memoria de la provincia de Cagayan," p. 21.

64. Calvo, "Memoria de esta provincia de Cagayan," fols. 211–212.

65. Nolasco de Medio, "Noticias de Cagayan," fol. 225; Tejada, "Memoria de la provincia de Cagayan," p. 28; Wickberg, *Chinese in Philippine Life*, p. 101.

Government control of its principal source of wealth probably arrested the process of social change in Cagayan. The strong Chinese push into the area after the abolition of the monopoly suggests that free enterprise in tobacco might have drawn them into the valley earlier. This assumes that the tobacco trade would have developed to the same extent even without the intervention of the government—an assumption which is not unjustified, considering the recognition that Cagayan tobacco already enjoyed prior to the establishment of the monopoly.

In opening up the valley to external, even alien, influences, abolition probably contributed to the process of social and political change taking place in the late 1880s. Fray Pedro Nolasco de Medio compared Cagayan under the monopoly to one large estate with the alcalde as the lord and the gobernadorcillos and cabezas as his retainers and overseers. The system conditioned the people to obey their chiefs blindly in everything, even working the fields of the principales upon command, without pay.[66] But Fray Agustín Calvo noted in 1886 political attitudes quite different from those described as prevailing under the monopoly.[67] In his view the post of cabeza had become the target of adventurers. Anyone who curried favor with the alcalde and was willing to do his bidding could get himself elected to office. The result was the election of men who did not know how to govern and whom the people could not respect. The traditional leadership, seeing that the office no longer carried any prestige, were retiring from public service of their own accord or losing out to those favored by the authorities:

> In other times and until not many years ago, the cabecerías in the province, which passed from fathers to sons, were, or were believed, hereditary; and the commoners regarded their respective cabezas and their families as people of a superior class, and respected, obeyed, and even loved them as their elders and fathers. And the principales or cabezas regarded and held their cabecerías as a thing of their own, which they tried to preserve and improve and, for the same reason, to guide and govern well. But now with the overthrow of the principales, and the nomination of selected cabezas, the contrary occurs.

66. Nolasco de Medio, "Noticias de Cagayan," fol. 236.
67. Calvo, "Memoria de esta provincia de Cagayan," fol. 214v.

The priests, Fray Agustín lamented, were powerless to prevent abuses in the electoral process because the alcalde no longer consulted them on the candidates. They were losing their influence even among the people, who were beginning to believe that the priest could no longer intervene to protect them from injustice.[68]

The complaints of Fray Agustín regarding the quality of the new crop of cabezas need not be taken at face value. To a great extent, these reflected as much on the fears of the friars that they were losing their grip over the people as on the abilities of the new leaders. But the period after the monopoly was obviously a time of transition. The changes in the social and political order which Fray Agustín so deplored—the displacement of the traditional native elite by a new breed of men with apparently sharper commercial instincts—recall those which the Central Luzon provinces had undergone a hundred years earlier.[69] The new opportunities for making money made possible by the system of papeletas and then by the abolition of the monopoly would help explain the origins of this new class.

Until its abolition in 1881, the tobacco monopoly more than any other single factor shaped the history of the Cagayan Valley. It reinforced native resistance to the government policy requiring them to settle within sound of the church bells. It also set the pattern of population movements. Emigration from the province in the late eighteenth century was a response to the monopoly's introduction. Similarly, Ilocano immigration into the province, beginning in the 1850s, was the result of government efforts to recruit tobacco farmers for the monopoly. These efforts did not begin to yield significant results until the 1880s, but by 1903 nearly one-third of the Christian population in the valley were Ilocanos.[70]

68. Ibid., fols. 214v–215.

69. The composition of the principalía class in Pampanga, and probably in other central Luzon provinces as well, had already begun to change in the second half of the eighteenth century with the rise to social and political prominence of a class of wealthy Chinese mestizos. See John Larkin, "The Evolution of Pampangan Society: A Case Study of Social and Economic Change in the Rural Philippines" (Ph.D. diss., New York University, 1966), pp. 76–89. The dissertation has been incorporated into a recently published larger study, *The Pampangans: Colonial Society in a Philippine Province* (Berkeley: University of California Press, 1972).

70. Keesing, *Ethnohistory of Northern Luzon*, p. 181.

Government administration of tobacco in Cagayan underwent four major transitions. From 1787 to 1800 the government prohibited tobacco cultivation in the valley. Persistent complaints from the missionaries that the ban was ruining the province and the need for a greater supply of tobacco persuaded authorities in the late 1790s to allow certain towns to grow the leaf for the monopoly. Between 1800 and 1830 tobacco cultivation became general throughout the province, and increasing deliveries from Cagayan began to attract the attention of the government. José Ferrer's visit to the province in 1830 and the reforms he worked into the rules drafted for the Cagayan colección laid the basis for a period of relative prosperity which lasted till 1863. The use of papeletas to pay farmers marked the fourth phase of the monopoly in the Cagayan Valley. During the period from 1863 to 1881 the monopoly inflicted on the region conditions even more miserable than those caused by the initial ban on growing tobacco.

The complex interaction of continuity and change, so central to Benda's interpretation of Southeast Asian history, is clearly evident in the events we have considered here.[71] Regardless of the impression standard sources have tended to give, the monopoly did not operate uniformly throughout Luzon nor did it persist unchanged from establishment to abolition.[72] The term "tobacco monopoly" itself implies an institutional solidity and consistency which did not in fact exist: we should rather refer, for accuracy if not elegance, to a succession of Spanish schemes to raise revenue from the tobacco industry, which had very diverse effects when applied to local social situations. It is

71. It is perhaps no accident that it was one of Benda's students who pioneered the movement in Philippine historiography away from "the tendency to treat society as a monolithic structure susceptible to outside influence and change at a uniform rate" (John Larkin, "The Place of Local History in Philippine Historiography," *Journal of Southeast Asian History* 8, no. 2 [1967]: 306).

72. See, for instance, Conrado Benitez, *History of the Philippines* (Boston: Ginn and Co., 1940), p. 315; Gregorio Zaide, *Philippine Political and Cultural History* (Manila: Philippine Education Co., 1949), 2: 28–31; and Eufronio Alip, *Political and Cultural History of the Philippines* (Manila: Alip and Brion Publications, 1952), 2: 49–50.

only when we are aware of this variety over time and place and can draw conclusions about its parameters and implications that we can begin to understand the real meaning for Philippine society of the monopoly and other aspects of the colonial experience.

Cagayan's response to the monopoly illuminates not only the situational variations in the enforcement of the system but also the elements distinguishing Cagayan from the rest of the Luzon provinces: its greater geographical extension but more limited resource base, its relatively undeveloped economy and undifferentiated society, its status as a frontier territory hemmed in by hostile *infieles*. These characteristics had limited Spanish interest in the province and permitted the indigenous principales, largely drawn from the preconquest ruling elite, to preserve their dominance over the rest of the population. From the beginning, the hegemony of the principales was complete: they held political office, social status, and economic power. However, the exercise of this supremacy was tempered by their recognition of two constraints, the poverty of the people and the openness of the frontier. With little to lose and much room to move into, the Cagayanes demonstrated a readiness to pack up and go, sometimes to adventure in another province, often simply to settle down beyond the reach of the colonial bureaucracy. Thus the extension to Cagayan of the ban on tobacco cultivation, which was the essential feature of the monopoly, threatened to erode the social order over which the principales presided. By depriving the province of its main economic resource, the Spaniards made the option of flight from the province easier for the cailianes to embrace. This development, in turn, made the position of the principales meaningless—what were patrons without clients?— and even dangerous since the government could hold them accountable for the tribute obligations of the deserters.

The establishment of Cagayan as a government colección saved the situation for the principales. It stemmed the drain of population from the province, thus protecting their access to a manpower pool. Income from tobacco deliveries gave them more prosperous and, presumably, more docile clients, and the bureaucratic controls entrusted to them by the monopoly permitted a closer supervision of the cailianes. With Cagayan's integration into the system of the monopoly, however, the prosperity of the province came to depend directly on the colonial government's ability to balance its budget, a task which became progressively more difficult as the costs of running the colony mounted and as political and economic problems in Spain itself forced Madrid to tap Manila for financial contributions. The consequence of this dependence became clear in the 1860s, when the colonial treasury began paying Cagayan farmers in papeletas. The move precipitated a serious decline in native welfare, but flight was no longer as feasible for the cailianes as it had been fifty years before, thanks to the monopoly's bureaucratic innovations.

Conservative in concept, the monopoly exerted in Cagayan a pressure for social conservatism. It reinforced the position of the principales within the society by using them to manage the colección. Their exclusive control over the region's main source of wealth left few opportunities to outsiders; it thus quarantined the valley from the social and economic forces which from the 1830s had begun to transform the other provinces of Luzon and protected the principales from external competition. The weakening of the monopoly in the 1860s and its abolition in 1881 exposed the Cagayan principales to these new forces. In the economic field, enterprising Chinese traders challenged them for control of provincial commerce. In politics aggressive parvenus, exploiting the opportunities opened up by free trade in tobacco, used their wealth to capture political office.

The dimensions of the changes which overtook Cagayan after 1881 require further study, but the abolition of the monopoly clearly marked a turning point. The speed of Chinese penetration of the valley and the evidence of shifts in power within the local elite suggest how effective the monopoly had been in holding the ring for the traditional ruling class and how little prepared it had left it for a changed environment. Thus at the same time that the specific policies of the tobacco monopoly reinforced the power of Cagayan's traditional elite, the broader involvement of the Philippines in a modern international economy, of which the tobacco industry was part, gave rise to social forces which were eventually to challenge and modify that elite's accustomed role. In this the relationship between local and central, and between intention and effect over time, reveals itself as a dialectic: we must consider not only central intent and local result but also the way in which different responses interacted to produce contrasts and pressures which braked, sped, and altered the course of change.

The Inscrutable and the Paranoid: An Investigation into the Sources of the Brotodiningrat Affair

On the night of 6 October 1899 a curtain was stolen from the house of J. J. Donner, Resident of Madiun territory in eastern Java. A tablecloth and a few other objects of little value also vanished, but the curtain was the clue. It had covered the window by which the resident sat, often in pajamas, for his coffee, and its theft, which infringed on the privacy and affronted the dignity of the highest official in the area, seemed clearly to be a demonstration against European rule. Summoning Raden Mas Adipati Brotodiningrat, Regent (Bupati) of Madiun, Donner told the regent the theft was definitely of a political nature, designed to make the resident look ridiculous, and ordered the culprit found forthwith.

For nearly a month the resident waited for the regent's inquiry to bear fruit while, instead, a series of thefts from other European houses in Madiun occurred. The local Dutch grew uneasy: never before had thieves dared enter the house of a European, and there was much nervous talk about the unrest of the times and a breakdown of law and order. The regent, summoned again by the resident, conceded blandly that criminality was on the rise in the town of Madiun and suggested

My study under the late Harry J. Benda at Yale University was made possible by grants from the Hazen Foundation, the Asia Society, and Yale University. The research for this essay was done primarily in the Netherlands during a Ford Foundation fellowship. I wish to express my indebtedness to all these institutions. I would also like to thank the staffs of the Koninklijk Instituut voor Taal-, Land-en Volkenkunde library in Leiden, the Leiden University Oriental Library, and the Colonial Archives of the Netherlands for their unfailing courtesy. Since my return to Indonesia I have been able to supplement the material on the Brotodiningrat affair through the imaginative assistance of the staff of the Arsip Nasional in Jakarta, for whom I feel special gratitude.

112

that the resident might meet the crisis by having the Europeans register all their servants and place lamps in front of and behind their houses. The resident flew into a rage, saying that such measures would sow panic in the European population and amount to an admission that the resident was unable to preserve law and order. By now Donner was more convinced than ever that the thefts were politically motivated, a deliberate attempt to secure his own downfall and weaken Dutch rule.[1]

Thus began the final act of what was perhaps the most spectacular quarrel between Dutch and Indonesian officials in the history of the colonial service. While the form of the quarrel owed much to the immoderate natures of the two protagonists, its tensions arose from the juxtaposition of Dutch and indigenous administrative power at the turn of the twentieth century. The gradual evolution of colonial rule following the last assertion of Javanese independence, the Java War of 1825–30, had brought about changes in the society at large and in the relationship between Dutch and Indonesian officialdom which were to threaten gravely the position of the regents, supposedly the kingpins of the Netherlands East Indies system of "indirect rule." The resolution of the Brotodiningrat-Donner quarrel marked a departure from the government's established policy toward the regents—a departure the government would later have cause to regret. But in order to understand the broader significance of the Brotodiningrat affair and its consequences, let us turn to the status of the regents and the structure of local authority seventy years earlier, before the Dutch assumed full control.

The region of Madiun had been part of the outer territories (*mancanegara*) of the kingdom of Mataram, i.e. part of those lands outside the core region (*negara-agung*) which was under the direct control of the crown. Ruling over the outer territories were bupatis, who had the official function of governors but in reality held their lands more like appanages. Madiun, even after its division into the principalities of Surakarta and Yogyakarta following the partition of Mataram in 1755, remained under this system of control until 1830.

1. For a short earlier account of the Brotodiningrat affair, see "De strijd om gezag in Madioen," *Indische Gids* 24, pt. 2 (1902): 1259–1262.

Though in some respects the Mataram system resembled that of European feudalism, there were fundamental differences in the legitimation and exercise of kingship. A Mataram king derived his royal position less from birth or election than from his possession of *wahyu* (divine inspiration) and *sekti* (supernatural power). His divine power was conceived of as a radiance (*cahya*) which spread out over the realm from the royal palace (*kraton*), its force diminishing with distance.[2] Essentially, wahyu was a divine gift, which might easily pass to another. Indeed, its possession was almost by definition transitory, for ultimately it was the product of ecstasy, the moment of mystical union between god and man. If therefore the king's policies faltered, if human or natural misfortunes threatened the prosperity of the realm, the people readily turned to speculation that the king's wahyu had deserted him, to be concentrated elsewhere, and began looking to others for signs of the kingly aura. Thus the kingship was unstable even in concept: the primary basis for succession to power lay not in a hereditary right but rather in a reincarnate phenomenon within the limits of divine predestination.

Royal power in this system was both absolute and fluid, and practice compounded the instability. Aside from rivalries within the royal family, the chief threat was posed by the bupatis of the outer realms. Maintaining residences (*kabupaten*) which were lesser replicas of the royal court, the bupatis commanded, if theoretically at the ruler's pleasure, an independent source of income and men from their appanages and enhanced their authority by claims to spiritual power. The Mataram kings tried to keep check on the bupatis by holding hostages from their families at court, forming marriage alliances with the more powerful, and destroying a bupati if necessary and possible. In regions that were particularly difficult to control, the court might even order whole populations moved in order to reduce the manpower available to their

2. Much of this analysis of the Mataram system is drawn from the brilliant work by Soemarsaid Moertono, *State and Statecraft in Old Java: A Study of the Later Mataram Period, 16th to 19th Centuries* (Ithaca: Cornell Modern Indonesia Project, 1968). For its relation to the general pattern of Southeast Asian state systems, see Robert Heine-Geldern, *Conceptions of State and Kingship in Southeast Asia* (Ithaca: Cornell Southeast Asia Program, 1956); for its application to modern Javanese attitudes, see Benedict R. O'G. Anderson, "The Idea of Power in Javanese Culture," in *Culture and Politics in Indonesia,* ed. Claire Holt (Ithaca: Cornell University Press, 1972).

bupatis. Above all, the kings diminished the position of the bupatis by increasing their number, a tactic that resulted in fewer individually powerful lords to contend with and more chances to play one off against another. By the time of the Dutch annexation in 1830, Madiun alone had twenty bupatis.

Within his territory the bupati assumed considerable independence. His position, reflecting the traditional political system, rested on his leadership over men rather than on claims over territory. The *lungguh* (appanage, or salary land as the Dutch translated the term) which the bupati held for the king was always expressed in the number of *cacah* (peasant families) or *karya* (peasant capacity of the land), not in areal extent. To his following the bupati was the chief, often invested with sacred authority, who protected his people, mediated their disputes, and in other ways acted as their patron in the close patron-client relationship of *kawula-gusti* (unity of god and man or of master and servant). Set apart from the *wong-cilik* (commoners) who had to work on the land for their livelihood, the bupati belonged to the *pryayi* elite (from *yayi,* the king's younger brother, denoting all royal officials) and exercised full rights to both the products of the land and the labor of peasants. His duties to the king were simple and few—save in time of war, which could be often. Once a year the bupati rendered tribute at court, also bringing to the king those of his peasants who were liable for liege-service, e.g. the construction and maintenance of roads, palaces, and irrigation works. Neither the liege-service nor the tribute ever reached very high levels, however, for the court was limited in its exactions by the poor state of communications and the plethora of regional chiefs. A bupati entrenched in the outer realm might defy the court, and it was too easy, with labor scarce and land plentiful, for peasants to avoid corvée by slipping over into the domain of another bupati, or another lord, certain of his protection in return for adding to his manpower.

Tribute and liege-service were imposed by the king—who in theory owned all the land in his realm—on peasants with rights to cultivate rice land. These peasants, referred to as *wong-sikep* (people who bear the burdens of the land), held the rice lands of a village, except for a small communal portion, as individual plots. Part of the communal portion was assigned as *tanah bengkok* (salary land) to village officials, who were usually members—or at least alleged members—of the founding families and who were of course sikep themselves. Also sharing by rotation in the village lands were some families which had no rice land of their own but had long been resident in the village; their right to share in the communal portion was preserved as a way of keeping within the village valuable sources of labor. Once granted land rights, though, such families became liable for duties to the state, and there was a tendency, whenever supravillage duties increased, to spread the burden by adding more communal owners. The non-sikep villagers were mainly *numpang* (dependents), the lowest class in peasant society. Numpang worked on the land of a sikep and were housed and fed in his compound, owing no supravillage duty because their labor belonged entirely to their master. The wealth and influence of a sikep were measured by the number of his dependents, for their labor made possible the extension of the land under his cultivation. Upon the establishment of a village, the bupati or the king would normally grant each sikep two or four *bau* of land.[3] By the end of the Java War in 1830, quite a few sikep peasants had holdings of more than ten bau.[4] These holdings were known as *tanah-pusaka* (inherited land) or *tanah-yasan* (self-cultivated land). With wealthier peasants able to control fairly substantial resources in manpower and land, village society developed a high degree of economic and social stratification.

The nonegalitarian nature of Javanese society and the mystical concept of power together produced a demand for brokers between the various social levels. To preserve the aura of sanctity and magic associated with their positions, the powerholders—whether village chief (*lurah*), bupati, or other district official—remained aloof in carrying out their duties as mediators between those higher in the hierarchy and those below or as mediators between the supernatural and man. It is not surprising, therefore, that there was a concomitant need for messengers between rulers and ruled. These brokers or messengers, who

---

3. W. B. Bergsma, ed., *Eindresumé van het bij Gouvernementsbesluit dd. 10 Juli 1867, no. 2, bevolen onderzoek naar de rechten van den inlander op den grond op Java en Madoera* (Batavia: Ernst & Co. and Landsdrukkerij, 1876-96), 3: 104. A *bau* (or *bahu*) is equivalent to 0.70965 hectare.

4. Ibid., 3: app. J, 143. For a more detailed discussion of rural relations in Madiun before and during the Dutch period, see Onghokham, "The Residency of Madiun: Pryayi and Peasant in the Nineteenth Century" (Ph.D. diss., Yale University, 1975).

possessed their own degree of charisma, handled administrative affairs, organized corvée, looked after the collection of tribute and fees, transmitted orders and regulations, and otherwise saw that affairs ran smoothly.

Relative distance from the formal focus of power also affected the exercise of authority in that those further down the line had less need for charisma and more scope for direct action. The bupati, for instance, acted publicly as leader and protector of his people and as judge, putting emphasis on himself as symbolic center. Insofar as his rule had to be identified with exactions, the bupati would endeavor to present the impression that, were it not for his influence at court and his efforts to ward off demands from the center, the people's burden would have been greater. Meanwhile, his right-hand man, the *patih,* and other henchmen would enforce the collections and take the brunt of criticism.

The particularly sharp social distinctions between commoners and the pryayi created another important area for mediation. If on a grander scale the bupati was the means of access to the king, the village headman was expected to provide the peasants with access to the pryayi world. Because many village headmen did not possess sufficient influence to be effective, the broker's role came in time to be performed principally by the *palang* (literally, junction), who in most cases was chosen by the headmen of a group of neighboring villages from among their ranks as the one best able to deal with the powers above.[5] The palang was a man of great local prestige, probably owning land in other villages as well as his own. From the bupati's viewpoint he was useful as a source of intelligence and control, someone who could keep negligent headmen in line and provide a check on the doings of lesser officials. At the same time, however, someone influential enough locally to do these things might become a source of trouble himself. Accordingly, the bupati did his best to see that the man selected as palang was one whose loyalty he could count on—a relative, if possible.

Both in theory and in practice the Javanese polity entailed a fluidity of wealth and power. The king's claim to the ownership of all land left the land and its resources relatively undemarcated, and the weakness of political centers made the control of population movement difficult. As

---

5. For a discussion of the role of the palang, see *Koloniaal Verslag,* 28 (1877): app. N, 7–9.

a result "public opinion" had some influence and was expressed on the village level by intercessors who arose from among peer groups to redress peasant grievances against the pryayi, just as bupatis might choose one from their ranks or someone close to the king to represent their interests at court in a dispute. The willing cooperation of those under his command was important to the bupati, palang, or village headman, not only to preclude the disgrace of rebellion or general flight by his people but also to provide evidence of his ability to command their loyalties and so strengthen his hand in dealing with excessive demands from above. Besides being accorded the traditional mystical attributes, those at the fulcrum of power were thought of as *kebal* (invulnerable)—had not these leaders dared to bargain with higher officials and gotten away with it?—and as themselves *digdaya* (powerful, possessing full authority). Thus the power wielder, whether high or low in the hierarchy, appeared to his own followers to be a *jago* (literally, fighting cock/champion) battling in their behalf, a hero deserving of their loyalty and obedience.[6]

There was another reason for attaching heroic qualities to the men of power: warfare was an inherent feature of the Javanese polity. Given the instability of the political centers and the expedient value of a large peasant following, bupatis and village headmen had to be able to exert both protective and coercive force to maintain their positions. One of their primary functions, of course, was to protect their villagers from outside threats, but the peasants also had to be kept from fleeing to other territories or leaving the established order by opening land in the woods. Where simple harassment failed, a bupati might thwart the movement of such peasants by creating unrest in nearby areas or by mobilizing their energies in raids on other bupatis' lands. The many uses of warfare made the men with special fighting abilities (*jagabaya,* which the Dutch translated as "police") highly esteemed by both bupatis and those dependent on their protection.

An ambitious jago would try to win favor with those higher in the

6. For a discussion of the role of the jago, see "Het recht en de Politie," in *Onderzoek naar de mindere welvaart der inlandsche bevolking op Java en Madoera* (Batavia: Landsdrukkerij, 1901–14), 8b: 123 (hereafter cited as *Mindere welvaart rapport*). For a description of the heroic attributes of people of power, see the contemporary chronicle of Pacitan (the residency's southern region), "Babadé Negara Patjitan," Ms. LOR 8991, Leiden University Oriental Library.

hierarchy by outperforming his peers in the service of his patron. A prince might offer to lead a particularly dangerous expedition, for example, or a village headman might volunteer more services and tribute than other headmen even dared ask of their people. Obviously the jago's roles as champion of his following and servant of his lord conflicted, but the strain was lessened by the fact that the main consideration in Javanese eyes was his closeness to the source of power. From power came protection, and the villagers felt a leader who was "in" with the powers above was more useful than one who set himself against the great. Their basic assumption was pessimistic: the leader was not there to improve their lot but to prevent, through his connections and pleading, a worse fate.

It was always possible that a popular jago fired by ambition or a just cause would turn in opposition to his patron, whether in his own name or in support of a rival lord's intrigues. To counter this danger the wise patron provided hope of preferment. The precolonial system, despite its emphasis on rank, allowed social mobility—even of commoners into the pryayi class. Entrance to the officials' class usually occurred through the *magang* system, under which pryayi, particularly bupatis, and occasionally a prominent villager surrounded themselves with young boys who by observation learned the ways of the world and the methods for handling the affairs of the powerful.[7] These boys would wait at table, accompany their master, deliver messages, do clerical chores, and hope for eventual appointment to an appropriate post. The magang of a bupati had, as might be expected, higher status than those of any other pryayi and could look forward to the higher offices their patron had in his gift. Bupatis tended to favor each other's kin, somewhat closing pryayi ranks against outsiders, but social lines were not strict. Personal favor outweighed the precedence of rank: boys of whatever origin, so long as their families were considered deserving, could be accepted as magang of a pryayi, and any magang who managed to win attention and favor might marry into the bupati's family and thus become eligible for a bupati post. A man who strove in his superior's interests might therefore hope not only for the rewards proper to his position in life but also for the great opportunity his advancement would bring to succeeding generations of his family.

7. The magang system is discussed in Moertono, *State and Statecraft in Old Java,* p. 95.

When the Dutch assumed control over Madiun in 1830 following the Java War, this traditional polity was in considerable disarray. For many years the Dutch had helped to prevent the emergence of a single strong ruler among the quarreling princes of Java by a policy of throwing their military weight to the weaker side in a conflict, thus compounding the inherent instability of the system. As the fortunes of local rulers rose and fell in quick succession, the emphasis on loyalty gradually diminished among the pryayi, who became inclined to render service at a price and within limits. Local chronicles of this period reveal the fairly opportunistic adjustments to changes of master and situation that seemed to be common among peasants and pryayi alike. There was also the divided loyalty of Madiun itself, part of its territory under Yogyakarta, whose Prince Diponegoro had led the rebellion, and the other part under the court of Surakarta, which had stood generally in opposition. Rival bupatis were appointed by the contending sides, the Dutch attempted to ensure allegiance by their own negotiations with bupatis, and in several places usurpers and village rebels took advantage of the confusion to overturn the established order. Under these conditions, the Madiun bupatis took on more than ever the aspect of petty chiefs, with uncertain loyalties and unstable followings. The influence of the courts, especially that of Yogyakarta, virtually ceased to exist.

Since the bupatis of the Surakarta sector for the most part remained allied to their court, and the chief bupati in the Yogyakarta sector, Raden Aria Prawiradiningrat, had taken the side of the Dutch, there was no cause for large-scale military operations in Madiun. Nonetheless, the area was sufficiently strategic and uncertain for the Dutch to garrison its major towns during the war and to reward cooperative pryayi with military rank and gold-embroidered uniforms. At the end of the war, with the courts in ruin, the princes in dire poverty, and neither the bupatis nor the people eager to return to royal dictate and long labor merely to restore princely living standards, the Dutch found little opposition to their assumption of permanent control over Madiun and the rest of the outer territories.[8]

8. For the role of Madiun in the Java War, see P. J. F. Louw and E. S. de Klerck, *De Java Oorlog, 1825-1830* (Batavia and The Hague: Landsdrukkerij, 1894–1900), 1: 525ff.; 6: 158ff.

In such manner did the Netherlands Indies become the successor state to Mataram. Its first priorities in its new role were to establish a stable order and to generate as expeditiously as possible a substantial income to bolster the stagnant Dutch economy. The governor general at this juncture, Count Johannes van den Bosch, saw the way to accomplish both through the bupatis. Netherlands rule, he reasoned, must of necessity be indirect, for though "a European has the highest authority, as a foreigner on alien land he would not know what went on in his immediate environment. It is a well-known fact that natives consider it the most detestable act to betray someone to a European."[9] The natural mediators would be the bupatis—called regents by the Dutch—for their power over the people was as much a reality as their need for a new basis of authority:

> The people's chiefs must henceforth be attached to our interests. For this a hereditary aristocracy possessing landed estates and receiving yearly subsidies is necessary. Such an aristocracy is incompatible with Eastern despotism, and we shall have nothing to fear from a conspiracy between them and the Sultan or Sunan. Their ally is the Netherlands government.[10]

Van den Bosch went on to argue that, because the wartime disruptions had greatly eroded their authority over the population, everything should be done to increase the pomp and circumstance surrounding the regents, "however heavily they are burdening the people, who prefer to see them thus."[11]

His recommendation to the Commissioners for the Regulation of the Principalities was, accordingly, to deal first with Prawiradiningrat, the chief bupati (*wedana bupati*) of Madiun, who had kept much of Madiun "loyal" and with whom the Dutch had already been in correspondence. "Promise him a fixed subsidy and estates," Van den Bosch urged. Prawiradiningrat, if willing to accept Dutch protection, should then be asked to approach the other bupatis, who would thereupon be contacted by the Dutch and assured of the government's good intentions. None of the bupatis rejected these overtures.[12]

9. Colonial Archives of the Netherlands (hereafter cited as CA), The Hague, Collectie J. van den Bosch, no. 220.
10. Ibid.
11. Ibid.
12. Louw and De Klerck, *De Java Oorlog,* 6: 158ff.

Under the Dutch the bupatis' magnificence did indeed increase re-markably. Their residences, usually of wood in the time of Mataram, became in the colonial period palatial affairs of stone; the etiquette of their courts became elaborate and fixed; and their retinues became grander. The Prawiradiningrats even boasted a company of bodyguards dressed as Dutch hussars.[13] Moreover, the gradation of their rank ex-panded, and the new regents could be accorded such lustrous titles as *tumenggung, adipati, aria,* or even the royal *pangeran.*

In the early stages of colonial rule, the regents provided the main point of access for the Dutch to the native population. Crimes against a regent's property became the occasion for deep concern among the Dutch, because on the regent's inviolability rested their own. Theoreti-cally the lower civil servants and villagers could go to Dutch officials with any complaint against the higher pryayi, but only in extreme cases would the Dutch fail to take the regent's side. There was, of course, a price: the regents' loyalty to Netherlands rule and their acceptance of a hierarchy of Dutch advisers under a resident with the prerogatives of an "elder brother."

Van den Bosch had also envisioned a fruitful relationship with the regents in economic management. The Cultivation System, which was introduced in 1830 and remained the principle of colonial exploitation until 1870, required villagers to devote a portion of their land and labor to the production of such commercial crops as sugar, indigo, and coffee. Regents, together with the Dutch residents, were responsible for super-vising the villagers' fulfillment of this obligation. Both European officials and Javanese, from regent to village headman, received as an incentive to push for higher production a percentage of their territory's output.

One wonders what would have happened to the development of this system in the Madiun area if the twenty regents had accepted landed estates in response to Van den Bosch's initial offer. The Dutch were soon to back away from the idea, realizing that private estates would give the regents independent economic power and endanger the efficient exploitation of Java under what was in effect a state plantation system. But to the regents of Madiun, and most of their colleagues elsewhere in Java, this reappraisal made little difference, for they did not share the European notion that the chief requisite of an aristocracy was the con-

13. *Tijdschrift van Nederlandsch Indië,* 21 (1859): 470ff.

trol of land. It was the peasantry, held in tributary relations with the courts and the pryayi, that had always been the basis of social, political, and economic power in Java. Land was still abundant. Probably the regents also felt that private landed estates would have been subject to inheritance laws, which would have diminished the value of regentship. In any case, the regents from the very beginning rejected landed estates, and even the later proposal of a combination of appanage lands free of land rent and a subsidy, in favor of a double monthly subsidy and no appanage lands.[14]

Their rationale in opting for this course—a course the Dutch were only later to realize was to their own maximum advantage—stemmed from their orientation toward the control of labor and the concomitant belief that the key to profit under the new Cultivation System would be the necessary manpower to work their lands. Because there was so much land lying fallow in neighboring regions depopulated by the Diponegoro war, the regents of Madiun had difficulty tying down their peasantry but used every possible means in their efforts to do so. The fact that their main income now came from a money subsidy made it possible to distribute their former appanage lands, hand out patronage more freely, and make loans to the peasants to form bonds of debt and loyalty. The old forms of gifts and tribute, whose retention was assumed, would provide income over and above that supplied by the Dutch.[15]

14. Quite a few regents elsewhere accepted direct landownership or grants of land in appanage. On the north coast of Java, some also held private estates granted by Raffles during the British interregnum (1810–1815) and subject to British laws of primogeniture; they derived large incomes from these lands. Among them were the regents of Tegal, Pemalang, Japara, Rembang, and Brebes. Some regents of the former western mancanegara, including those of Banyumas, Bagelen, and Purwakarta, opted for grants in appanage, though they profited less from the lands than did the regents of the north coast. See CA, Schaarsbergen, Verbaal 24 October 1865, no. 1 (a collection of reports from the residents on the income of regents in Java); also CA, The Hague, Geheime Missive, 12 January 1902, no. 835; Onghokham, "Residency of Madiun," pp. 139–140, n. 69; and, for the general relationship of the regent's position to colonial economic development of the time, D. H. Burger, *De ontsluiting van Java's binnenlanden voor het wereldverkeer* (Wageningen: H. Veenman & Zonen, 1939), pp. 124–125. The system of appanage lands was replaced in the early 1860s by increased salaries.

15. How much such contributions amounted to is something of a mystery. An important regent of Madiun, needing more than 2,000 picols of rice a year for his

To the Madiun regents, therefore, the new system seemed to be simply a more favorable version of the old. Their overlords were different, but the foreign new ones promised to be even more dependent on their cooperation than the traditional rulers had been—certainly the foreigners were eager in their wooing. Already the regents had seen their positions become in principle hereditary, their privileges and status increase, and their income grow without sacrifice of their old sources of tribute. The Dutch, for their part, confidently expected to make the regents the linchpin of their rule. But that is not the way things worked out. By the end of the century the regents' power had been fatally weakened, and it was, ironically, the policies embarked on by the Dutch that did it.

A number of factors contributed to the decline in the regents' strength, one being the shift in the balance of power as the Dutch replaced the princes at the center. With the Dutch in control of all Java and able to call on greater resources, unity, and organization to enforce their rule, the regents could no longer resort to defection to another patron or serious contemplation of rebellion as maneuvers for fending off excessive demands from above. Furthermore, the image of the warrior chief gradually gave way to one of a functionary in a bureaucratic apparatus, detracting from the leadership role that had secured popular loyalties. Had the regents opted for land rights, they might have acquired the interests and ideology of a landed gentry and gained recognition in that role. As it was, the money subsidy led eventually to their

---

family, dependents, and public festivities, could get it with no indication that he ever bought rice; CA, Schaarsbergen, Verbaal 24 October 1865, no. 1. An ordinary family would need some 25 picols a year. However, the regent had to hold public feasts on such occasions as installations, awards of promotions and medals, and the yearly *lebaran* and *suro* festivals. In addition, he was expected to entertain many visitors, especially neighboring regents and their retinues and Dutch officials. On the other hand, regents do not seem to have supplied food to the laborers called to do corvée for their households. Permanent servants and a few relatives were not provided with food but rather given portions of the regent's salary land (where this existed) to provide for their support. Some of the north coast regents used their money income to pay the poll tax of the local peasantry to the Dutch, the peasants repaying in rice; in this way the regents controlled the local rice market. This is not reported for the regents of Madiun, but it is unclear whether the omission is due to the absence of the practice or to poor reporting by the residents concerned.

relegation in Dutch eyes to the status of salaried bureaucrats, honored cogs in the colonial machine. Though continuing to look to the old sources of tribute and corvée for part of their income, the regents grew increasingly dependent on the subsidies and share in agricultural production granted by the Dutch to pay for the heightened splendor of the *kabupaten* courts and a newly acquired taste for European furnishings. All this alienated the populace, and the Dutch, coming to regard the regents as civil servants, saw the regents' exactions from the peasantry for luxuries as a corrupt use of office.

The new balance of power between the regents and the center had a further consequence. Whereas Mataram had used a policy of divide and rule to keep the outer territories from falling under the sway of any one leader, the Dutch preferred to deal with larger units, thereby simplifying administration and reducing the burden of support from the colonial exchequer and the local population. Their policy therefore was to promote only a few pryayi families and establish only a few regents; these were, however, to be elevated far above all others in position and income. Gradually, from 1830 to 1876, the number of Madiun regents was reduced from twenty to five, and through no accident these five— Madiun, Magetan, Ngawi, Ponorogo, and Pacitan—were the regencies in whose chief towns the resident and his four assistant residents had been stationed. The hereditary principle yielded to the perceived interests of colonial administration at other points too, particularly as the number of regencies shrank and that of high-status pryayi families without adequate position grew. Usually the Dutch minimized resistance to a regency's abolition by waiting till an incumbent died and then pensioning off the family or offering its members other pryayi positions. The remaining regents happily acquiesced in this policy, for the official income from the subsidies and production shares of abolished regencies was added to theirs and there was always the hope that the abolished regencies' territories would also be redistributed. In only a few cases did deposed regent families fight back with success; one such instance occurred in Pacitan in the late 1830s when the regent family prevailed against an assistant resident who had tried to prevent the succession of its heir.

In the late 1840s an effort was made to speed up the consolidation of regencies in Madiun, and several of the lesser regents managed to convey their alarm to The Hague, which instructed Batavia and the resident not to abolish regencies in the future without consulting the Ministry of Colonies. This interference in local colonial affairs by the metropolitan government was rare for the time and effectively postponed abolitions for several decades.[16] Even so, by the end of the Cultivation System in 1870 only six regencies remained, and of these only two were in the hands of bupati families that had held them since the beginning of Dutch rule.[17] In the ensuing Liberal period, with its business-minded principles and expanded administrative activity, the process of transforming the regents from "native chiefs" into freely interchangeable functionaries proceeded yet more swiftly. Perhaps the only reason the hereditary principle was retained at all at this point was that, there being no other way to select a bupati, it was a convenient bureaucratic routine.

The administrators of the colonial civil service (*Binnenlands Bestuur* or BB) could scarcely be blamed for wanting to work through able Indonesians, and as Batavia usually accepted the advice of the administrators on appointments and promotions these showed a strong bias in favor of European-style bureaucratic expertise. BB members did not, and did not try to, understand the complicated workings of Javanese society, leaving largely to the pryayi the business of preserving their traditional status and power. It was to Dutch opinions, needs, and criteria—not "native" ones—that the ambitious pryayi increasingly had

16. CA, Schaarsbergen, Geheim Verbaal 4 December 1852, no. 438.

17. In 1870 the Prawiradiningrat line came to an end as regents of Madiun, to be succeeded by the bupati of the abolished regency of Purwadadi. About a decade later the Jagakarya family was replaced in Pacitan by a clerk's family brought from Semarang around 1830. Ngawi had practically always had outsiders as bupatis. Of the other three regencies—Magetan, Sumoroto (abolished 1876), and Ponorogo—only Magetan and Sumoroto had an unbroken line of bupatis of the same family. In Ponorogo the family could be called old and of local elite origin since it descended from Kyayi Imam Besari II of the free-village Tegalsari, which had a famous religious school; but the bupatis of Ponorogo were not descendants of regents. These changes in personnel do not seem to have had a traumatic effect on local relations. The hereditary principle was, after all, a Dutch-imposed one. For the history of some of the main regent families of Java, see Heather Sutherland, "Notes on Java's Regent Families," *Indonesia* 16 (October 1973): 113–147; 17 (April 1974): 1–42. For the general context of Dutch policy toward the regents, see Heather Sutherland, "Pangreh Pradja: Java's Indigenous Administration and Its Role in the Last Decades of Dutch Colonial Rule" (Ph.D. diss., Yale University, 1973), pp. 80ff.

to conform. Enhancement of pryayi influence over the peasantry, as called for by colonial policy, took the form of bureaucratic backing. For instance, the pryayi got strong Dutch support through the colonial legal system, especially the police courts (*politie-rol*), which fined and sentenced peasant defendants on the basis of cursory interviews. The regent was made head of a well-organized native civil service (*pangreh praja*) consisting of his right-hand man (*patih*); technical services supervisors (*mantri*) for such areas as irrigation, forestry, coffee and sugar production, storehouse management, and police; district chiefs (*wedana*); and subdistrict chiefs (*camat*). Moreover, the Dutch reserved the positions in this expanding civil service for the pryayi. But by exalting European values, the BB administrators acted to detraditionalize Javanese society and thus unwittingly undermined the foundation of the regents' hold on the population.

Aggravating the tension for the regents, already caught between trying to control the population according to the traditional system and trying to conform to the expectations of alien overlords, were the expanding technical demands of the colonial administration. Very early, the need for such skills as the ability to write Malay, the language of colonial government, had brought the addition of outsiders to the Madiun bureaucracy.[18] With the growth of the administrative structure and the communications network under the Cultivation System and particularly after the development of large-scale private plantations in the Liberal period, the range of new functions and services became so great that the regents often found themselves unable to supervise all activities in the sphere of native administration. By the end of the century this dual role of conservator of tradition and principal channel for change had put the office of regent under heavy strain. Those who could not or would not fulfill completely the modern bureaucratic role were likely to retreat into the "native" world of ceremony and tradition or seek to renew their charismatic appeal by mystical practice. As can be imagined, such conduct diminished their usefulness to the colonial administration as points of access to the population, and despite official policy the residents and other Dutch officials began, especially as technical services acquired their own chain of command, to quietly sidestep the regent.

18. See, for example, the account of the early colonial order in the "Babadé Negara Patjitan."

This gradual alteration of the regent's role was paralleled by profound changes taking place in village society. A principal form of peasant leverage against exploitation, flight to another region, had virtually vanished upon the establishment of order, and regents, their authority backed by the Dutch, could now enforce the full traditional panoply of imposts. The villagers' main prospect for relief was reduced to hoping for the appointment of a new regent from outside who might not become acquainted immediately with all the possibilities for extraction which local custom provided. The Dutch, though they complained loudly of the native elite's gross exploitation of the peasantry, themselves placed considerable burdens on the villagers. Heavy labor demands were imposed both for corvée to maintain expanding road and irrigation systems as well as official establishments and for the production of export crops under the Cultivation System. One portentous development related to the tax on land use.

In the Mataram period land had often been used to produce corvée laborers under a system whereby Javanese princes granted peasants land in compensation for their liege-service (*herendiensten* in Dutch). The regents' distribution of their lands to the peasantry had the same motive, to tie the people to their corvée. The exaction of labor in return for land rights reached new proportions, however, under the colonial regime. The Dutch claimed as successors to the Javanese kings the right to land rent, i.e. a tax on land use, and then under the Cultivation System commuted the tax to corvée. In other words, instead of collecting a land tax and paying wages to the peasants for their work on the plantations, the Dutch counted the one against the other. Indeed, the whole bookkeeping of the Cultivation System rested on a fictive base as far as wages and tax were concerned, for fictive land tax was collected and fictive wages were paid. Peasants were considered to be in arrears on their taxes if not enough labor was rendered to the plantations—and alternately were kept in a constant state of arrears by their lack of cash from wages. Consequently, to the peasant the land tax and corvée were identical and, since labor was reckoned in the government's bookkeeping at a very low cash value, the exaction was heavy.

The substitution of corvée for the land tax put the entire burden on landowning peasants and threw the sikep class in particular into a quandary. Although the sikep had heretofore been able to meet corvée requirements by sending their numpang, their relationship to these dependents had changed. The Java War had caused much fertile land in the areas bordering Madiun to be abandoned, and the availability of this land together with the fact that in Madiun itself the regents were distributing land to tie peasants to corvée greatly strengthened the bargaining power of the numpang, who could now effectively threaten to leave a sikep unwilling to share his land. Most sikep eventually chose to give their numpang land rights, seeing in this course the additional benefit of a lighter corvée obligation because a larger number of people would be liable.[19]

The pressure from the landless below was augmented by pressure from the officials above. Both Javanese and Dutch functionaries found dealing with individual landowning peasants a cumbersome process that did not always produce sufficient labor for the needs of the Cultivation System and so began to set requirements on a village basis.[20] This accelerated the designation of common land in the villages and finally led to the revival, with Dutch encouragement, of the ancient practice of subjecting all land in a village to annual redistribution. Village heads did not usually lose, being secure both in their percentage of the production for the Cultivation System and in their ability to retain, with the help of other local officials, a good portion of the best fields as salary land, but the rest of the village families suffered a sharp leveling. Having thus

19. For a discussion of the burden placed on the landholding peasants in the colonial period, see CA, Schaarsbergen, Mailrapport 1888, no. 54, especially chaps. 1 and 2. This is a manuscript report of more than 1500 pages on the results of an investigation in the late 1880s by Resident Wiselius into the land rights in Kedu, part of the western mancanegara of Mataram; it includes a brilliant account of the historical development of landownership and its relation to social structure. It was the demand for their labor rather than their land that weighed on the peasants of Madiun. Theoretically the Cultivation System required that 20 percent of the lands be given over to plantations, but in Madiun only 2 percent were. Of course, this represented a higher proportion of land in cultivation and encompassed the most fertile, best irrigated fields; see Onghokham, "Residency of Madiun," pp. 176–203. Robert Van Niel, "Measurement of Change in Java, 1837–1851," *Indonesia* 14 (October 1972): 98, concludes that in general the land area used for plantations in Java was small but that 70 percent of peasant families were involved in working them.

20. Thus Resident Wiselius of Kedu noted that the government and the pryayi between them managed to raise the forms of corvée from above twelve categories in precolonial times to between forty and eighty in 1888; CA, Schaarsbergen, Mailrapport 1888, no. 54.

transformed the pattern of landownership from one of individual plots to one of communal property, the colonial government proceeded slowly to herd the rural population, which had traditionally lived in scattered groups of a few families and their dependents, into well-structured settlements centered on the headman's house—the large peasant villages typical of Java today.

Through this and related policies the Cultivation System set in motion the process that effectively stifled peasant initiative and ultimately bred the "shared poverty" still characteristic of rural Java. During the Liberal period the Dutch, zealously applying their new ideology, tried to restore individual peasant landownership only to run into opposition from pryayi and village headmen, who had become accustomed to dealing with the villages as territorial units and who, furthermore, enjoyed the greater prominence communal landholding gave their positions. In any case it was too late. The sikep had so completely disappeared from the Javanese experience that the very term had faded from common parlance, replaced by the word *kuli* (from the British Indian *coolie*) referring to all peasants.[21] Although in theory the Liberal system was less demanding of corvée, in fact it exacted much. Taxes were calculated in money and, while the landowning families found payment in money a

21. Similarly, the old word for communal village land, *tanah lanyah* (possibly from *wilayah,* meaning territory, or from *ulayat,* meaning working right) was supplanted by *tanah kongsèn* (from the Chinese *kongsi,* meaning cooperative or joint effort), a term probably imported from the north coast residencies; see *Eindresumé,* 2: 200–201. Some idea of the relative burden the colonial economic system imposed on the peasantry can be gained by comparing the labor and land use demands in Madiun generally with those in the *perdikan-desa,* the villages that by tradition were exempted from state exactions in exchange for their support and maintenance of local religious institutions and sacred places. The sharp difference is evident in the pattern of Tegalsari and Banjarsari, both sites of famous religious schools, where individual land rights continued, and the villagers even kept a register of their claims with the headman. Not all perdikan-desa villagers succeeded in retaining individual land rights, though, as illustrated by the perdikan-desa of Kauman in Ngawi; when a new mosque was built there and its officials needed appanage lands for their maintenance, they persuaded the peasantry to adopt the communal land system; *Eindresumé,* 2: 202; F. Fokkens, "De priesterschool te Tegalsari," *Tijdschrift voor Indische Taal-, Land- en Volkenkunde uitgegeuen door het Koninklijk Bataviaasch Genootschap van Kunsten en Wetenschappen* (hereafter cited as *TBG*) 24 (1877): 310–377; Pangeran Koesoemojoedo, "Schets van den rechtstoestand der perdikan desa's in het Regentschap Ponorogo," Ms. 1926, Koninklijk Instituut voor Taal-, Land- en Volkenkunde, Leiden.

relief from the labor exactions of the Cultivation System, the scarcity of cash among the peasantry and the very low valuation of labor and rural produce forced the peasants to borrow the necessary funds at considerable cost.

Therefore despite a staunchly traditional appearance—especially to those Dutch observers who imagined that anything so unmodern as communal landholding must be the old way of things—the Javanese village had experienced what amounted to a social revolution. Superior status within the village was now concentrated in the village head and his assistants; there were still many fine gradations of status based on land control, but the former connotations of power were gone. As tanah-bengkok and cultivation percentages provided village heads (*lurah*) with economic security, and with tenure of office more dependent on government favor than on local support, it became common practice for lurah to keep the office in the family and to identify with the powers above rather than the people below. All this narrowed the opportunities for other villagers to rise socially through relationships with pryayi patrons.

The same forces that had widened the gap between ruler and ruled in the regencies did so in the new-style villages, where the lurah was now in charge of a large administrative unit. His lieutenant, the *kebayan,* became the channel of communication linking lurah and villager, while the lurah himself, following the way of the real powerholder, remained aloof from worldly matters and things that caused pain to his people. The kebayan was a man with land rights and usually a relative of the lurah—though the headman would never appoint his son or intended successor to the post because the kebayan risked unpopularity with the people in carrying out his duties of directing the village police, organizing corvée, and, especially, collecting taxes. The lurah did not tarnish his image by demanding taxes himself, waiting at home instead for his lieutenant to bring back the revenue. Individual grievances and village quarrels were heard and adjudicated by the lurah, but anything that might give his office the appearance of being an agency of exploitation was avoided as far as possible.[22] The kebayan acted only on orders

22. L. W. C. van den Berg, "Gemeentewezen op Java en Madoera," *Bijdragen tot de Taal-, Land- en Volkenkunde van Nederlandsch-Indië uitgegeven door het Koninklijk Instituut voor Taal-, Land- en Volkenkunde* (hereafter cited as *BKI*) 52 (1901): 34ff.

from the lurah, of course, and these orders came only after the lurah had carefully balanced the expectations of the regent against the productive capabilities of his clients.

As the colonial system and Dutch thinking became dominant, some key elements of the old rural power relationships fell into disuse. The jago role was one for which the new bureaucratic ethic had no place. Indeed, with the multiplication of regulations and demands on villagers and the narrowing of channels for protest and social advancement, jago-desa came to be regarded by the colonial authorities as potential leaders of dissent, and the term *jago* began to acquire a flavor of illegality it had never had before. Even the important and respected role of palang assumed, at least in Dutch eyes, an illegitimate character. Nevertheless, these intermediaries seem to have proliferated under the Cultivation System to fill the need for communication between the population and the pryayi, and the new village structure did not always destroy the old patterns of patron-client bonds. To the Dutch, however, there was no need for any nonbureaucratic leadership above the village level: the palang was an unnecessary expense if not also a probable source of local resistance to needed reforms. Regents who made much use of such intermediaries were suspected of scheming to extract excessive tribute from their villagers or, worse, of attempting to build an anti-Dutch power base.

The Dutch never placed the palang (*tussenhoofd* or intermediary chief in colonial terminology) on the official list of functionaries of the Indies and eliminated even informal recognition of the office after the end of the Cultivation System. Yet the regents needed intermediaries more than ever before as channels of communication to the major social levels. True, the regent now had a more fully structured administration and could rely on his patih and other members of the pangreh-praja. But it was not this official hierarchy or its less developed earlier forms that enabled the regent to control his people, useful though these officials might be. His power over the peasantry had always lain in his informal manipulation of rural leaders, the jago-desa, and now this system of patron-client relationships had been severely curtailed.

His control of village society was imperative in view of his responsibility to the Dutch for the maintenance of order and production, and regents who felt their lower officials and headmen were insufficiently industrious or loyal continued to turn to local intermediaries. The peasants, meantime, had developed the attitude that village administration was coercive, precisely because of its bureaucratic setup and its many regulations and orders. Consequently, the village leader or jago had to tread a fine line, careful to preserve the traditional image of patron to his clients and careful to prevent his protests in their behalf over bureaucratic "legalism" from looking like incipient opposition to those above. Not backed by colonial authority as the regent and other pryayi were, the jago resorted to the only practicable way to get the protection from the regent that his difficult dual role required: the jago became the regent's spy (*weri*). The absence of organized police forces was used to justify the employment of jago as spies and strong-arm men to keep the peace, and by the beginning of the twentieth century there were an estimated four to five thousand weri in Madiun residency.[23] Many were villagers of substance, some even headmen, but the ambivalence of their role as local political bosses, informers, and extortionists, plus their lack of prospects for advancement into the official class, meant that there was little moral or material check on their doings. As a result, a need developed in rural Madiun for brokers not only between the hierarchical levels of the social system but also between legality and criminality, and the jago gradually moved into the penumbra of these overlapping spheres.

Another aspect of Javanese society affected in significant ways by the Dutch presence was religious leadership. From Mataram days the pryayi life style and Islam had always been in loose coexistence, and the bupati, with a few notable exceptions, had tended to be little involved in matters of Muslim teaching and jurisprudence. The Dutch, however, having discovered during the Java War how easily Islam could become a rallying point for opposition, were anxious to link religious leaders to colonial interests. Thus at the village level under the Cultivation System the *modin* (muezzin) was given a share of the produce along with the secular officials. At the same time, the regents were given a greater role in religious affairs, being treated as the final arbiters in questions of Islamic law, though a regent who evinced particularly strong religious leanings came under grave suspicion: was his religious penchant a reasonable expression of devotion and of desire to guide the religious ele-

---

23. W. T. L. Boissevain (Resident of Madiun, 1902-1907), *Memorie van overgave*, p. 40 (CA, The Hague).

ment in the approved manner or did it spring from fanaticism and the intent to mobilize the populace against the Dutch?

The problem was particularly acute in Madiun residency, where a number of religious centers had been established under famous *kyayi* (religious teachers) during the Mataram period. To support the *pesantren* (religious schools) where these men taught, certain villages were made exempt from state exactions and their tribute diverted for this purpose. The areas around these villages—especially those in the regency of Ponorogo—became important foci of religious activity. In Madiun, therefore, the Dutch, unable for reasons of both Muslim and Christian ideology to assume religious authority themselves, were even more concerned to subordinate religious leadership to the regents, and the regents were encouraged to behave in a worldly fashion. After all, a secularized regent was an easier chap to get on with, besides being unlikely to embrace the "fanaticism" the Netherlanders so dreaded.

Yet, however pleasing secular behavior might be to the Dutch, the regent's hold on his people lay in religious legitimation, if not from orthodox Islam then from the pre-Islamic *agama Jawa* which still provided the main spiritual authority for the courts and the principal orientation of much of the population. His high estate, the outward trappings of power were meaningful to the people only in the appropriate traditional context, and this, given the restricted modes remaining open by the late nineteenth century, meant display of the spiritual attributes of power. The proper bearing called for aloofness (from the Dutch as well as the common mass), ascetic practice or at least patronage, and an evident personal association with the wellsprings of mystical power. By no means were all regents ambitious enough or otherwise able to follow this pattern, but only the more prescient or xenophobic who did retained any leverage at all against the Dutch.

The people, even as late as the end of the nineteenth century, continued to look to the regent as the most powerful figure in their lives—the focus of ritual, the source of justice and redress, the one who with the help of strong-arm men and spies maintained law and order. To the Dutch his key role as agent of extraction lost all relevance with the end of the Cultivation System and the introduction of private estate agriculture, and it seemed likely that before too long the Netherlanders would conclude that the regents were no longer essential to colonial rule, placing the future of their families and their culture in jeopardy. Indeed, since the advent of the Liberal period there had been a visible movement in that direction. As part of their modernization of the administrative and taxation systems, the Dutch had been gradually converting the pryayi's income to salary alone, stripping away the system of gifts and tribute. Although a regent was paid equally as well as the resident, who was expected to live in the magnificence appropriate to an "elder brother" of the regent,[24] a regent had the additional expense of providing for a very large family and following and of giving patronage and public feasts. Without their traditional sources of income, the regents' purses became greatly strained, and soon there was a rising clamor from the Dutch about overspending, indebtedness, and illegal exactions by regents. Eventually their spending would be markedly reduced with a concomitant diminution of their social rule. One potentially attractive alternative—participation in the burgeoning development of Java as private entrepreneurs—was discouraged by the colonial authorities, who prevented the relatives of regents from entering business enterprises as a guard against possible corruption of office. Thus were the pryayi stifled in any inclination toward a capitalist solution for their financial problems.

If the regent's situation at the end of the century could be described as in crisis, so too could the resident's. Housed in rival splendor, the resident relied on his own hierarchy of assistant residents and district officers (*controleurs*) working alongside the hierarchy of pryayi officials, whose activities their Dutch counterparts supervised. The resident was the link with Batavia, and his responsibilities to his Dutch superiors included the preservation of order, the delivery of taxes, and the supply of labor from the population. All this had to be accomplished through the regents, for the resident had no police force and only a minimal

24. The "elder brother" analogy of the relationship was written into the *Regeeringsreglement* of 1854, the Indies constitution. The regent may have been financially better off, as he was entitled to greater corvée and tributes. Both, however, received percentages of the export crop yield under the Cultivation System until percentages were abolished for European civil servants in 1863. For the resident of Madiun, the percentage amounted in 1860 to somewhat over 5,000 guilders (on top of a salary of 15,000 and allowances of 3,000); CA, Schaarsbergen, Verbaal 25 October 1865, no. 21, section on "Bestuurshervormingen." There was a considerable difference in salary income between the lower ranks of the pryayi and the lower ranks of the BB, which encouraged the pryayi as a whole to rely on nonsalary forms of income.

European staff. The sole Javanese official reporting directly to the resident was the chief *jaksa* (public prosecutor), whose assistants and weri provided the resident's only source of intelligence. Such intelligence had to be evaluated with care. The chief jaksa was, like the regent, part of the local pryayi world with expectations of staying in the area for life, whereas the resident would be there no more than five years.[25] Heedful of his local attachments and interests, the chief jaksa was as likely to use the resident as the resident was to use him. At the same time the chief jaksa's close relationship to the highest Dutch official exposed him to opportunities for advancement in the colonial order, making him a somewhat suspect figure in the eyes of the pryayi and villagers. Nevertheless, if a regent and the jaksa stood together on an issue, there was little the resident, ignorant of local customs and language, could do except seek conciliation.

Compounding the precariousness of the resident's status vis-à-vis pryayi officials was the insistence of Batavia that the prestige of the regents be maintained at all costs. Sometimes this protection extended to their close relatives too, as in Ponorogo in 1885 when the brother of the regent came under suspicion during an investigation of a messianic movement. The regent's brother, who had been passed over for the succession upon the retirement of their father, was not exiled or otherwise punished—which might tarnish the name of the regent family—but was instead appointed patih in faraway Gresik.[26] What happened if a resident rashly impugned a regent's honor is illustrated by an incident in Magetan five years later. The newly appointed resident, C. Donker Curtius, having heard rumors that the regent of Magetan was involved in opium smuggling, decided to investigate and assigned the chief jaksa of Madiun to look into the matter. Alarming information from weri was

25. As we shall see below, his term of office could be much shorter, notably in the case of Madiun in the 1890s. The major source of continuity was the *memorie van overgave* which an outgoing resident presented to report on his tenure of office. But the resident or lesser official who hoped for promotion was careful to follow the guidelines from Batavia and the Ministry of Colonies in The Hague in writing his reports and policy recommendations. As a result, one often finds that such reports largely ignore the politics of the local pryayi in favor of descriptions of local colonial administration and development. Reassuring as this may have been to the higher authorities, it is unlikely to have been of great aid to the new incumbent.

26. CA, Schaarsbergen, Mailrapport 1886, nos. 8a and 8b.

duly forthcoming, and the resident, unaware that he had become en-
snared in the chief jaksa's own intrigues against the regent, ordered the
kabupaten searched. No opium was found. After an ensuing investigation by neutral outside officials, ordered by Batavia, resulted in the
complete exoneration of the regent, Donker Curtius was dismissed from
service, guilty of the cardinal sin.[27]

Nonetheless, a change was in the air. The very fact that the resident
had dared invade a regent's house, whatever the state of his proof of
wrongdoing, was evidence of this. There were other signs, too, that the
Dutch were beginning to tire of their dependence on the pryayi and to
seek direct control of the society. As early as 1885 Batavia's Adviser for
Native Affairs, L. W. C. van den Berg, had inquired into the books of
Arabic sermons read in the mosques of Madiun, thus busying himself
with one of the last fields in which the regents were still allowed complete say. He was prudent about it though, pretending to be only a
scholar.[28] But when in 1889 Christiaan Snouck Hurgronje assumed the
advisership and on his tour of Java came to the residency of Madiun,
such caution was no longer necessary. Investigating conditions openly,
conversing with anyone at will, Snouck felt no compunction about
reporting on the mismanagement of religious affairs by the regents or
even about contradicting their rulings on matters of Islamic law.[29] A
similar shift in attitude was apparent in Batavia, where high officials
had begun to question the once inviolable principle of the regent's
public inviolability.[30]

The new mood was part of the imperial self-confidence which generally possessed the colonial powers at the end of the nineteenth century.
Moreover, the influx of Europeans in the Liberal period following the
development of the private plantation economy, the improvement of
communications, and the extension of technical services all served to
lessen the former isolation of the Dutch administrators and to solidify
their feeling of superiority to the "backward" native official class. Cul-

27. CA, Schaarsbergen, Mailrapport 1890, nos. 152 and 384. The bupati was
R. M. A. Kerto-adinegoro; the investigating official was the Inspector of Opium
Affairs, H. te Mechelen.

28. CA, Schaarsbergen, Mailrapport 1888, no. 148.

29. C. Snouck Hurgronje, "Aanteekeningen," ms. in Leiden University Oriental
Library, pp. 1132–1133.

30. CA, Schaarsbergen, Mailrapport 1889, no. 207.

tural complacency and their growing numbers drew the Europeans together in a world of their own surrounded by an opaque Javanese
society. Yet greater Dutch power did not still their sense of unease. Just
as fear of the "yellow peril" was tempering Western imperial self-
confidence elsewhere, the Dutch were nagged by the thought that the
natives might not calculate as rationally as Europeans the impossibility
of defying Dutch rule. Consequently, the colonial administrators were
only too sensitive to any hint of disaffection—by "fanatical" Muslims,
"treacherous" native chiefs, or the "rebellious" peasantry.

Unable to fathom the inner workings of Javanese society, the Dutch
ignored the regime of weri in the countryside and put their emphasis
on the strict maintenance of the outward signs of an orderly society.
The neatness of a village was equated with its security. In Madiun there
were regulations on the height and thickness of the fences that could be
built around houses or along the roads. The cattle had to be put in communal stables at night and guarded. Villagers also had to take turns at
night patrolling the village itself, the roads, and the waterworks. Travel-
ers needed identification papers and sometimes even special travel
passes, neither of which provided a guarantee against official harassment: a stranger was a source of suspicion, and as such could be arrested
at will and sent back to his place of origin. Guests in the village had to
be reported to the authorities. Close relatives of a criminal suspect were
taken as hostages for use by the police in unraveling the crime or forcing
a confession. Moreover, house searches could occur at any time, and
their purpose was not always to trace criminals. Often the house search
was carried out, with its accompanying abuses, as "preventive punishment" to persuade the population to be more vigorous in preserving
order.[31]

On the surface, then, Madiun appeared like all Java to be at peace.
What weighed heavily on the mind of the resident, who was ultimately
accountable for law and order, was the haunting thought that all might
not be well beneath. His resources, as we have seen, were few, and the
growth of the local European community had both distracted his attention from Javanese affairs and brought great pressure to react strongly
to every imagined threat. Not surprisingly, one resident cracked under

31. "Het recht en de politie in de Residentie Madioen," in *Mindere welvaart
rapport*, 1: 8–9, 17; "Recht en politie," ibid., 8a: 48ff.

the strain. And it was under these circumstances that the Brotodiningrat affair took place.

The Brotodiningrat family had been regents of Sumoroto, now a district of Ponorogo, since the seventeenth century. Family tradition has it that the first Brotodiningrat to be bupati carved out a territory for himself and his followers and only after this recognized Mataram's sovereignty. Like most Madiun pryayi families, the Brotodiningrats claimed descent from the first Muslim proselytizer of the area, the local saint Batoro Katong. After the division of Mataram in 1755 into the sultanate of Yogyakarta and the sunanate of Surakarta, the family gave their allegiance to the latter and, still in power at the time of the Java War, found themselves allied to the Dutch.[32]

When in the 1840s Sumoroto was put on the list of regencies to be abolished and integrated with Ponorogo, the then bupati protested and, as mentioned earlier, succeeded in winning the intervention of the colonial ministry in The Hague.[33] A scandal that rocked the family in the early 1850s led to the exile of the incumbent bupati, and in 1856 the ruling Brotodiningrat died, leaving a six-year-old son, Raden Samadikun, as heir. Either occasion might have served the Dutch as an opportunity to end the line.[34] But Sumoroto, although small and isolated, was allowed to continue as a regency until 1876, perhaps in part because of the coffee plantations there.

Raden Samadikun, who would later rule as R. M. A. Brotodiningrat,

32. L. Adam, "Geschiedkundige aanteekeningen omtrent de Residentie van Madioen," *Djawa* (Tijdschrift van het Java Instituut) 20 (1940): 341ff.

33. CA, Schaarsbergen, Geheim Verbaal 14 December 1852, no. 438.

34. In 1850 the bupati became involved with the wife of the penghulu of Ponorogo, whereupon his concubine poisoned the lady. The regent tried to cover up the crime, but the penghulu and the regent of Ponorogo would not let the matter rest. In the ensuing scandal the Sumoroto bupati was replaced by his son, Raden Tumenggung Brotodirjo, father and predecessor of the Brotodiningrat who is the subject of our story. See CA, Schaarsbergen, Verbaal 29 August 1860, no. 11. The Dutch had a very high opinion of Brotodirjo (CA, Schaarsbergen, Geheim Verbaal 9 June 1855, no. 303) and this probably contributed to their decision to appoint the patih of Ponorogo acting regent for Sumoroto until the majority of his son.

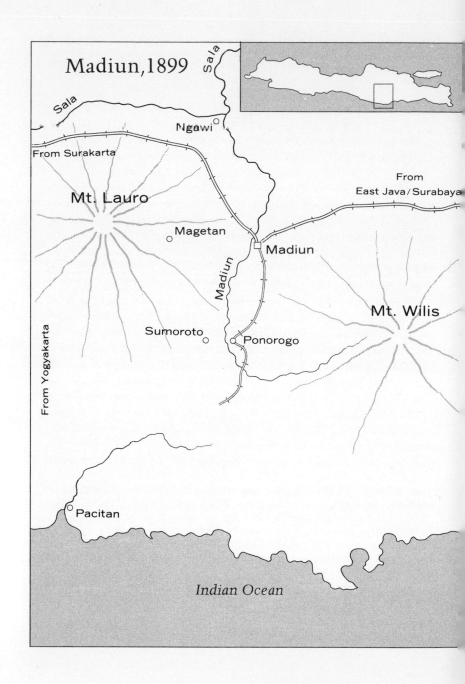

Madiun, 1899

Sala

Sala

Ngawi

From Surakarta

From
East Java/Surabaya

Mt. Lauro

Magetan

Madiun

Madiun

Mt. Wilis

From Yogyakarta

Sumoroto

Ponorogo

Pacitan

Indian Ocean

was brought to the court of Surakarta in 1856 by his widowed mother, daughter of a prince and granddaughter of Susuhunan Paku Buwono V. The young Samadikun became a magang at Surakarta, then the grandest of Java's courts and one where the resident still took a relatively humble stance toward the monarch. In 1866 at age sixteen Samadikun left this life of grandeur to begin his career in Dutch service as an apprentice government clerk (*mantri negeri*) in Madiun at thirty guilders a month. His rise was rapid, as only a bupati's heir could expect: appointment a year later as wedana of Magetan at eighty guilders a month and in 1869 installation at age nineteen as bupati of Sumoroto with a monthly income of a thousand guilders, the office having been held vacant pending his return.[35] Just seven years afterward, when the Dutch abolished the regency and assigned Sumoroto's lands to Ponorogo, the bupati was appointed regent of Ngawi. According to the Dutch, this new post represented a promotion, for Ngawi was more important than Sumoroto, and so the new regent was granted the title and name of Raden Mas Tumenggung Brotodiningrat.

Brotodiningrat himself was a bit unhappy about the appointment. His family line counted for little in Ngawi and, more to the point, his ambition had been to become the regent of Ponorogo—or at least have one of his relatives in the post.[36] For years he continued to intrigue toward this goal. In 1883, for instance, Brotodiningrat reported to the Dutch that the wedana of Caruban, son and successor of the regent of Ponorogo, had been imposing taxes too strictly on the local peasants, causing great numbers to migrate to Ngawi. The charge was dismissed as groundless, but in 1885, when the wedana was made regent of Ponorogo, a messianic rebellion broke out, whereupon Brotodiningrat apparently declared publicly that with a more capable regent such a thing would not have happened. This episode brought relations between the two families to their nadir.[37]

35. On the arrangements for Samadikun's education and succession, see CA, Schaarsbergen, Verbaal 8 March 1899, no. 25.

36. Ngawi was outside the area where Batoro Katong ancestry counted, for according to tradition it had been converted to Islam by saints from the north coast, notably Sunan Kali Jaga. In fact, family origins of any sort seem to have counted for little in Ngawi because it had long had as regents career officials from outside the area.

37. Arsip Nasional Republik Indonesia (hereafter cited as ANRI), Missive, Regent of Ponorogo, 24 January 1900, in Besluit 22 July 1900, no. 1. When in 1884

Brotodiningrat was also piqued by the gradual erosion of the regent's authority since the end of the Cultivation System in 1870. His first conflict with the colonial administration came in 1883 after the Dutch, without prior consultation, replaced his patih with a new one. Brotodiningrat's sharp protest to the resident regarding the procedure elicited instead of an explanation a reprimand from Batavia calling for the display of more respect in the future toward his Dutch superior.[38] Yet it was as regent of Ngawi that Brotodiningrat, perhaps intent on finding countermeasures, greatly expanded his power base in the residency of Madiun. When the local assistant resident, a man of Liberal economic principles, decided to encourage the application by Javanese for land rights in this relatively sparsely settled area, Brotodiningrat not only made use of the opportunity himself to obtain approximately a hundred bau, which he held more or less as private property, but urged his *guru* (spiritual adviser) to apply for some uncultivated land too.[39] The guru, Kyayi Kasan Ngalwi, took the advice and settled with 110 of his followers on about a hundred bau of Ngawi land.[40]

In 1886, after a little less than ten years in Ngawi, Brotodiningrat was appointed regent of Madiun. This again was a promotion, in that Madiun

---

or 1885 the old regent of Ponorogo retired, Brotodiningrat tried unsuccessfully to have his uncle, Raden Brotodirjo, the wedana of Keniten, appointed regent of Ponorogo. Relations between the regents of Madiun and Ponorogo only improved after 1890 when Brotodiningrat's relations with the regent of Magetan became really hostile. The material on the Brotodiningrat case in the ANRI is stored as the Brotodiningrat Papers and consists mainly of three bundles of government decisions which include all the papers used in the deliberations.

38. ANRI, Missive, Regent of Ngawi, 7 October 1883, in Besluit 1899, no. 5.

39. Many other upper class Javanese took advantage of this opportunity, especially Central Javanese princes (such as the Mangkunegara) and rich *haji*. There were 650 bau of land in Javanese private ownership in Sepreh and 950 in Gendingan, with plot sizes ranging from 20 to 140 bau. Brotodiningrat and his guru were the only ones in Madiun residency to hold relatively large land parcels; most of their land was turned over to plantation cultivation of rice. See J. Hofland (Resident of Madiun, 1907–1914), *Memorie van overgave*, pp. 53ff. (CA, The Hague).

40. Ibid. Kyayi Kasan Ngalwi, born in 1844 at the village of Karang Gebang in Ponorogo where there was a famous religious school, had become an influential local figure with a reputation for invulnerability, the power to charm people (*ilmu pengasian*), and skill in the martial arts. For more on his influence, see CA, The Hague, Verbaal 1902, no. 835 (report of the Regent of Ponorogo).

was the main town of the territory, but the thirty-six-year-old regent had now risen as high as a Javanese official could under the colonial system. All that remained were such ceremonial honors as the *adipati* title and the right to be shaded by the golden umbrella, both of which were bestowed on Brotodiningrat in due course. His conduct as a public servant won rather high praise from the Dutch: a capable official who was expert in agriculture and excellent in solving police problems as well as a hard worker and, according to his first Dutch superior in Madiun, an extremely scrupulous financial manager (a very great rarity among the pryayi).[41] His personal character elicited less favorable comment: he was considered obstinate, difficult to control, and jealous of his prerogatives as regent, especially in affairs relating to the mosque. It was hoped that his appointment to Madiun, where he would be under the direct supervision of the resident, would help him to master these defects. Indeed, his first resident, Mullemeister, seems to have been able to handle and even to like Brotodiningrat. The end of Mullemeister's term in 1890, however, ushered in a period of instability in the office of Madiun resident during which there was a quick succession of seven incumbents in as many years, beginning with C. Donker Curtius, whose sudden dismissal was recounted earlier. Throughout these years of flux, Brotodiningrat grew in power and arrogance even as Dutch patience with regent pride was growing shorter.

Though probably aware of this stiffening disposition toward regents, Brotodiningrat made no concession to the fact in his behavior under the residents who came and went, and all filed reports critical of the Madiun regent. One resident who appeared particularly meddlesome provoked Brotodiningrat to remark that "nowadays residents no longer trust their bupati, whom they think of only as weri."[42] His chafing under resident supervision stemmed in part from his conviction that the regents actually had the upper hand and could always, through their control of the pryayi, frustrate a difficult resident. Brotodiningrat liked to remind the pryayi and village headmen that regents remained their rulers for life whereas residents rode on a passing wave, not even staying as long as

41. CA, The Hague, Exhibitum 14 August 1902, no. 16; CA, Schaarsbergen, Verbaal 8 March 1899, no. 25.

42. ANRI, Missive, Resident of Madiun, 11 September 1896, in Besluit 22 June 1900, no. 1.

coconut trees bear fruit.[43] It is little wonder that the Madiun regent was reprimanded two more times during these years for insolence toward his superiors.

Friction between the regents and the now secure imperial Dutch over traditional prerogatives surfaced in Madiun with Snouck Hurgronje's visit there following his appointment as Adviser for Native Affairs. Alarmed at the Islamic scholar's inquiries into religious matters, Brotodiningrat asked whether Dr. Snouck "is also entitled to investigate affairs which are the bupati's [sole province]."[44] Snouck seemed correspondingly startled by Brotodiningrat, commenting that never in his experience had he met such a regent as the regent of Madiun. According to Snouck, Brotodiningrat had a very high opinion of himself and a rather low one of all except a few of the European officials, his haughtiness with newly arrived Dutch administrators bordering on contempt.

Snouck also noted that the regent of Madiun acted variously as a tyrant of old toward his own subordinate pryayi, as the wise old Javanese grandee with Europeans, and as the modern colonial administrator in court circles.[45] This chameleonlike behavior reflected his marginality in the society of the day and the contradictions in the position of regent. Brotodiningrat was a man of high noble status yet also a mere official of the Netherlands Indies, a despot encircled by restrictions. From his ability and experience as an official came a feeling of being able to replace the Dutch in modern administration, a notion that would help unite the nationalists who arose in the next generation. Moreover, as we shall see, he had the orientation toward modern means of communication and the cosmopolitanism of discourse that was to characterize nationalist propaganda. But the political base was not the same. The founders of the nationalist movement were outsiders who had no power within the colonial establishment. The Madiun regent had

43. Ibid. Brotodiningrat must have felt, though, that with the Dutch mistrusting him his control over his own pryayi was threatened. How much he thought a Dutch show of confidence would increase his effectiveness as regent is evident in his requests for his own promotions; ANRI, Missive, Regent of Ngawi, 7 October 1884, in Besluit 19 May 1899, no. 5.

44. CA, Schaarsbergen, Verbaal 26 October 1900, no. 23.

45. C. Snouck Hurgronje, *Ambtelijke adviezen,* ed. E. Gobee and C. Adriaanse (The Hague: Martinus Nijhoff, 1957), 1: 579–580.

a great deal. His "marginality" was the very product of his being so far inside both the colonial bureaucratic and traditional aristocratic worlds.

J. J. Donner, about fifty years old at the time of his appointment as resident of Madiun in 1896, had a good but not spectacular record in the colonial administration and had served in two places regarded as restless—Banten under Van Ravenswaay and Madura during the divestiture of the powerful Cakraningrat dynasty. His first and unpleasant task upon assuming office was to transmit to Brotodiningrat the government's displeasure at the regent's behavior toward the former resident. Donner, an emotional and not always consistent man whose pomposity was matched only by Brotodiningrat's arrogance, did his best to smooth over the matter, observing that Van Ravenswaay was indeed a difficult boss and offering to forget past events. The new resident soon discovered, however, that the regent was involved in all sorts of petty quarrels with members of the local Dutch community, including the local judge and several other officials. There was, for instance, his refusal to contribute to the support of the local Dutch music corps (which was dear to the Europeans) because of a clash with the Dutch music director. When Donner himself reproached Brotodiningrat about the intransigent tone of his letters and reports, so unlike those from other regents, the regent of Madiun retorted that his letters were different "because I'm no old woman."[46]

There was to be no surcease in the contention between the two officials. At one of Donner's big receptions, Brotodiningrat is said to have remarked loudly that Resident Mullemeister used to give much better parties and had really known how to win the hearts of Madiun society. Donner was deeply stung by the slur, for the residents prided themselves on being accepted by the native hierarchy and local notables. Nor did Brotodiningrat let any opportunity go by to humiliate Donner through his relatives. A local sugar mill which employed Donner's stepson De Kock lost a dispute over irrigation rights against another factory owned by a wealthy Chinese concern after a hearing before the regent of Madiun.[47] For his part, Donner apparently countermanded some of

46. CA, Schaarsbergen, Verbaal 26 October 1900, no. 23. Most of Donner's observations and opinions of the regent of Madiun in their first encounters are contained in this document.

47. R. M. A. Brotodiningrat, *Na 31 jaren regentschap in de Residentie Madioen* (Jogjakarta: Privately printed, 1902). The regent's view of the events can also be found in several published petitions.

Brotodiningrat's orders and otherwise tried to curb his peremptory style. Moreover, the regent's uncle, the wedana of Keniten, was suddenly transferred to an unimportant post, and Donner began urging the European community to go to the feasts of the Magetan regent rather than those of Brotodiningrat in an attempt to prove the Madiun regent's unpopularity.

A high point in their quarrel came during the festival for the coronation of Queen Wilhelmina in 1898. Rumors that Brotodiningrat was complaining about Dutch plans to keep to themselves a celebration paid for by the people forced Donner, who headed the festival committee, to spend considerable time assuring the Javanese that this was not true and that everybody would participate. Then Brotodiningrat proposed that the regents of Madiun, the only possessors of ceremonial cannon, would fire the gun salute at their own expense, a move the resident nullified by announcing that the army would fire the regents' cannon. The real issue, of course, was the place of the regents in the celebration, and Donner became convinced that Brotodiningrat was preparing to sabotage the festival or at least steal the limelight. When Brotodiningrat announced to the press and to his people that he would lead the prayers at the mosque on coronation day, Batavia reacted with alarm, whether because of Christian scruples or because of the possibility such assertiveness might set a dangerous constitutional precedent for pryayi behavior. On the eve of the festival, Donner called Brotodiningrat to the residency and explicitly forbade the gesture. The still recalcitrant regent departed with the words, "and if I nevertheless do it?"—to which the resident replied that he should then accept the consequences. It was with great relief that Donner found Brotodiningrat and the rest of the pryayi in the local church the next morning rather than in the mosque.[48]

Thus matters continued till 1899 when, on the occasion of Brotodiningrat's thirty-year jubilee as regent in the Netherlands Indies service, Donner tried to get the government to award the regent some honor as an appeasement, perhaps the *aria* title or even membership in a Dutch order. The Council of the Indies turned down the request with the stern advice that the government did not deal in this way with insubordinate regents and that the resident should himself handle the problem.[49] It

48. CA, Schaarsbergen, Verbaal 26 October 1900, no. 23.
49. ANRI, Besluit 15 June 1899, no. 5.

was a fateful message: Donner, though embarrassed by his blunder, saw a sign that Brotodiningrat was in disgrace in Batavia and could now be suppressed with impunity.

Yet moving against the regent must be done circumspectly, because many pryayi in the residency had come to regard Brotodiningrat as a powerful figure with great influence in Dutch circles, and his support in obtaining promotions and other favors was eagerly sought. The one important exception was the regent of Magetan, who not only eschewed Brotodiningrat's support but was his bitter rival. Donner recognized an opportunity and, on his special recommendation, the regent of Magetan was raised in 1899 to the *adipati* rank. To show his partiality to this particular pryayi, the resident sent out special invitations to all high Javanese officials for the ceremony (a thing which had never been done before) and published a statement extolling the dynasty of Magetan as the oldest and the least blemished by irregular succession. Brotodiningrat did not attend the ceremony for the regent of Magetan.[50]

Donner's next step was to try to isolate the regent of Madiun from administrative affairs by forming alliances with Javanese officials who could be persuaded to cooperate, a tactic Brotodiningrat had himself used repeatedly against European officials. The two selected by Donner for special trust were the newly appointed patih of Madiun and the chief jaksa, Raden Hadiputro. Brotodiningrat quickly took the occasion of a Muslim feast to humiliate his patih in public, by first inviting him to sit at the gaming table and then, after his flustered refusal, ordering him to go to the mosque and join the pious in their prayers. In addition to thus making the patih look ridiculous in the eyes of the local pryayi, the regent of Madiun bypassed his faithless lieutenant to put the irrigation chief (*mantri ulu-ulu*) effectively in second-place command.

The chief jaksa presented a different kind of problem for the regent in that Raden Hadiputro, as the only pryayi who reported directly to

50. R. M. A. Brotodiningrat, *Memorie van toelichting op de aan de Neder-landsche Volksvertegenwoordiging ingediend rekest* (Jogjakarta: Privately printed, 1902). The rivalry between Brotodiningrat and the regent of Magetan had started in their youth when both were magang at the resident's office in Madiun. Kerto-adinegoro refused to attend any of Brotodiningrat's receptions and forbade his pryayi to do so. Their feud gave the Dutch an opening: Brotodiningrat seems to have helped Donker Curtius in his opium case against the regent of Magetan. ANRI, "Nota betreffende de verhouding tusschen de regenten van Magetan en Madioen," Besluit 22 June 1900, no. 1.

the resident, had his own useful Dutch connections and could be considered a potential rival. Brotodiningrat therefore dealt with his disloyal chief jaksa by keeping him at a distance and giving him no cooperation at all in police affairs. The powerful regent of Madiun could afford to do this, for he had his own efficient organization of informants among the weri. His spies under surveillance, Raden Hadiputro could no longer fulfill his duties properly and turned bitterly against Brotodiningrat. To Donner this outcome merely enhanced the trustworthiness of the chief jaksa, whose influence over the resident eventually became so great as to be detectable in every decision and appointment Donner made.[51]

As the turmoil attendant on these intrigues grew, demoralizing the Madiun pryayi and disrupting administration, something like a power vacuum arose. The bolder and less scrupulous took advantage of the situation to act for their own gain; the rest stood aside, hoping to save themselves by inaction. It was at this point that the curtain was stolen from Donner's house.

After the resident's second interview of the regent in the course of the investigations, an escaped prisoner named Suradi was recaptured by Brotodiningrat's agents and the resident's tablecloth recovered from somewhere in Ponorogo. The regent blamed Suradi and his companions for all the thefts of recent weeks, assured the resident that "peace and order" would now return to Madiun, and asked for medals for his agents. The resident rejected the request for rewards and asked in disbelief how a lowly convict could have robbed the residency without assistance. Brotodiningrat replied that Suradi was "a powerful (*digdaya*) and dangerous criminal who can take the form of a dog and enter houses undetected"—a Javanese retort that the resident did not understand.[52] Anyway, Donner was much more inclined to believe the chief jaksa's report that Suradi had escaped from prison only after the theft of the curtain and so could not have been the culprit. Calling the regent's account a lie, the resident sent Suradi and his companions off to Ponorogo

51. *De Locomotief,* 9 October 1901.
52. ANRI, Geheime Missive, Resident Donner, 21 December 1901, no. 112, in Geheime Missive, Gouvernement's Secretaris, 30 December 1901, no. 386.

for questioning to foil any attempt by the regent to influence the proceedings. Only later did Donner realize that Brotodiningrat had agents in Ponorogo as well and had managed to bribe the alleged thieves to confess that their stealing had been masterminded by Raden Hadiputro, the chief jaksa.

Finally resorting to his ultimate weapon, the resident charged in a missive to Batavia that the regent and his irrigation official had deployed their spies—former criminals more powerful than any police—in an anti-Dutch intrigue.[53] The government agreed to Donner's proposal to relieve Brotodiningrat temporarily of his post. After the regent and his family had been removed under guard from Madiun to Padang on Sumatra's west coast, the resident was given the task of conducting an inquiry into the whole matter. Here was a major break with past policy: in the Magetan affair the suspension of the regent came only after the *fait accompli* of the search of the kabupaten and even so Batavia went to elaborate lengths to preserve his dignity and position. Now Batavia's intent was to humble a too proud regent, and the official least likely to spare the regent's reputation was chosen as judge.

Donner found one person, also a former convict and according to the regent a very unreliable fellow, willing to testify on all the wrongdoings of Brotodiningrat and his henchmen—their illegal detention of witnesses and suspects, their physical intimidation of some and bribery of others.[54] We do not know, much less the people at the time, exactly what happened and who did what. Nor was anybody then interested in finding out. Consequently, Donner succeeded in putting all the blame for the series of thefts on Brotodiningrat.[55] In the purge that followed, many pryayi were dismissed or transferred. Several officials close to the suspended regent asked for sick leave or simply failed to show up.

The inquiry had also extended to the regent's influence over the mosque and its treasury, especially his contacts with gurus and other spiritual leaders, but none of these were purged. Nor for the moment were the spies, whom Donner felt could be neutralized by the appoint-

53. ANRI, Geheime Missive, Resident Donner to Governor General, 23 November 1899, in Besluit 7 January 1900, no. 3.

54. Snouck Hurgronje, *Ambtelijke adviezen*, 1: 584.

55. *Semarangsche Courant*, 5 November 1901, had a long account of the events and suggested that the thefts might have resulted from a bet among the weri on who could steal the resident's curtain and make shirts of it.

ment of a European police chief and a new modern police force for the township of Madiun. Donner may have had other reasons as well. For example, a former convict named Kartorejo, then living in Madiun and suspected of running a brothel and dealing in opium, was mentioned in the report as Brotodiningrat's chief spy. Verifiable details of his life and career are scant, but his local renown as writer of petitions for the peasants and others would indicate literacy and some education as well as good standing in the community. Apparently his career as informant began when Brotodiningrat's uncle, the wedana of Keniten, sought his help in tracking down the source of the many sugar cane fires in the area. Kartorejo, who had many contacts, was thereafter employed personally by Brotodiningrat and enjoyed a rather intimate relationship with the regent. At the time of the inquiry, Brotodiningrat took special pains to point out that Kartorejo was paid from the resident's police funds with the resident's full knowledge.[56]

On 20 March 1900, some five months after Brotodiningrat's removal from Madiun, Donner reported his findings to the government.[57] The governor general, the director of the civil service, and the members of the Council of the Indies all seemed to be impressed with the report and convinced that the regent was indeed extremely arrogant and untrustworthy and that his henchmen formed the underworld of Madiun. The resident's recommendation was that Brotodiningrat be dismissed without honor, given a small pension in recognition of his thirty years of service as regent in the Netherlands Indies government, and forbidden to settle in the residency of Madiun or in those principalities where he had many contacts.

Not of a disposition to take such a decision peaceably, and, unlike most previously disgraced regents, knowledgeable about the way to maneuver in the Dutch bureaucratic system, Brotodiningrat turned to his powerful friends among the Europeans. One of these was his former superior, Mullemeister, who rallied to his support and may have persuaded Hora Siccama, a Councillor of the Indies, to give a dissenting opinion during the deliberations on the Brotodiningrat matter.[58]

Also making use of new modes of publicity, Brotodiningrat presented

56. ANRI, Geheime Missive, Gouvernement's Secretaris, 22 February 1902, no. 76.

57. CA, Schaarsbergen, Verbaal 26 October 1900, no. 23.

58. CA, The Hague, Mailrapport 1901, no. 38.

his case to a wide spectrum of the modern educated public by publishing appeals to the queen, to the States-General (parliament) of the Netherlands, and to the minister of colonies. One of the first Indonesian journalists to emerge, Raden Tirtoadisuryo of the *Pembrita Betawi,* and the influential Indies editor, Brooshooft, took up his cause, which became the subject of considerable argument in the Dutch-language press—argument that was by no means always in favor of the resident. Furthermore, stopping in Batavia on his way to Padang, Brotodiningrat contacted some lawyers.[59] If Batavia and The Hague were going to insist on adherence to Dutch legal practice in their closer supervision of local Indonesian affairs, the regent would take advantage of that too.

His lobbying had mixed results. Governor General van der Wijck finally decided to retire Brotodiningrat honorably on a pension of 250 guilders a month, allowing him to return from Padang (but with oral instructions not to live in Madiun) and promising him that one of his sons would later succeed to the regentship.[60] This decision had its motives, for a dishonorable removal would have given the ex-regent more legal grounds and greater incentive to appeal against the judgment, along with a stronger case for attracting supporters. The government did not want to stir up questions about Donner's conduct of the investigation. It was now the resident as the representative of Dutch power, not the regent, whose prestige must be upheld at all costs. This shift in policy reflected Batavia's increasing reliance on the European bureaucratic apparatus, which was henceforth encouraged to handle problems with the pryayi as routine administrative matters rather than subjects for diplomatic negotiation.

Yet the affair did not end here. Much to the discomfiture of the resident of Madiun, the ex-regent settled in neighboring Yogyakarta, and Donner resumed his persecution of Brotodiningrat's followers and relatives. Anyone connected with the ex-regent could expect to be rejected for public office, even for such a humble post as forest ranger. A brother of Brotodiningrat trying to visit another brother in Pacitan was ousted from the district by force on orders from Donner, who ostensibly acted on advice from the assistant resident of Pacitan that the Brotodiningrat

59. ANRI, Geheime Missive, Gouvernement's Secretaris, 30 December 1901, no. 386.

60. ANRI, Geheime Missive, Gouvernement's Secretaris, 11 February 1902, no. 58.

family were "rebel chiefs" (*kepala kraman*).[61] Brotodiningrat implored
the Indies government in several petitions to protect his family.

Because of his pending appeals to the Netherlands and his audience
with the governor general, the ex-regent probably felt reasonably con-
fident of his ultimate vindication, and the many people who went to
Yogyakarta seeking his help against Donner and others found him burning with curiosity about events in Madiun. One visitor was Kartorejo,
and soon after his visit a series of robberies by *kecu* and *kampak* gangs
(large and violent robber bands), especially of rich villagers, erupted in
Ngawi and Magetan, with a few incidents in Madiun and Ponorogo.[62]
These robberies, which continued from 1901 to 1902, were accompanied in some places by the cry, *"Gusti mesti menang, residen mesti
kalah"* (The bupati must win, the resident must lose).[63] Fearing that
the unrest might reach the residency's capital, the new regent, R. M. T.
Kusnodiningrat, an experienced official and scion of the old Prawiradirja
regent family, increased the night patrols. But Resident Donner, seized
by panic, distributed arms to all European citizens and sent a warning
to Batavia that a new Java War was in the making. The resident accused
Brotodiningrat, of course, of being behind the robberies and cast a wide
net for his sympathizers. Kartorejo was arrested in November 1901 in
a roundup of some sixty people that included an assistant wedana, ten
village policemen, eight gurus (one being Kyayi Kasan Ngalwi), and
many weri. This was but the beginning, for the shadow of Donner's suspicion eventually fell on a number of wedana, village headmen, and
patih and even on the regents of Ponorogo and Ngawi. Donner proposed
that twenty-two people—on a list headed by Brotodiningrat, Kartorejo,
Kasan Ngalwi, and the other gurus—be exiled from Java. The government concurred after excepting Brotodiningrat.[64]

Understandably hesitant to exile the retired regent at this time,
Batavia finally sent Snouck Hurgronje, the Adviser for Native Affairs, to
make an impartial investigation, cautioning him to be as inconspicuous

61. ANRI, Geheime Missive, Gouvernement's Secretaris, 30 May 1902, no. 194.
62. *De Locomotief,* 9 October 1901.
63. ANRI, Geheime Missive, Gouvernement's Secretaris, 12 December 1901, no.
112.
64. CA, The Hague, Geheim Exhibitum, 26 May 1902, no. 62; CA, Schaarsbergen, Verbaal 7 August 1902, no. 11, and Verbaal 26 August 1904, no. 60; and
De Locomotief, 26 November 1901.

as possible in order not to embarrass the resident. As Snouck himself admitted, his stay in Madiun from February till March 1902 was too short to uncover any plot, but this time he sided with the regent, describing the resident as overworked and ready for retirement. Snouck felt that the new wave of unrest was, like the first series of thefts, probably only a reflection of the general demoralization and deterioration of local administration that had accompanied the Brotodiningrat-Donner conflict. Moreover, by dismantling the police apparatus of a regent without arranging for its replacement, Donner had created a situation in which followers of the former regent might have acted on their own to cause trouble or bad elements might simply have made use of the chance to plunder. Snouck found no evidence at all of a conspiracy between Brotodiningrat and the regents of Ngawi and Ponorogo, noting that these families, though related through the intermarriage of their children, were in fact at odds with each other.[65]

The government was not able to make up its mind about Snouck's advice, for acceptance of his judgment would have meant the removal of an official whose prestige it had gone so far to maintain. Inaction in Batavia left the battle in Madiun unabated, with Brotodiningrat now shrewdly attempting to reorient his case to one against Donner personally. His first move in this direction was to file libel suits against the resident, the chief jaksa, and the assistant resident of Pacitan for calling him a "rebel chief."[66] Donner on the other hand continued to shower Batavia with ever more fantastic reports of plots by the ex-regent and a widening circle of prominent Javanese families—in particular, those families living in Madiun who had been blacklisted at one time or another by the Netherlands Indies government, such as the descendants of Sentot Ali Basya of the Java War.[67] As the charges and countercharges mounted, the whole pryayi corps became divided into two camps and routine duties were neglected.

In December 1902 the government sent again for Snouck Hurgronje, who repeated his opinion that the resident, now obviously on the verge of a nervous breakdown, should be retired.[68] The question had acquired

65. Snouck Hurgronje, *Ambtelijke adviezen*, 1: 578–588.

66. ANRI, Geheime Missive, Gouvernement's Secretaris, 30 May 1902, no. 194.

67. ANRI, Geheime Missive, Resident Donner to Governor General, 15 March 1902, no. 30, in Geheime Missive, Gouvernement's Secretaris, 3 April 1902, no. 122.

68. Snouck Hurgronje, *Ambtelijke adviezen*, 1: 588–602.

new urgency following a report by the Hoofdinspecteur der Cultures that a widespread rice-plant disease, *hama patek,* had caused an exceptionally bad harvest in Magetan; as one Councillor of the Indies pointed out, bad harvests had often in the past led to unrest among the people.[69] Donner was sent home on sick leave and never returned to the Indies. There was to be no letup in his attacks on Brotodiningrat, however, and in Holland the resident bombarded the Ministry of Colonial Affairs with memoranda about an anti-Dutch plot by the ex-regent. The culmination of his feud was probably the publication of a pamphlet in 1908 alleging that the Brotodiningrat affair was part of the conspiracy of the whole non-Western world against Christian and Western civilization—the "yellow peril" incarnate.[70]

Brotodiningrat himself remained a source of controversy as long as he lived. His libel suits put the government in a quandary, for it was felt that the case, even if Brotodiningrat lost, would attract too much attention and do more harm than good. The government tried to dissuade the attorney for Donner from pursuing the resident's plan to lay bare in court all the ex-regent's "plots" and ultimately got the libel suits set aside after warning the ex-regent that his legal action might be interpreted as an attempt to undermine government authority and thus become grounds for his exile from Java.[71] Upon Donner's retirement, Brotodiningrat sought to reenter government service but was told to remain quietly in Yogyakarta in the interests of his children's careers. In 1905, with Madiun to all appearances well in hand again, the Dutch allowed the ex-regent to settle in Ngawi on his own estate; before long Brotodiningrat was again being accused of building an anti-Dutch power base there with the help of his former weri, the village headman of Ketanggi. None of his children would become regents during Brotodiningrat's lifetime; it was not till the late 1930s that one of his sons became a regent, and even then more through the efforts of his father-in-law than because of his own ancestry.

In Madiun the new resident, W. T. L. Boissevain, dismissed Donner's chief jaksa, reinstated the purged pryayi, assured Javanese officials of their status, and did everything else in his power to regain pryayi confidence, declaring after six months that peace and order had been

69. ANRI, Besluit 11 May 1902, no. 45.
70. J. J. Donner, *Een tienjarige strijd* (Epe: Privately printed, 1908).
71. ANRI, Geheime Missive, Gouvernement's Secretaris, 30 May 1902, no. 194.

restored.[72] The tranquillity of the pre-1900 years never returned, however, for attacks on property, though below the record level of 1902, remained more frequent than before. A new and insistent popular demand for cash income, the developing shortages of land, better communications, and the loosening of the old social bonds had all contributed to the erosion of the old order, but the administrative paralysis of the official class during the Brotodiningrat affair had precipitated an acute form of this gradually deepening malaise.[73] By 1900 the expansion of the Netherlands Indies bureaucracy, with its emphasis on legal and administrative norms rather than the time-honored method of manipulating village leaders, had so alienated the people from their government that the traditional jago-desa was no longer able to bridge the gap. At first the general unease was expressed as it always had been in times of disorder, but the appearance a little more than a decade later in Madiun, as in many other parts of Java, of the earliest Indonesian mass organization, the Sarekat Islam, gave the people a new outlet. For a brief hopeful span, peasants would look to the Sarekat Islam leaders for the protection and redress of wrongs formerly provided by the jagos and pryayi—and follow their new leaders in blaming the Dutch for their distress.

In retrospect it is clear that the bupati's preference for larger money incomes over private landed estates led to a fatal weakening of the very basis of their power. Lulled by solicitude for the symbols of their almost sacred status as traditional rulers, the pryayi did not recognize

72. Boissevain, *Memorie.*
73. In 1902 there were 149 cases of sugar field arson (i.e. attacks on Dutch property) affecting more than 425 bau, as compared to 12 cases affecting 39 bau in 1897. There were 17 kampak robberies where there had been none before, numerous small crimes, and some murders. These statistics are from Boissevain, *Memorie,* p. 40. For the general official concern at the disorders of 1902, see CA, Schaarsbergen, Verbaal 7 August 1902, no. 11, Verbaal 26 August 1904, no. 60, Geheim Verbaal 17 May 1902, no. 68, and Geheim Verbaal 18 June 1902, no. 70; and CA, The Hague, Geheim Exhibitum, 26 May 1902, no. 62. After 1902 the sugar cane burnings remained under 100 cases every year, affecting less than 200 bau; cattle thefts amounted to less than 100 cases; and kampak robberies were under 10 per year. See Boissevain, *Memorie;* J. Hofland (Resident of Madiun, 1907–1914), *Memorie;* CA, Schaarsbergen, Verbaal 5 December 1914, no. 8.

that the Dutch would usurp real power and bestow the paraphernalia of office as their own interests might dictate. There was little concern in the government for the difficulties the bupati faced in holding their personal power bases—the intrigues, the fluctuating loyalties of their followers, even the willingness of the peasantry at times to accept a change of bupati as a potential relief from some traditional bonds of tribute. Erosion of a bupati's power over his people meant greater dependence on the colonial administration, and gradually the pryayi were reduced to mere salaried officeholders who could be removed from office and whose regency could be abolished. The government would have met more effective resistance to these encroachments on traditional rights had the bupati families been in possession of private landed estates, as the Brotodiningrat family demonstrated. Secure in their land in Ngawi, the Brotodiningrats retained their prominence despite loss of office, intermarrying among the elite families of Java. It was also in their village of Paron in Ngawi, where Brotodiningrat was an intermediary for the distribution of land, that the unrest was most troublesome to the Dutch. Private landed estates would also have put the pryayi in a position to exploit the opportunities for profit in the later development of a modern economy as some princely families, notably that of the Mangkunegara, were to do. Instead, the great majority of the pryayi, without capital to invest, wound up more as victims than as masters of the changes to come.

For some time the Indies authorities continued to move away from reliance on the regents to reliance on their own bureaucracy. During the Ethical period of Dutch colonial policy in the early years of the twentieth century the position of the pryayi was further challenged by champions of social welfare and democracy who saw injustices in such aspects of the bupati office as the patron-client system and hereditary succession. But in the 1920s the voices of these reformers were drowned by a contrary call for restoration of the old pattern of authority: what was needed if the Netherlands was to preserve its hold on the Indies was not greater administrative efficiency or democracy but a bolstering of the traditional social bonds. By the end of the decade the tide of reform was in full ebb and the government, spurred by Communist-led revolt, rushed to restore the prestige and power of the regents through programs to decentralize territorial administration and "detutelize" the regents.[74] Freed from close European supervision and once again given full backing for maintenance of their traditional status, the bupati would, it was hoped, regain their authority over the population and provide a loyal and conservative native leadership to check the anti-colonial unrest.

Administrative policy in the last decades of Dutch rule was largely devoted to this retraditionalization, but it was by then far too late. Attitudes at both the pryayi and popular levels had greatly changed, and in the continuing rapid economic development of Java the old basis of social relations seemed less and less valid. It was not possible to go back around the corner that had been turned when Resident Donner triumphed over Regent Brotodiningrat. The old pathways were becoming overgrown, and when the Japanese invaded during World War II the last traces vanished.

74. For a discussion of the motives for and effects of detutelization and decentralization, see Harry J. Benda, "The Pattern of Administrative Reforms in the Closing Years of Dutch Rule in Indonesia," *Journal of Asian Studies* 25 (1966): 589–605.

The Capampangan Zarzuela: Theater for a Provincial Elite

JOHN A. LARKIN

As our understanding of the events of the Philippine Revolution broadens, the problem of determining the meaning of nationalism in that era becomes more complex. Unsettled conditions at that time gave rise to numerous movements not immediately associated with the main political and military struggle against the Spanish overlord and American interloper. Regional activists and peasant rebels pursued goals other than the establishment of an independent, centralized Philippine state, and diversity of aims often presented enormous operational difficulties for the fledgling Malolos government. Such movements, small beside the formal opposition to colonialism, not only illustrate the class and ethnolinguistic cleavages of turn-of-the-century Philippine society, they also attest to the multifaceted nature of nationalism then.[1] Historians wishing to fathom that nationalism will first have to learn much more about its component parts.

The purpose of this study is to identify, describe, and evaluate just one of the many movements which proliferated during the Revolution, the Capampangan zarzuela theater. It is significant for it speaks to the aspirations of an influential group in Philippine society, the recently

I wish to express my deep gratitude to the staff of the Filipiniana Section, University of the Philippines Main Library, in particular Mrs. Namnama Hidalgo, Mrs. Yolanda Granda, and Miss Tita Ruiz, for seeing that I gained access to scarce materials vital to the preparation of this essay.

1. Examples of this variety of purpose can be found in Ma. Fe. Hernaez Romero, *Negros Occidental between Two Foreign Powers, 1888-1909* (Bacolod: Negros Occidental Historical Commission, 1974), pp. 69-278; Reynaldo Clemeña Ileto, "*Pasión* and the Interpretation of Change in Tagalog Society, ca. 1840-1912," (Ph.D. diss., Cornell University, 1974), passim; David R. Sturtevant, *Popular Uprisings in the Philippines, 1840-1940* (Ithaca: Cornell University Press, 1976), pp. 96-136.

emergent Pampangan elite—wealthy Chinese mestizo farmers, intellectuals, and professionals whose participation in the revolutionary struggle fluctuated considerably. Elsewhere I have discussed the extent of that involvement;[2] here I wish to take up their attitude toward the social and political changes going on about them. In the absence of recorded personal statements I have chosen to examine all the extant sources about this drama for evidence of Pampangan sentiment, since the zarzuelas were written and performed by local artists expressly for the elite who frequently attended them in the major towns.

The zarzuela, a Spanish form of operetta or light comedy, was imported into the Philippines in 1879 and flourished most prominently in the Manila area. Traveling companies took it to the larger provincial towns of the Archipelago, but only in Pampanga did a local theater movement develop. This province claimed a rich educated class who, though they could and did frequently travel to nearby Manila, nevertheless patronized their own regional theater performances of Spanish plays. By the turn of the century only the Pampangans and Tagalogs possessed the audiences, talent, and resources to launch a real dialect theater movement. In other regions further from Manila, its theater life, and the war—e.g. Ilocos, Pangasinan, and the Visayas—the development of dialect theater lagged behind and did not really begin until well after 1904 when revolutionary passions were already on the wane. But though other regions did not contribute comparable dialect theater between 1900 and 1904, enough differences existed between the content and intent of the Capampangan and Tagalog zarzuelas to indicate real variations in attitude and sentiment toward the Revolution. Whereas Tagalog drama took up mainly political themes such as anticolonialism, independence, and nation-building, reflecting that region's predominant involvement in and commitment to the Revolution, Capampangan plays protrayed domestic life, which revealed the locally strong interest in purely social and cultural change.[3]

2. John A. Larkin, "The Place of Local History in Philippine Historiography," *Journal of Southeast Asian History* 8 (September 1971): 306–317.

3. On dialect zarzuela theater in regions besides Pampanga and the Tagalog area, see Tomas C. Hernandez, *The Emergence of Modern Drama in the Philippines, 1898–1912* (Honolulu: Asian Studies Program, University of Hawaii, 1976), pp. 110–111, 149–174. I am indebted also to Mr. Alfred McCoy for information on the Ilongo zarzuela taken from his own current research.

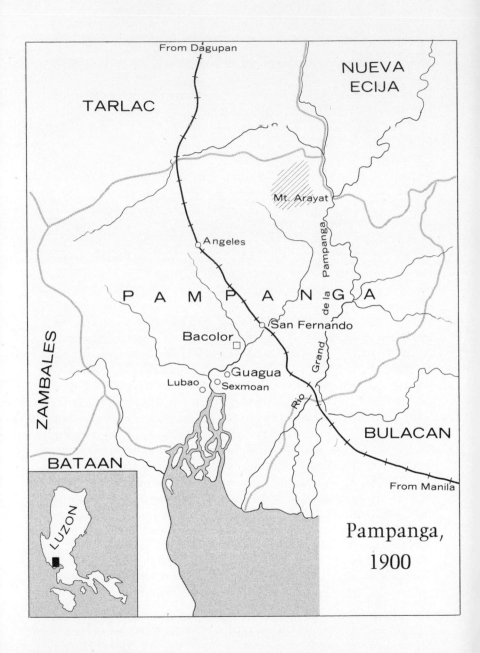

From Dagupan

NUEVA
ECIJA

TARLAC

Mt. Arayat

Angeles

P A M P A N   G A

de la Pampanga

San Fernando

Bacolor

Guagua

Lubao   Sexmoan

Grand

Rio

ZAMBALES

BULACAN

From Manila

BATAAN

LUZON

Pampanga,
1900

The Capampangan zarzuela movement began in a time of great stress, while United States forces fought republican troops for control of the countryside, destroying many of the province's villages and fields. It proliferated for the next four years while the provincial elite, confronted with rampant guerrilla warfare, faced a crisis of political allegiance. The growth of the frequently light and frivolous dialect zarzuela, in both its versions—operetta and comedy sketch—in the midst of so much agony offers only a seeming paradox. It gave voice to the social and cultural ideals of this provincial upper class during a time of transition, and revealed the central focus of their political loyalty: the perpetuation of their own class. For most Pampangan leaders interest in the development of a nation-state only came after the crisis of Revolution had passed and the zarzuela movement had already peaked in creative terms and in audience enthusiasm.

Pampangans had resided in the lower portion of the Central Luzon Plain for centuries before the coming of the Spanish conquerors in the late 1500s. Their interaction with the colonial masters over the next 330 years eliminated most of what had been their original unique culture, and their way of life in 1900 had come to look like that of most lowland Christian Filipino peoples with its blend of Spanish and native customs. In manners, dress, architectural style, and town planning Pampangans could scarcely be distinguished from, for example, their surrounding Tagalog neighbors. Yet in one respect Pampangans continued to be set apart, for their language, Capampangan, one of the Malayo-Polynesian dialects, was quite different and provided speakers with a clear identity. A great majority of them clustered within the boundaries of a single province of 850 square miles, Pampanga, and several bordering towns. Contiguity thus combined with linguistic distinctiveness to create a sense of separateness that characterized the Pampangans' behavior throughout much of their history.[4]

In social structure, Pampangan society broadly resembled that of other Filipino groups. The Pampangans belonged to an agrarian society

4. The basic information on Pampanga province and the Pampangan people comes from John A. Larkin, *The Pampangans: Colonial Society in a Philippine Province* (Berkeley: University of California Press, 1972). It should be noted that the term "Capampangan" refers exclusively to the language.

based on wet rice and sugar cultivation in which two classes flourished: a landowning group consisting of perhaps between 10 and 15 percent of a population of 250,000; and the rest who provided labor services, mainly, though not exclusively, through a system of share tenancy. On holdings ranging from several hectares to many hundreds of hectares, the bulk of farmers toiled for a small return in kind and cash, but also for a relatively high degree of social security. A rather tight symbiotic relationship held tenants and landlords together. In exchange for their services, tenants received from landlords assistance in their old age, subsistence and consolation through harsh times including bleak harvests and illness, guidance with personal and religious problems, and aid in raising their children. The relationship, obviously an unequal one in terms of distribution of power and financial rewards, still offered, in that era at least, a sufficiently high degree of satisfaction for both parties. Ritual kinship (the so-called *compadrazgo* system), occasionally real kinship, and often generations of interaction further cemented these ties. Elsewhere in the Philippines other systems of labor may have prevailed and worked equally well, but none could have provided greater solidarity than that of the Pampangans.[5]

With the rapid advance of Philippine commercial crops into the world marketplace after 1820, sugar replaced rice as the major export of the province. The switch in emphasis precipitated an agricultural revolution which pushed the cultivated zone onto the forested reaches of upper Pampanga and lower Tarlac and multiplied annual sugar yields manyfold. Increased acreage and improvements in the techniques of sugar processing made the area the second leading producer in the

5. Currently several able young scholars are working to complete local histories which will add appreciably to our understanding of agrarian developments in the Philippines and provide data for a far more sophisticated comparative analysis of labor systems in the Islands. Areas being studied include: Nueva Ecija, Cebu, Panay, Bicolandia, the Cagayan Valley, Negros, Ilocos, and Samar. For an outstanding work on the dynamics of a modern-day tenant system see Akira Takahashi, *Land and Peasants in Central Luzon: Socio-Economic Structure of a Bulacan Village,* I.D.E. Occasional Papers Series, No. 4 (Tokyo: The Institute of Developing Economies, 1969). To place the Pampangan experience in the wider context of Southeast Asia see James C. Scott, "The Erosion of Patron-Client Bonds and Social Change in Rural Southeast Asia," *Journal of Asian Studies* 32 (November 1972): 3–37.

Archipelago and earned its planters a reputation, mostly justified, for great wealth. It was native Pampangan landowners rather than outsiders who initiated this expansion and benefited most by acquiring large sugar haciendas in the north. The taming of virgin land came about mainly through a system whereby entrepreneurs sent their tenants to the jungle, supported the latter while they did the initial clearing and planting, and then registered the land as their own. Hence the two-class society of landowners and tenants was simply transferred to the new territory, and the moving frontier brought the peasants only minimal opportunity for socioeconomic advancement.

If the old two-class structure persisted through the agricultural expansion of the nineteenth century, the composition and lifestyle of the upper segment did not remain static. Decades of intermarriage between the native Pampangan elite and immigrant traders produced an upper class of aggressive Chinese mestizo entrepreneurs who operated the new sugar estates and machinery, in large measure controlling agricultural life. They shared economic power only with the Chinese merchants who monopolized retailing as well as the buying and exporting of provincial produce. Politically the mestizo elite (collectively referred to as the *principalia*) held all local offices up to the rank of municipal mayor (*gobernadorcillo*), higher provincial administration being reserved only for Spaniards. Socially, too, they fit on the scale just below the tiny group of peninsular and insular-born Spanish and Spanish mestizo families resident in the province; and the most prominent and wealthiest principales, known as the *ilustrados,* mingled freely with the Europeans. Only the restraints imposed by a colonial regime prevented Pampanga's Chinese mestizos from obtaining unrestricted leadership of their society. A small number of ilustrados, including notable figures like Mariano Alejandrino and Ceferino Joven, protested the Spanish order by joining such movements as the clandestine Masonic Order or the Liberal party of the martyr Father Burgos; however, the overwhelming majority found their status quite acceptable. Pampanga had few Spanish inhabitants other than Augustinian parish priests and a small corps of officials, and the Europeans did not possess enough acreage to pose any threat to the native position in agriculture, as was the case in the Tagalog provinces. Furthermore, many members of the native elite admired, studied, and enjoyed Spanish culture.

One direct result of the nineteenth-century economic transformation of Pampanga was the increasing Europeanization or, more properly, Hispanization of elite society. There were visible signs of such a change in the greater adoption of Spanish dress, especially the latest fashions, and the importation of European furniture, carriages, and other accoutrements. Foreign visitors, and also Filipino writer José Rizal, remarked after experiencing the renowned Pampangan hospitality on the lavish spending of the principalia and their possession of things occidental. But the acceptance of Spanish culture went deeper and many, particularly the ilustrados, mastered the colonial language. To do so they often pursued their secondary and university level education in Manila and, occasionally, at institutions of higher learning in Spain itself. Those among the principalia who possessed neither the social prominence nor the wealth of the ilustrados, those most likely to take over early management of family property, usually learned the rudiments of Spanish in grammar schools and private secondary schools, or *colegios,* within the province. The colegios, frequently operated by a single teacher, or *maestro,* sprang up to meet the demands of principal families for Western education, and like so many other institutions in Pampangan society received their patronage and financial support. One of the traditional customs not lost in the new social transformation was elite sponsorship of local cultural and charitable activities.

The population center, or *población,* in each of the twenty-one municipalities served as the focal point where colonial and native cultures met, for a need to conduct government business in the *municipio* (town hall), or to consult the parish priest at the big church, or to buy and sell in the local market brought principales and their families to the plaza area with some regularity. Wealthier families took to maintaining their chief residence, or at least a second home away from their holdings and tenants, in the poblacion in order to participate in the social, educational, and cultural activities clustered there; other principales unable to do so themselves made long visits with relatives living in town. Three poblaciones were especially popular for this purpose. Bacolor, an historic town, had served as the seat of Spanish authority during the British invasion of the 1760s. As provincial capital it offered the inducement of being the hub of governmental activity and attracted many influential ilustrado families, who erected some of the most beautiful homes in Pampanga. Guagua, the main riverport leading to Manila, stood as a key financial center where Chinese and mestizo merchant families congregated and profited from the bulk trade that passed along its wharves. And, finally, San Fernando boomed in the nineteenth century as a regional collecting point for sugar, especially after 1892 when the completion of the Manila-Dagupan Railroad turned it into a transportation and communications core for the entire province.

A new group of native professionals and artisans, created out of the business and social demands associated with the onset of commercial agriculture, located in the poblaciones. Salaried or deriving a livelihood from services rendered, these newcomers did not enjoy the same social standing as did landholders; nevertheless, their occupations as government clerks, pharmacists, lawyers, craftsmen, teachers, merchants, and middlemen provided them ample opportunities to mingle and some-times intermarry with the gentry—or even, given a measure of talent, ambition, and good fortune, acquire their own land and the attendant prestige. These townsfolk became avid participants in the developing urban culture, and from their ranks sprang the four major playwrights of the dialect zarzuela movement, as well as many of its performers, in the years during and following the Philippine Revolution. The release from Spanish supervision, particularly that of the clergy, stimulated much literary output, mostly in theater, journalism, and poetry, which, in addition to its artistic satisfactions, boosted the social standing of its creators.

Occurring as it did in the midst of so many social changes, the Revolution caught the province largely unprepared to take sides. Pressing competition for agricultural land as well as for social and political position which so divided the Tagalogs and Spaniards had not yet developed to any serious degree in Pampanga with its expanding frontier and small number of colonials. Generally, the elite chose to adopt a position of neutrality, before the actual presence of contending factions from both the republican and colonial armies forced them to take sides. Not until June of 1898, almost two years after struggle began in the Manila area, did Pampangans in significant numbers start to participate, first against Spain and then against the United States.[6]

6. Studies of the Philippine Revolution are legion but the following offer a good overall view of the struggle: Teodoro M. Kalaw, *The Philippine Revolution* (Manila: Manila Book Co., 1925); James A. LeRoy, *The Americans in the*

166 JOHN A. LARKIN

Once committed, Pampangans fought bravely enough in the open warfare, which came directly to the province during the rainy season of 1899, and in the guerrilla campaign which began in November of that year. Commitment exacted a high price. In the first phase much property was destroyed and the planting season lost, thus assuring a rice shortage the following year. The guerrilla campaign induced a crisis of divided loyalty—some officials deciding realistically to acquiesce to the new American overlords, others patriotically holding out—and the issue of collaboration generated severe repercussions. Loyalists threatened, kidnapped, injured, or killed the Americans' supporters; the colonial army ran to ground those who stayed faithful to the idea of the Republic. The worst part of the struggle came in 1900 when most of the terror occurred, but isolated incidents of violence erupted until 1903. Even after then the ill feeling persisted and remained a political issue of some importance as late as 1909.

The divisiveness of this period involved mainly the elite of the province, those men of wealth and political power who concerned themselves with national affairs, and their retainers. Peasants generally stayed out of such matters, looking after problems of survival so urgent during the war and the economic depression which ensued.[7] Certainly no interclass rivalry developed at this time of stress. The Pampangans emerged from the war scarred by the physical damage but with their social system and sense of group loyalty unaltered.

On 13 September 1900, while guerrilla warfare raged and native officials suffered intimidation, the one-act play *Ing Managpe* (The Patcher) by local playwright Mariano Proceso Pabalan premiered at

Philippines, 2 vols. (Boston: Houghton Mifflin, 1914); Teodoro A. Agoncillo, *The Revolt of the Masses* (Quezon City: University of the Philippines, 1956); Cesar Adib Majul, "The Political and Constitutional Ideas of the Philippine Revolution," *Philippine Social Sciences and Humanities Review* 22 (March–June 1957): vii–212.
7. The depression had its origins in the 1890s when unfavorable world market conditions caused a severe drop in the price of Pampangan export sugar. War exacerbated the difficulties and American tariff barriers prolonged the crisis until 1909.

El Teatro Sabina in Bacolor.[8] The plot revolved around a domestic quarrel between an unsatisfied, jealous wife and her hard-working, tired, but innocent spouse. A maid eventually patches up the rift (hence the title) after the presentation of several scenes and musical numbers by stock comedy players. The frivolity of plot scarcely seemed to suit the historical importance of the occasion: the first performance of a zarzuela in a native Philippine dialect.[9] The Pampangans possessed an old and extensive body of native literature, including poetry and drama, and the Spanish zarzuela had already found an audience in the province by 1900; but the wedding of dialect and play form represented a breakthrough in keeping with the spirit of the revolutionary era.

Little is known concerning the roots of Pampanga's literary heritage, except that, as in other regions, native forms were altered from early on by the Spanish influence brought by friar missionaries. The oldest remnants, lullabies (*tumaila*) and folksongs (*basulto*) sung by parents

8. The most extensive and authoritative information on Pabalan comes from Ely V. Javillonar, "The Significance of Mariano Proceso Pabalan in Capampangan Dramatic Literature" (Master's thesis, University of the Philippines, 1961). She not only possesses the largest collection of Pabalan's manuscripts but has included in an appendix three of his most important plays: *Ing Managpe* (The Patcher), *Oita pa, eh!* (Here We Are Still, Alas!), and *Apat ya ing Junio* (The Fourth of June). See also her article, "The First Vernacular Zarzuela," *Philippine Studies* 12 (April 1964): 323-325. For additional information consult E. Arsenio Manuel, *Dictionary of Philippine Biography*, 2 vols. (Quezon City: Filipiniana Publications, 1955-1970), 1: 298-299.

9. Some claims and evidence challenge the notion that *Ing Managpe* was the first zarzuela in any Philippine dialect. See Raymundo C. Bañas, *The Music and Theatre of the Filipino People* (Manila: By the author, 1924), pp. 40, 43-44; Jean Edades, "Filipino Drama of the Past and Present," *Theatre Annual* (1947), 32; Amelia Lapeña-Bonifacio, *The "Seditious" Tagalog Playwrights: Early American Occupation* (Manila: Zarzuela Foundation of the Philippines, 1972), pp. 45, 50; and Paula Carolina Malay, "The Zarzuela," *Weekly Women's Magazine*, 28 February 1958, pp. 15, 29. On the other hand, Javillonar, "Mariano Proceso Pabalan," pp. 56-60, makes a strong case for Pabalan's play being the earliest. The difficulty in resolving this question lies in the paucity of early manuscripts remaining and the failure of authorities to specify the difference in date between when a play was written and when it was first produced. In any case, and what is most important for this article, Pabalan believed his was the first vernacular zarzuela. He prefaced the script of *Ing Managpe* with the notation: "It was Pampango, before any other native language, that first adopted the *zarzuela* form"; Javillonar, "The First Vernacular Zarzuela," p. 323.

to their children, go back in oral tradition to remote times, and legends and folk tales, too, have come down from undetermined origins.[10] But Pampangan drama derived more directly from public and participatory literature; poetic games and jousts, recitative religious literature, and romantic epic poetry frequently spoken aloud in the nineteenth century. The long evenings of wake following a family death created the opportunity for many literary games and contests which promoted the poetic tradition in Pampanga. The *bulaclacan* (flower game) played between young men and women called for proper answering of a series of questions, with recitation of poetry as one of the possible penalties for improper replies. Similar consequences might be invoked in the riddle game, *bugtungan*. The less spontaneous *caragatan* differed from the games for the younger set, being almost staged performances in the house of mourning. Accomplished combatants, both women and men, declaimed verse lines, often memorized, which constituted the heart of jousts on such subjects as love, courtship, and honor.[11] Players holding a large stock of responses and a quick wit achieved reputations in the caragatan and many times were invited to participate.

10. One of the most helpful sources on Capampangan folksongs is Luther Parker's unpublished essay "A Brief Study of Pampangan Songs," located in the Luther Parker Collection (hereafter cited as LPC) in the Filipiniana Section, University of the Philippines (U.P.) Main Library. In his essay, Parker has included a sampling of different folksongs with their partially inaccurate translations. The Historical Data Paper volume on Pampanga (hereafter cited as HDP), found in the Philippine National Library, Filipiniana Section, is a valuable source of riddles and folksongs, ancient and modern. For a general overview of Capampangan folk literature, see Ricardo E. Galang, "Ethnographic Study of the Pampangans" (unpublished MS in the possession of Mr. Mauro Garcia, Manila, 1940), pp. 74–130.

11. Information on the various poetic games, some of them still played in Pampanga, came from talking with residents of the province and from the following other sources: Juan S. Aguas, *Juan Crisostomo Soto and Pampangan Drama* (Quezon City: University of the Philippines, 1963), pp. 5–8; "Historical Data of the Town of San Fernando, Pampanga, Barrio Del Carmen," HDP, p. 21; Rosalina Icban-Castro, "Exploring Pampango Literature," *Sunday (Manila) Times Magazine,* 29 June 1969, p. 18; Alfredo Panizo, O.P., and Rodolfo V. Cortez, "Introduction to the Pampango Theatre," *Unitas* 41 (March 1968): 132–134; Ignacio Manlapaz, "Filipino Drama: A Sketch," *Philippine Magazine* 28 (November 1931): 259; Jean Edades, "The Earliest Beginnings of Filipino Drama," *Philippine Educator* 3 (August 1948): 27–28. A text of a caragatan entitled "Pamañguang lisensia ybat sulip" (Seeking permission starting from the ground floor) is located in LPC.

The grandfather of Juan Crisostomo Soto, Pampanga's best-known playwright, became famous as a versifier in these debates.[12]

Public recital, so widespread as diversion in the nineteenth century, did not include just temporal material but religious as well. The Passion of Christ, or *Pasion,* a major part of Holy Week ritual, went beyond a mere translation into the dialect from European Catholic sources of one of the four major gospel versions of the death of Jesus to present, in metric stanzas of five lines, his life from birth to resurrection with additional material on moral precepts and early events from the Book of Genesis.[13] Through a process of adaptation as old as the Spanish conquest itself, the Pampangans had taken an element of Iberian tradition, lovingly and insistently transmitted by Augustinian friars, and transformed it into a usable and artistic aspect of their own culture. Though written down and published,[14] Pasion were repeated aloud in singsong fashion, usually from memory, by older members of the community before elaborately festooned altars in churches, chapels, and temporary barrio structures. The dramatic qualities of the lines and presentation drew large audiences seeking both religious experience and entertainment.[15]

Medieval Spanish epic poetry, which included such classics as *El Cid,* provided sources and inspiration for two other kinds of Capampangan literature, the *curiru* (dramatic poem) and *cumidia* (moro-moro drama). Heroic tales of knights, princesses, and infidels attracted

12. Galang, "Ethnographic Study," p. 122.
13. On the Capampangan Pasion and the Pasion in other Philippine dialects see: Mariano A. Henson, *The Province of Pampanga and Its Towns,* 4th ed. rev. (Angeles, Pampanga: By the author, 1965), p. 188; Edades, "Filipino Drama," pp. 19-21; Dionisio Salazar, "Filipino Drama during the Spanish Period," in *A Short History of Theatre in the Philippines,* ed. Isagani R. Cruz (Manila: Philippine Educational Theatre Association, 1971), pp. 74-77; and Ileto, passim. Anyone interested in studying the Spanish influence upon Philippine vernacular literature of all groups would do well to begin with Harley Harris Bartlett, "Survey of Vernacular Literature," in *Encyclopedia of the Philippines,* ed. Zoilo M. Galang, 3rd ed., 20 vols. (Manila: Exequiel Floro, 1950-1958), 1: 1-24.
14. Around the turn of the century the main publisher of vernacular literature was Cornelio Pabalan, brother of the playwright. See Galang, *Encyclopedia,* 3: 507; Aguas, *Soto and Pampangan Drama,* p. 4.
15. My own attendance at a recital of the Pasion in Angeles, Pampanga, during Holy Week of 1964 leads me to believe that Pampangan audiences still react to it with the same intensity as that described in the literature for earlier times.

audiences in Pampanga long after they ceased to do so in Spain. When or how these sagas arrived in the province has yet to be determined, but by the nineteenth century printed curiru circulated there, read and recited aloud as popular literature.[16] These long poems appeared in eight-syllable lines with rhyming couplets and took for their setting Europe and other exotic lands. The Philippine Archipelago never became the scene of action in spite of the fact that Pampangans had long made the curiru their own through translation and adaptation. Stylistic alterations naturally occurred in the transformation of Western epics into dialect poems; but, additionally, different episodes from various Spanish originals were sometimes combined to create new stories, and characters suitable to the Pampangan heroic ideal invented to carry out the action.[17] Dramatic content might be simplified (and usually was) in the process of adaptation, but the ending always contained the triumph of good over evil and Christian over infidel. Given the power of the Church in the Philippines, these tales never strayed far from their original medieval European religious themes and thus the curiru and its close relative the cumidia functioned as literary vehicles for the encouragement of Catholicism.

The term *cumidia,* though derived from the Spanish word *comedia* meaning play or drama in general, had the very specific definition of moro-moro play in Pampanga. Characters in these melodramas, Christian and Muslim royalty and soldiers, acted out the recurrent classic struggle of the medieval world. In fact, curiru frequently served as

16. Bartlett, pp. 7–8; Galang, "Ethnographic Study," p. 120; "Historical Data of the Town of San Fernando, Barrio San Juan," HDP, p. 11; Manlapaz, "Filipino Drama," pp. 259–260.

17. Copies of curiru can be found in scattered places. A full text of one, *Bernaldo,* is located in LPC. Another, *Corrido qñg bierang delanan ning conde Irlos ila ning condesang asauana qñg cayarian Francia* (Story of the way of life of Count Irlos and his wife the Countess in the Kingdom of France) (Manila: J. Fajardo, n.d.), was given by H. H. Bartlett to the University of Michigan Library and is kept in the Worcester Collection. Other sources listing curiru are the catalogue of the Harley Harris Bartlett Collection in the American Philosophical Society Library in Philadelphia; and the List of Titles of the H. Otley Beyer Collection. For further information on the latter group of materials, which, sadly, have now been allowed to leave the Philippines, see Letter from Gabriel Bernardo, Librarian, University of the Philippines, Manila, to Thomas F. Currier, Assistant Librarian, Harvard College Library, 7 June 1937. This letter and the List of Titles can be found on microfilm at the U.P. Library.

scripts for cumidia. At barrio fiestas all over Pampanga local actors in flashy costumes declaimed heroic speeches and simulated bloody battles on newly constructed stages.[18] Often plays took two, three, or more nights to complete, but spectators would return to share in the mythical triumph of true religion. The action unfolded in a world of fantasy: the characters always belonged to a distant time and place, e.g. the infidels would be Moors from such remote areas as Turkey, Albania, or North Africa rather than the fierce and feared Moros of the Southern Philippines. Plain, straightforward ideas, action and pomp, familiar plots and music, plus an inevitable just ending appealed to barrio folk, peasant farmers who appreciated escapism after the reality of a season of hard work. Annual barrio fiestas, the occasion for most moro-moro plays, were a time of release as well as celebration of the community's patron saint. In staunchly Catholic Pampanga, Augustinian parish priests could readily approve of such dramas, most often sponsored by a local landowner, which combined amusement and indoctrination. Not surprisingly, Anselmo Fajardo, a Pampangan priest, wrote *Gonzalo de Cordoba*, the province's most renowned cumidia, performed as early as 1831 in Bacolor and on numerous subsequent occasions all over Pampanga.[19]

By late in the nineteenth century, then, the Pampangans already had a strong literary heritage dominated by folk and religious elements

18. Information on the cumidia and its productions can be found in the following sources: Manuel L. Carreon, "An Account of the Moro-Moro As It Is Given in Pampanga Province" (*ca.* 1910), Beyer Collection, pp. 1–7; Consuelo Barrera, "Origin and Development of the Pampangan Drama" (*ca.* 1910), Beyer Collection, pp. 1–3; "History and Cultural Life of the Town of Minalin, Barrio San Francisco," HDP, p. 38; Edades, "Filipino Drama," p. 23; Galang, "Ethnographic Study," p. 121; Henson, *Pampanga*, p. 189; Felicidad Mendoza, "The Moro-Moro," in *A Short History*, pp. 100–122. A full script of a cumidia, *The Emperor Saladin*, handwritten in nine composition books can be located in LPC. Moreover, a rare translation into English of the first two notebooks is included.

19. For information on Padre Fajardo and his cumidia see Faustino P. Gutierrez, *Parnasong Capampangan* (Capampangan literature) (San Fernando, Pampanga: Ing Catimawan, 1932), pp. 47–52; Galang, "Ethnographic Study," p. 128; Bartlett, "Vernacular Literature," p. 21; and Aguas, *Soto and Pampangan Drama*, pp. 8–11. A printed copy of the play can be found in the Bartlett Collection. To confirm that the cumidia was merely one example of a Spanish Empire-wide phenomenon, see Robert Ricard, "Une fiche supplémentaire sur les fêtes de 'Moros y Cristianos,'" *Bulletin Hispanique* 61 (April–September 1959): 288–289.

and enjoyed by all classes. The zarzuela offered a startling contrast.
The form, secular, urbane, and highly developed by this time, came
from the popular Spanish stage, where the term *zarzuela* referred to
a special type of play combining musical numbers with the spoken
word. Its origins under that label reached back to the seventeenth
century, to the time of Lope de Vega and Calderón de la Barca. Indeed,
the later's two-act *El Jardin de Falerina* is often considered the first
zarzuela, although others point to the former's *La Selva sin Amor.*[20]
In any case, the genre became definitely established during the reign
of Philip IV and continued as part of Spanish theater from that time
on, even though it was largely eclipsed in Iberia by Italian opera during
the eighteenth and first half of the nineteenth century. Around 1850
a group of Spanish playwrights began to resuscitate the zarzuela, first
in a three-act form referred to as the *zarzuela grande* and later in a
short one-act version, the *genero chico,* which proved more successful
at drawing audiences and became the most frequently staged. Although
both blended songs and dialogue, the two differed somewhat in style.
The zarzuela grande resembled in many ways the operetta, with themes
from either the fantasy world of princes and princesses or from modern
life. The mood was romantic and melodramatic, and the ending could
be either happy or sad. The genero chico featured farce comedy,
modern scenes, and, often, satirical elements, strung together by song
and dance routines. By the late nineteenth century the contempora-
neity of the genero chico coupled with certain economic advantages in
production led to the decline of the zarzuela grande in Spain; it did,
however, flourish in the Philippines.

Along with the winds of liberal change the zarzuela arrived in the
Archipelago, the first performance occurring in Manila in 1879.
Throughout the 1880s and 1890s, both forms of the zarzuela flour-
ished, not only in Manila where theaters were eventually constructed to

20. The most authoritative and complete source on the history of the zarzuela
in Spain is Emilio Cortarelo, *Historia de la zarzuela, o sea el drama lírico en
España, desde su origen a fines del siglo XIX* (Madrid: Tipografía de Archivos,
1934). See also N. D. Shergold, *A History of the Spanish Stage from Medieval
Times to the End of the Seventeenth Century* (London: Oxford University
Press, 1967), pp. 316–320, 334–335; and J. E. Varey, "Zarzuela," in *The Oxford
Companion to the Theatre,* ed. Phyllis Hartnoll, 3rd ed. (London: Oxford
University Press, 1967), pp. 1024–1025.

accommodate them but also in the provinces where it appealed to Spanish-speaking principales.[21] Plays by European authors remained popular, but Philippine writers started to write zarzuelas too. Even so, the genre showed few signs of domestication by the end of the century; Spanish continued as the language of dialogue and lyrics and Spaniards as the main characters of the plays. Brought to the provinces by traveling troupes, the worldly zarzuela with its secular themes and modern Spanish style provided a sharp contrast to the folk and religiously influenced literature which had been sanctioned before. The popularity of these plays, and their occasional inclusion of such risqué elements as the cancan, indicated something of the changing atmosphere in the Philippines of the late nineteenth century, a time of growing disagreement over Church control as a newly rising native elite sought a greater role in the leadership of the colony. Never did the local zarzuelas exhibit the kind of protest found in the Propaganda literature being produced by Filipino intellectuals in Europe at the time—colonial officials would never have tolerated such dissent—yet the acceptance of such plays did reveal new attitudes and tastes among the population, particularly city dwellers and rural landowners. And the zarzuelas exerted an influence on a young generation of Pampangan writers who viewed them at home and in Manila during school days. For instance, the performances of a traveling company in San Fernando inspired Juan Crisostomo Soto to become a playwright, the most prolific in the dialect.[22]

Although the reason for the lag remains unclear, it took more than a decade after the introduction of the Spanish zarzuela for the first in Capampangan to be staged in the province. Certainly facilities for such a production existed. Even before the end of the Spanish era a Pampangan group of players, *La Compañia Limjuco,* performed zarzuelas in San Fernando, and some actors from this company in later years moved to the neighboring town of Bacolor to appear in dialect plays.[23] Fur-

21. On the Spanish zarzuela in the Philippines see W. E. Retana, *Noticias histórico-bibliográficas de el teatro en Filipinas desde sus orígenes hasta* 1898 (Madrid: Librería General de Victoriano Suarez, 1909), pp. 96–171 passim; and Malay, "Zarzuela," pp. 12–15.
22. Alejandro P. Capitulo, "Crissot Acknowledged Best Poet Ever Produced in Pampanga Province," *(Manila) Tribune, Pampanga Carnival Supplement,* 22 April 1933, p. 6; and Manuel, *Dictionary,* 1: 421.
23. Javillonar, "Pabalan," pp. 18, 44–45, 105, 110.

thermore, the playwrights who ultimately provided the majority of scripts for Pampanga's most admired period of theater (the opening years of the twentieth century) were not too immature to have written such plays before 1900, when *Ing Managpe* opened for the first time. By then Pabalan was thirty-seven, Felix Galura thirty-four, and Jacinto Tolentino thirty-five. Soto, at thirty-three, had already translated into the vernacular and staged several plays including *Romeo and Juliet, Faust,* and Hartzenbusch's *The Lovers of Teruel.* Aurelio Tolentino, also thirty-three, had composed in 1891 a long cumidia, *The Vengeance of Robdeil.* Availability of both capable companies and authors preceded by some time the coming of the first vernacular zarzuela.

Why the delay? The answer probably lies somewhere amid several possible explanations. First of all, in an era when theater troupes barely survived financially, few producers could gamble on an untried drama form. Spanish-language plays already commanded a following among the elite of the province and the poor preferred the cumidia in Capampangan, so these forms represented no economic risk. Secondly, the repressive atmosphere of the 1890s scarcely offered any incentive for theatrical experimentation. As the issues which finally led to revolution slowly came to a head, government and the Church kept tight surveillance upon the native population, looking for signs of deviation. In 1892, for example, a number of Pampangans had been arrested or exiled when the regime crushed a budding Masonic movement in the province. This action made permanent Philippine patriots of many local leaders—one notable case being the exiled Mariano Alejandrino's son José, who became a general in the army of Aguinaldo—and turned others against the Church establishment. Nervous Spanish priests might well have been reluctant to sanction potentially subversive theatrical performances in dialect dealing with contemporary native life, and only in 1898, when all Spanish friars were permanently removed from the province, was this inhibiting influence eliminated. And, finally, but perhaps most importantly, the notion persisted that Capampangan was not suitable as a language for the zarzuela, supposedly a purely Spanish art form. Though some native leaders might question Spanish authority, the elite almost unanimously believed in the superiority of Spanish culture, and many used the Spanish language among themselves as a sign of position, education, and breeding. Indeed, this vestige of a colonial mentality outlasted the old regime itself and forced Pabalan, in 1900 at the time of the premier of *Ing Managpe,* to justify to his scoffing critics the use of Capampangan instead of Spanish.[24] But that barrier broken by the success of his play, the vernacular zarzuela proliferated, and, like the cumidia, became a form of native culture.

Pampangan zarzuela theater reached its zenith between 1900 and 1904. These years saw the completion by the province's outstanding authors of their most innovative and remembered plays. Traveling professional troupes staged productions throughout Pampanga and the Capampangan-speaking towns of neighboring Tarlac.[25] Two theaters, one in Bacolor and the other in Guagua, provided permanent showcases where many of the zarzuelas appeared for the first time, performed by more or less resident companies. In addition, amateur drama clubs sprang up in some of the larger communities for the performance and enjoyment of zarzuelas by local playwrights.

Mariano Proceso Pabalan not only initiated this period of intense activity but also supplied, before his death in 1904, many of the best plays in the genero chico style, which he preferred to all others and used in almost all of his ten or so original works.[26] The titles of several of these suggest something of their farcical nature: *Atlu Bagut* (Three Wives), *Ing Alimpungatan* (The Sleepwalker), *Magparigaldigal* (Killing Time), *Adua Tata* (Two Fathers), and *Oita pa, eh!* (Here We Are Still, Alas!). Their humor revolving around chance happenings and much action, these plays might best be described as situation comedies with

24. Gutierrez, *Parnasong Capampangan,* p. 57.

25. Pabalan's *Oita pa, eh!* (Here We Are Still, Alas!), since it is a play about actors seeking employment, offers revealing details about local show business and, allowing somewhat for literary license, is a good source on theater life in this era. It is really the only contemporary document on the zarzuela movement.

26. For a list of Pabalan's plays see Clemente Ocampo, "Datos históricos sobre el Pueblo de San Fernando, cabecera de la Pampanga, I.F.," LPC, pp. 29–30. Javillonar, "Pabalan," pp. 91–108, gives summaries of four plays and provides original texts and translations in an appendix of three others. Three more are readily available, though without translation, at the U.P. Library: *Ing Alimpungatan* (The Sleepwalker), *Atlu Bagut* (Three Wives), and *Ing Mamaligo* (The Distractor). Pabalan also translated Chivot and Duru's play *La Mascota,* but a manuscript of this work is no longer available.

music. The province served as the setting and Pampangans as the characters in all of Pabalan's zarzuelas, while his subjects, topical and contemporary, often included such family matters as parental consent for marriage, wifely responsibilities, marital fidelity, and inheritance.

The single, major exception to this pattern was his patriotic one-act drama *Apat ya ing Junio* (The Fourth of June), commemorating the day in 1898 when many villagers of Bacolor first cast their lot with the revolutionary cause by attacking a Spanish garrison in town, an act followed by much destruction. In this play with music, his only venture into political drama, Pabalan revealed a somewhat ambivalent attitude toward Philippine nationalism in exploring the idea of commitment. While most characters in the play take a nationalist stance, at least two—a wise old man named Pedro and a volunteer, Casimiro—are cynical of the dedication and thoughtfulness of revolutionary leaders whose actions caused the wasting of Bacolor. Casimiro complains:

> Everybody wants to lead, to be noble, royal; no one wants to follow . . .

> They say they shall be saviors of the suffering country, the harbingers of happiness and peace. But look at what has happened. Because of their impetuosity, not a hut now stands in town.

> Personally, I don't lose anything. But I cannot stand this dictatorship. Forcing others to join a lunatic project. Why, they can't compel me to die like they do their stupid recruits!

> I think it will be best to go home—the whole thing nauseates me.[27]

In the end, however, love of country prevails and in a closing speech the Pampangan heroine, Leona, promises her revenge upon the Spanish:

> Oh, all you sons of Bacolor, if you have ears, have pity on your unfortunate brethren who perished in this struggle. They are the real Martyrs of Bacolor! Except their wives and kin, who know their names, their faces? . . .

> And let us go, young and old, men and women, and make them pay for this calamity.[28]

27. Javillonar, appendix, pp. 56–57.
28. Ibid., appendix, p. 79.

Despite his successes, Pabalan, perhaps the best craftsman of all the Pampangan playwrights, never gave up his job as a secondary level teacher of Spanish, Latin, and English, which provided necessary support for his wife and six children.

Music for the dialect zarzuelas often came from amateur songwriters, musicians, and bandmasters. Although Pabalan later relied heavily on melodies from the Spanish song literature and Italian opera, his inaugural show, *Ing Managpe,* was scored by a local physician and amateur composer, Amado Gutierrez David. Felix Galura relied on Gutierrez David for much of the music of his early works but later collaborated with other provincial composers. Member of a prominent professional family, Gutierrez David wrote zarzuela tunes as a sideline until his death during the cholera epidemic of 1902. Pablo Palma, another provincial composer for the zarzuela, was called to the stage for a bow along with the playwright when Galura's first work, *Jues de Paz* (The Justice of the Peace), premiered in Bacolor in November 1900. Pampangan composers also supplied the music for all of Juan Crisostomo Soto's famous works.[29]

Soto, usually referred to by his pen name Crissot, wrote a total of 50 plays before his death in 1918; nevertheless, by 1904 he had already finished his most respected works including *Alang Dios!* (There Is No God!) which established him as the master in Pampanga of the zarzuela grande. His peers and later critics, while appreciative of his many one-act comedies, preferred his longer pieces, usually melodramatic, which dealt with unfulfilled love and romance ruined by circumstances. Crissot made Pampanga the setting for his dramas and, even more so than Pabalan, introduced elements of provincial life into his story lines. There was talk about local towns and customs, and the lead characters, though stereotyped in a heroic and romantic mold, were motivated by accepted norms of behavior. These plays contained a wealth of information about existing social values and ideals, and, if occasionally the author disputed some of these values, he attempted still to portray them faithfully. The merit of his work resided in the presentation of atmosphere and beauty of language rather than in the uniqueness of plot or subtlety of characterization.[30]

29. Ibid., pp. 41–43; and Manuel, *Dictionary,* 1: 427–428.
30. Two major lists, both of them practically complete, of Crissot's works exist: Aguas, *Soto and Pampangan Drama,* pp. 62–64; and Manuel, 1: 430–436.

As a soldier Crissot knew the hardship of war and drew upon that experience in several of his dramas. He portrayed a number of his major male characters as participants in the Revolution, including Julio in *Julio Agosto,* Armando in *Perlas, Zafiro, Rubi* (Pearl, Sapphire, Ruby), and the general in *Ing Anac ning Katipunan* (Child of the Katipunan). Usually, however, the wartime experience of these characters figured only incidentally in the story. In *Alang Dios!* for example, the second male lead, Ramon, admitted to having gone to jail because he had "had some clash with the past administration,"[31] but the event was never mentioned again and had no bearing on either the outcome of the play or Ramon's actions. Expressions of patriotism were common in his plays but in only a very few, such as *Ing Anac ning Katipunan* and *Balayan at Sinta* (Country and Love), the latter written while Crissot was a prisoner of war, did the Revolution become the subject matter. The joys and tribulations of love overwhelmingly dominated as the major theme in his plays.

Before the Revolution and in the last few years of his life, Crissot earned his living in government service. During his most productive period, however, from about 1898 to 1913, he managed to maintain himself and his family by working as a reporter and editor for several provincial newspapers and staging his plays regularly at El Teatro Sabina during the dry season from October to the beginning of Lent.

El Teatro Sabina and its company of players owed their existence to the patronage of Pampanga's most prominent citizen, Don Ceferino Joven, a wealthy landowner, Philippine patriot, and first governor

---

Manuel's includes helpful summaries of nine plays, while Aguas, who translates all the titles, has attached a complete translation of *Alang Dios!* (pp. 68–138). The U.P. Library has manuscripts in Capampangan of seven of his plays: *Ing Anac ning Katipunan* (The Child of the Katipunan); *Ing Sultana; Julio Agosto; Perlas, Zafiro, Rubi* (Pearl, Sapphire, Ruby); *Ing Perlas qñg Burac* (A Pearl in the Mud); *Ing Caviteña* (The Girl from Cavite); and *Kiki-Riki. Delia,* a one-act play, translated by Aguas, can be found in "A Study of the Life of Juan Crisostomo Soto with Special Reference to *Alang Dios!*" (Master's thesis, University of the Philippines, 1956) appendix C, 1–26. Manuel, 1: 420–430, provides the most thorough information on Crissot's life and theatrical career, but Aguas, *Juan Crisostomo Soto,* pp. 17–32, adds some helpful information. See also Ricardo C. Galang, "Crissot," *Philippine Magazine* 35 (August 1938): 382–383; and Gutierrez, *Parnasong Capampangan,* pp. 72–83.

31. Aguas, *Juan Crisostomo Soto,* p. 86.

under the American regime. His career in politics stretched back to the early 1890s when he became one of the first Pampangan Masons. This act put him in jeopardy with the Spanish government and nearly led to his arrest in 1892. The whole experience made him anti-Spanish, especially antifriar, and turned him into a strong advocate of the separation of church and state.[32] He held office in Aguinaldo's government, but his prestige was so great that the Americans chose him for provincial governor in 1901, and fellow citizens elected him to that office in 1902. Where his interest in theater sprang from remains unclear, but he did have strong ties with the Pabalan family. Several of its members worked as overseers on his properties, and Cornelio Pabalan, Mariano's brother and himself a prominent printer of Pampangan literature, was Joven's godson. Whatever the reason, Joven became a real enthusiast. Actors rehearsed in his house, he himself did bit parts, and his daughter performed juvenile roles in several plays. At extraordinary events, like his own inauguration or the visit of influential insular dignitaries, Joven would arrange a special showing of a zarzuela.[33] He helped support the orchestra, acted as official sponsor for the whole endeavor, and, perhaps most crucial of all, in 1900 supplied funds to convert a warehouse into El Teatro Sabina, the home of Pampangan zarzuela drama.

The actual appearance of the theater, named for one of the governor's relatives, is unascertainable because original plans and early photographs can no longer be located, and no traces of the building exist in Bacolor today. One can, however, depend to some extent on Manuel's description of the place, which coincides with that found in other sources:

> This showhouse was constructed in 1901 [sic] with mixed materials—adobe and sawali walls, galvanized iron roofing, and wooden floors and posts; it had an accommodation of one thousand people, but this figure is probably overestimated. The management usually charged an entrance rate of one peso during the first showings, two pesos for orchestra seats, and fifteen to twenty pesos for box seats

32. On Joven's career, see Larkin, *The Pampangans*, pp. 97, 109–110, 118n, 125–126, 163, 180.

33. Punu, "History of Bacolor, 1746–1908" (handwritten in Capampangan without numbered pages, *ca.* 1910), LPC.

of six chairs in the balcony. Upon second showing the rates were reduced.[34]

Whatever the capacity of the theater may have been, it proved sufficient to provide Crissot with a livelihood and actors and musicians with some remuneration, although most were only semiprofessionals or pure amateurs who had to supply their own costumes. Wealthier players could depend on family income, while poor ones supplemented their pay by taking such jobs in town as salesclerk, baker, and dressmaker. By contrast, the touring companies were made up exclusively of professional players who would hire a theatrical agent to arrange engagements and funding. In a takeoff, the plot of Pabalan's *Oita pa, eh!* revolved around the desperate search of such a group of actors to find a manager.

Bacolor claimed recognition as the center of Pampangan theater because of El Teatro Sabina and three famous playwrights—Crissot, Pabalan, and Felix Galura. Though he wrote a number of popular zarzuelas, Galura also earned a reputation as a grammarian, author of religious literature, and newspaperman. Indeed, his contributions in furthering the use of the dialect led some of his contemporaries to refer to Galura as the "Father of Capampangan" (*Ibpa na ning amanung Capampañgan*).[35] Furthermore, he capped off an illustrious career by serving as municipal president of his hometown from 1909 until 1918, the year before his death.

Just a single manuscript by Galura has survived and one must depend upon old lists, incomplete and sometimes inaccurate, to gain some idea about the content and style of his dramatic works.[36] Of his dozen or

34. Manuel, 1: 426-427. The date of 1901 is probably incorrect, and elsewhere Manuel puts it at 1900 (1: 298), as do most other sources. A ground plan of the theater has been reconstructed by Mr. Aristedes Panopio and Mrs. Josefina Gutierrez Dyoco of the Bacolor School of Arts and Trades. One copy of the plan is located in the U.P. Library.

35. Gutierrez, *Parnasong Capampangan*, p. 67. For additional information on Galura's life, see Galang, *Encyclopedia*, 3: 473.

36. While scattered references to Galura's work can be found in a number of sources, Ocampo, "Datos historicos," pp. 25-29, supplies the most complete, if slightly inaccurate, list of his plays, with a brief description of each. Ocampo also adds the names of Galura's musical collaborators, some information about the productions, and Spanish translations of each title. For a list, again inaccurate, of the few plays Galura wrote after 1908, see Berrera, "Origin of Pampangan

so zarzuelas, at least five written before 1904, almost all were in the genero chico style, and a sampling of the titles suggests their resemblance to those of Pabalan, i.e. light and satirical situation comedies: *Ing Magasasamaiz* (The Quack), *Ing Camarinayan* (The Embarrassment), *Ing Balitcayu* (The Disguise), *Ing Adua Bola* (The Two Balls), and *Ing Carnaval* (Carnival). A rare contemporary description of one of these short plays gives a good indication of their mood and style:

> [A zarzuela] in one act and in verse entitled *The Disguise* is a satirical work which brings to the stage a Spanish friar enamored of a young wife whose husband disguises himself as a woman and goes to a rendezvous with the friar who is also disguised, as a juggler. With Spanish music.[37]

But Galura possessed a wider concept of the function of drama than either Crissot or Pabalan. In addition to zarzuelas written mainly for entertainment, there were dialect plays such as *Ing Sufragio* (The Vote) and *Ing Divorcio* (Divorce) which utilized the stage to discuss issues of contemporary relevance and others like *Patawaran yang Micasala* (To Pardon One Who Errs), *Ing Sabla qñg Salapi Minurung* (Everything Retreats before Wealth), and *Alang Utang a Esana Mibayaran* (No Debt Goes Unpaid) which offered the audience moral lessons. Galura also wrote several religious plays, including *Ing Belen* (Nativity Scene), *Ing Mala ning Virgen* (The Miracle of the Virgin), and *Ing Casaquitan at Camatayan Jesus* (The Agony and Death of Jesus) to dramatize important biblical events and illuminate religious experience. In all these other plays he exhibited a desire to shape public opinion and attitudes— an impulse which probably helped spur him ultimately into politics. Unlike his colleague Crissot, Galura did not find that devotion to the theater alone sufficiently satisfied his ambition.

While Bacolor, the acknowledged cultural center of Pampanga, took a clear lead in the development of the vernacular zarzuela, the nearby commercial town of Guagua played a role in fostering its growth as well. As the area's chief port offering access to Manila Bay, Guagua possessed a large merchant community and the only other permanent

---

Drama," p. 4. The one manuscript extant is *Ing Mora* (Moslem Girl) in the U.P. Library.
37. Ocampo, "Datos historicos," p. 26.

theater in the province, El Teatro Trining, named for its patron from
an ilustrado family, Doña Trinidad Gonzales. Here were performed,
among others, the plays of the Tolentino brothers, the town's most
famous authors. Jacinto, the older of the two, in 1901 completed four
Capampangan zarzuelas—one genero chico and three of the longer
type. After this flurry, however, he ceased writing dramas and devoted
himself to assisting the career of his younger brother, Aurelio, then
becoming one of the most outstanding Filipino authors of his era.[38]
Aurelio's fame rested on his Tagalog dramas, very nationalistic in
tone, which found their most appreciative audiences in the Manila
area, for, although the Tolentino brothers were born in Guagua, their
parents came from the Tagalog region and the boys spent much of their
young adult life going to school in Bulacan and Manila. With rare
exception, Aurelio's Capampangan plays represented mere translations
from Tagalog originals, perhaps because of his greater facility in that
language, but also because of his deep commitment, the strongest of
any Pampangan author, to the revolutionary cause. He joined that
struggle at its inception, passing out the Propagandists' newspaper
La Solidaridad, and participated in every phase thereafter, even in the
abortive uprising of Artemio Ricarte in 1904. His intense feeling led
him to write a very different kind of zarzuela, one filled with nationalist sentiment designed to arouse an audience in favor of Philippine
independence.[39] The most famous work, *Kahapon, Ngayon, at Bukas*
(Yesterday, Today, and Tomorrow—*Napun, Ngeni, at Bukas* in the
Capampangan version), was an allegorical rendition of Philippine
history, unabashedly patriotic and hostile to the American regime.
So hostile in fact that shortly after its opening in Manila in May 1903
colonial authorities arrested both brothers—Aurelio, the author and
an actor in the production, and Jacinto, who served as prompter—for
violation of a sedition law then in force. Shortly afterward, Jacinto
returned to his prerevolutionary job with the Manila Railroad Company

38. On the life and work of the Tolentinos, see Manuel, 1: 454–455, 2: 371–
432; Gutierrez, pp. 63–65, 84–93; Isabel B. Yumol, "A Critical Study of Aurelio
Tolentino's Novel *Ang Buhok ni Ester*" (A Lock of Esther's Hair) (Master's thesis,
University of the Philippines, 1955). Yumol presents a complete translation of
the novel, and Manuel includes a Tagalog version of Aurelio's most famous
play, *Kahapon, Ngayon, at Bukas* (Yesterday, Today, and Tomorrow).

39. The most complete work on nationalist drama of the Tagalog theater is
Lapeña-Bonifacio, *The "Seditious" Tagalog Playwrights.*

and never wrote another play. Aurelio spent the next seven years in court, in jail, or on probation and, as a result, modified his scripts considerably, presenting thereafter only watered-down versions of his militant zarzuelas in Guagua and Tagalog theaters. The plays in Tagalog, Capampangan, and Spanish written after his release from prison had none of the nationalist fire of before. Nevertheless, these zarzuelas dating from about 1908, along with some of his novels, produced enough income to support a quiet retirement, mainly in Manila, until his death in 1915, long after the great era of Capampangan zarzuela theater had faded away.

Although no one clear event marked its decline, the zarzuela movement showed noticeably less ingenuity and verve after 1904. Among the probable factors was the death of Pabalan that year and the harassment of the Tolentinos, who never fully rebounded from their experience with colonial repression. Crissot continued to write, but nothing innovative came from his pen after 1904, and the same was true of Galura, who eventually turned to politics.[40] Moreover, none of their successors proved either especially ingenious or particularly productive. Modesto Joaquin, originally an actor with La Compañía Sabina and a budding playwright, gave up the theater to study law and become a politician and newpaperman. Felino Simpao, physician and municipal president of Guagua, did only a few plays as a sideline, and Monico Mercado of Sexmoan, Pampanga, perhaps the most talented of the new generation, devoted most of his energies to Nacionalista party affairs.[41]

40. Galura became actively involved in Nacionalista party affairs and a supporter and friend of the then rising young star Manuel Luis Quezon. In 1918 Galura, still something of a rebel, came into conflict with the Executive Bureau and its chief over a matter of separation of church and state; however, his friendship with Quezon kept him from serious trouble. On this matter see "Session of the Provincial Board, Honorio Ventura Presiding and Pablo Angeles David Present, 21 August 1918," Pampanga Province, Manuel Quezon Papers; and Letter, Manuel Quezon to Felix Galura, 18 May 1918, General Correspondence, Manuel Quezon Papers (Collection located in the National Library of the Philippines).

41. For information on Simpao, Joaquin, and Mercado, see Gutierrez, pp. 101-124; Larkin, *Pampangans*, pp. 185, 190-192, 226, 269; and Manuel L. Carreon, "Poetry in Pampanga Province" (*ca.* 1910), Beyer Collection, p. 3.

Later authors showed even less inclination to promote a creative theatrical tradition, and the zarzuela form petrified in its early mold. Around 1915 vaudeville and silent movies started to draw audiences away from the zarzuela in the larger towns of Pampanga. Only in some of the more remote communities of the province did the form find a haven. Well into the post-World War II era, at occasional barrio fiestas, traveling companies and local amateur groups performed zarzuelas on portable stages for appreciative rural folks.[42] The zarzuela, first performed for a Spanish-speaking elite, then in native dialect for those who could pay for tickets, found its final audience among the people of the barrios. But here in the backwashes of Pampanga the musical play had to compete with the cumidia, still the more favored entertainment among the peasantry;[43] moreover, the zarzuela manuscripts, composed by obscure local authors, exhibited little quality. In the 1960s, Ely Javillonar, the leading literary authority on the Capampangan zarzuela, traveled about the province in an attempt to locate an alive and imaginative zarzuela theater. Her findings read like a sad epitaph for the once flourishing movement begun and forwarded by Mariano Proceso Pabalan, Felix Galura, and Juan Crisostomo Soto:

> So, for months we read manuscript after manuscript, handwritten or typewritten, in the hope of discovering at least a hint of a gem—until we suddenly realized that we were reading the same stories under different authors. Still we persisted. We spent hours and hours sitting in mosquito-infested fiesta presentations, thinking, hoping to find the *zarzuela* on the boards better than the one on paper. We shook hands and talked with all kinds of people . . . hoping we would find some explanation for the phenomenon of mass repetition that we were painfully reading through.
>
> But we were disappointed in our "search for theatre" in Pampanga. Today, we find her vernacular drama deplorable, if not pitiable.[44]

42. Benigno Fajardo, "Social Life in Lubao," Beyer Collection, pp. 3–7; and Isagani R. Cruz, "The Zarzuela in the Philippines," in *A Short History*, p. 136.
43. Cruz, p. 151. A survey of references in HDP, rich in information on cultural life in the barrios, suggests a preference for the cumidia by the rural people, and the lists of local authors indicate many more of them composing moro-moro drama than doing zarzuelas.
44. Javillonar, "Pabalan," p. vii.

Zarzuela theater lost much of its originality as the years passed and talented writers turned to other endeavors. Instead of coming up with inventive and amusing new situations, authors of later genero chico persistently relied on slapstick, and on stock stories, and on gags utterly familiar to the audience. The zarzuela grande quickly crossed the boundary from serious drama into work of high sentimentality, and the longer play form became just one appendage of a growing body of romantic literature, and later cinema, in the Philippines. Love stories from these plays, endlessly repeated, could also be found in popular novels, magazines, and true-romance comics of several dialects.[45] As new writers employed more sentimentality to create a mass market for their plays, the zarzuela ceased to serve as entertainment mainly for the elite of the cities and the larger towns.

Financial exigencies contributed to this development. Some time in the first decade of the new century, perhaps as early as 1904, La Compañía Sabina lost the patronage of its chief angel, Don Ceferino Joven,[46] and no person of wealth followed to underwrite that company or any comparable group. Henceforth players had to depend on their own drawing power for support. Further, the spirit of experimentation which had launched the zarzuela movement dried up because few writers enjoyed the luxury of devoting full time to their craft. Crissot managed to live as a writer until 1913, when the competition of films and additional family responsibilities forced him once again to take a government job. Aurelio Tolentino remained an author exclusively until his death in 1915, but did so by following such expedients as writing novels and doing plays which advertised certain businesses, including the Germinal and La Yebana tobacco companies. The competition of cinema and vaudeville finally made such independence

45. Tolentino's *Ang Buhok ni Ester* provides a good example of the kind of transition occurring. Written in 1911, the novel is really a zarzuela in an altered form. Emphasis favors action and sentimentality rather than realistic plot and setting, although the author still attempts some serious character delineation. The book, designed to reach as wide an audience as possible, shies away from the revolutionary sentiments which marked the author's earlier works.

46. In this period in the Philippines when politics still cost candidates money rather than yielding them large profits, Joven spent considerable sums. During 1904 and 1905 he had to sell substantial amounts of his land and this was a likely time for him to have ceased supporting the zarzuela theater movement. See Larkin, *Pampangans*, p. 186n.

impossible for others and most authors cranked out plays in between more mundane activities. Moreover, the American colonial regime, through its systems of public education and elective government, offered young people with literary potential alternative occupations in the professions and politics. A number of articulate people who, like Felix Galura, did not possess sufficient family wealth to make them economically independent, followed his example and forsook full-time writing in order to find advancement in public life. It became something of a pattern in Pampanga for an ambitious person to earn a reputation as an author and then head into a government career. Monico Mercado, Modesto Joaquin, and José Gutierrez David (later a justice of the Supreme Court) were just three of the earliest to follow this path. In a later generation, Diosdado Macapagal did some writing and acting in his father's theatrical troupe, La Compañía Lubeña, before going on eventually to become the fifth president of the Philippine Republic.[47] Alternate employment simply drained literary talent away from playwriting.

But financial stringencies only partially account for what happened to the early zarzuela movement. It petered out due to a much more basic cause: it had lost its reason for being. The Capampangan zarzuela began in the midst of revolution, a fundamental fact of its existence, and at its inception represented both a gesture of protest against and a celebration of victory over Spanish domination. In cultural terms the writing and initial staging of *Ing Managpe* came forth as a revolutionary act of defiance against the vaunted superiority of the Spanish language. At that time Pabalan defended a production in his native language by declaring:

> Yes, Spanish is sweet and soft, our language hard and stiff. But is only Spanish fit for music? Are Italian, French, English, and German also hard because they are not Spanish, and not fit, therefore, for music?[48]

He clearly identified one of the major aims of the dialect movement when he spoke through a character in a later play, an actor named Jacobo:

47. [Pampanga High School], *Alumni Golden Jubilee Yearbook, 1912-1962* (Manila: Executive Committee Alumni Golden Jubilee Homecoming, 1962), p. 155.

48. Gutierrez, *Parnasong Capampangan*, p. 57.

More beautiful, more precious than silver are [a] thousand claps
and honor heaped on us by the public. Especially with us of the
Capampangan zarzuela—because the honor of our language is obtained side by side with our personal triumph—our language of
old which is unknown to most and which is looked down upon
by some who know a smattering of the language of those bam-
boozling them. Yes, we try to propagate our beautiful language
which a few stupid ones try to stifle.[49]

The success of Pabalan's first play brought Capampangan a greater
measure of literary equality with Spanish and made the dialect thence-
forth the language of legitimate theater throughout Pampanga. Those
who followed Pabalan not only wrote in the vernacular but drew their
themes and characters from provincial life and society, thus indicating
a growing recognition among audiences of the intrinsic worth of local
norms and values. Heroes and heroines no longer needed to come
from foreign lands and Pampanga itself provided dramatic enough
setting for the plays. This feeling of pride underlying the Capampangan
zarzuela movement can be sensed in the following lyrics from *Alang
Dios!*:

> The young Pampangan maiden
> Is pure and true and faithful.
> Hers is an Oriental haven,
> She's a dear and precious pearl.
> She has beauty and diligence,
> She is a tender fragrant flower;
> Young swains desire her loveliness,
> They rave to deserve her favor
> And to covet her tender care.[50]

The new self-consciousness of the Pampangans, so apparent in the
dialect zarzuelas, emerged as a necessary facet of the rejection of
friar-dominated Spanish colonial society. Before the style and values
of the new American order had had time to intrude, native society,
particularly the elite part, rejoiced in its cultural liberation. Later in
the first decade of American occupation, growing concern with national
level politics, interest in the independence and tariff issues, and the

49. Javillonar, appendix, p. 111.
50. Aguas, *Juan Crisostomo Soto*, p. 111.

increasing prestige of English blunted the original appeal of the dialect zarzuela. Its celebration of the triumph of Pampangan language and culture became less germane even though the elite still spoke the dialect and Capampangan literary groups, dramatic clubs, and newspapers continued to exist. Philippine identity gradually began to supersede provincial identification among its former audience.

Revolution brought social change to Pampanga, and the triumph of the new order found expression on the stages of Bacolor and Guagua. In the nineteenth century the native upper class had had to share its social standing and moral authority with a small but extremely influential group of Spanish priests, officials, and landowners who enjoyed a special prestige derived from colonial domination. When war swept almost all the foreigners from the province, the Pampangan elite stood alone at the social pinnacle, free from the uneven competition of before. The zarzuelas noted this victory by delineating the new social order in the cast of characters. Very frequently the dramatis personae listed some or all of the following major parts: the ingénue, pure and innocent, from a wealthy native family; her rich and influential parents, misguided perhaps, but ultimately benevolent in intention to children and servants alike; the young hero, talented and true, sometimes wealthy but always of "good stock"; a series of loyal retainers, comical and complaining on occasion, yet constant to the command of their masters; and a villainous person intent upon upsetting the just order. Only rarely was a Spaniard portrayed—and then very unsympathetically. Little room existed in these plays for outsiders or anyone else who might seriously question the status quo.

The zarzuelas not only assumed the rectitude of the new social order, they helped perpetuate it by glorifying the paternalism of the wealthy and by praising the faithful service of the poor. On the premise that the existing order produced the greatest well-being for all, an assumption designed to satisfy the conscience of the rich and mollify the poor, the plays provided examples of correct behavior between master and servant. The prevailing ideal was expressed most explicitly, again, in a song in *Alang Dios!* sung by the laborers on the estate of the benevolent Don Andres:

> We the masses
> Through sweat, tears, and sacrifices

Allow the rich the chance
To live in abundant peace.
Happy are those
Whom wealth has favored.
Happier still are the poor
Whom wealth has yet to spoil.[51]

The vernacular zarzuela paid tribute to the social triumph of the native elite and the immutability of the economic order while encouraging the poor to remain within their station.

If the zarzuela movement reflected the attitudes of the Pampangan elite about social, cultural, and economic matters during a time of revolution, it also demonstrated, if somewhat negatively, political feelings as well. The plays showed a distinct lack of interest in the notion of Philippine nationhood. Occasional anti-Spanish and antifriar remarks cropped up, but almost no comment blamed Americans for stamping out the Republic. One might attribute the absence of anti-American or pro-Republican sentiment to the government censorship of the time, except that just then writers in Tagalog like Aurelio Tolentino, Severino Reyes, and Juan Abad were turning out and producing their most patriotic plays in Manila right under the noses of colonial authorities. Crissot, Pabalan, Galura, and Joaquin all fought in the Revolution, showing no less bravery than their Tagalog counterparts, but they did not feel sufficiently strong about the cause of the Republic to make it a serious part of their theater. Nor, apparently, did their audience demand such sentiments from them. The Revolution in Pampanga sought to establish the preeminence of the native elite and bring new recognition for Pampangan culture—these proved goals enough. What nationalist feeling prevailed took the form

---

51. Ibid., pp. 98–99. One finds echoes of this sentiment elsewhere in the literature of the era. In *Ang Buhok ni Ester*, for instance, the following passage appears without intended irony: "'Long live Kapitan Luis!' shouted the servants at the top of their voices. 'Long live the father of the poor!'"; Yumol, appendix, p. 4. A full study is needed on the inability of Filipino authors of this era, from José Rizal through people like Soto and Tolentino, to write sensibly about the plight of the poor. Not until the 1930s and 1940s generation of Socialist writers like Amado V. Hernandez and Carlos Bulosan does a realistic picture of Philippine poverty appear.

of a kind of Pampangan group chauvinism largely, though certainly not completely, satisfied by the time the war ended.

During its heyday the Capampangan zarzuela mirrored the beliefs and aspirations of a native elite in crisis and transition. Once the province returned to a more settled condition, that ruling class, its position now assured by the new regime, turned to the business of governing and coping with the serious agricultural depression then raging. No longer the chief means of expressing elite feelings, the zarzuela became just one more form of entertainment, though no doubt filled for some with memories of more stirring times. By 1904, other diversions had started to absorb the attention of the Pampangan upper class: electoral politics now offered not only spectacle but ample rewards as well. A new form of theater, far more serious in intent, sent the zarzuela to the back roads of the province from where it never returned.

Communal Conflict in the Burma Delta

DOROTHY HESS GUYOT

> May we be spared the misfortune
> arising from a change of kings.

This Burmese prayer, voicing the folk wisdom of a people historically familiar with interregnal tribulation, must have been on many lips during World War II as the forces of the Japanese emperor displaced those of the British king. Afflicted immediately and directly were the one and a half million people in towns that were bombed or lay along the invasion route. The lasting affliction occurred in the Irrawaddy delta, a backwater of the military campaign. Here, in this triangle of land one hundred miles wide and one hundred miles deep, the British regime quietly disintegrated at the end of February 1942 but the Japanese did not establish control until late June. During this change of kings, a totally unforeseen communal war erupted between Burmans and Karens and continued until suppressed by Japanese force. There had been no previous Burman-Karen riots or attacks. Tolerance laced with suspicion, not ethnic hatred, had characterized Burman and Karen attitudes toward each other. The dynamics of the origin and escalation of the conflict will be examined for Myaungmya district in the heart of the delta, where the hostility was at its worst and the record is the clearest.[1]

In this essay I have benefited from the penetrating criticisms of my far-flung colleagues Michael Adas, John Cady, F. K. Lehman, Gerald McBeath, and James C. Scott. My thanks also go to the assembled colleagues of the 29th Congress of Orientalists who commented upon an earlier version. The Ford Foundation Foreign Area Training Fellowship Program and the Research Foundation of the City University of New York provided the supporting research grants. Special thanks are due the archivists of the Defense Services Historical Research Institute, Rangoon, and the many citizens of Burma who shared their experiences with me.

1. Myaungmya was the only town the length of Burma which published a newspaper during the turbulent months of the interregnum. A member of the town governing committee preserved not only nine of the seventeen issues of the news-

First it is necessary to elucidate the latent conditions of the social upheaval.

In the Irrawaddy delta of lower Burma remarkable economic and social development occurred between 1852 when the British annexed lower Burma to their Indian Empire and 1910, by which time cultivators had transformed seven million acres of swamp, grass, and jungle into rice fields.[2] Rice exports climbed from 280,000 tons in 1862 to over 3,000,000 tons annually in the 1930s.[3] To explain this striking agricultural expansion is to recount the development of a plural society, where distinct ethnic groups met in the marketplace, were controlled by the same government, but established no sense of community.

At the outset of British rule the delta had a thinly distributed population of about one million who raised rice for subsistence, any incentive for hacking out paddy fields from the malarial jungle having been stifled by the Burmese law forbidding the export of rice from the kingdom. Mons, whose early kingdom had transmitted Buddhism to the Burmans, were in the final stages of cultural assimilation by the Burmans. Karens, who had migrated from the hills to the east, lived in scattered villages across the delta, away from the major waterways. Burmans comprised perhaps half the population in the north of the delta but only about a third in the central part stretching from Myaungmya to Rangoon.[4]

---

paper but handfuls of leaflets issued by the administration of Myaungmya and neighboring towns. The Defence Services Historical Research Institute preserved both a file of letters from the Myaungmya administration to the Burma Independence Army Headquarters and testimony taken in the court-martial of the Myaungmya commander. One must bear in mind that all of these documents were written by BIA members, issued under BIA auspices, or received by BIA members.

2. Michael Adas, *The Burma Delta: Economic Development and Social Change on an Asian Rice Frontier, 1852-1941* (Madison: University of Wisconsin, 1974). Adas provides an outstanding analysis of the dynamics of development which I draw upon here supplemented by Burma, *Report of the Burma Provincial Banking Enquiry Committee, 1929-30,* vol. 1, *Banking and Credit in Burma* (Rangoon: Government Printing, 1930); and Burma, Commerce and Industry Department, James Baxter, *Report on Indian Immigration* (Rangoon: Government Printing, 1941).

3. Cheng Siok-hwa, *The Rice Industry of Burma, 1852-1940* (Kuala Lumpur: University of Malaya Press, 1968), p. 206.

4. Adas, pp. 50-53, estimates the ethnic and geographic distribution of the population based on Burma, *Report on the Administration of Pegu, 1856-57,* app. W.

After the British opened the delta to the world rice market, two separate streams of migrants flowed in—one from upper Burma, one from India. A highly complex division of labor within the monocrop economy developed in the last quarter of the nineteenth century and would persist basically unchanged until the Japanese invasion. The great majority of delta Burmans and Karens were cultivators carrying out all phases of the agricultural cycle in adjacent villages but with little common contact. Indians performed complementary functions, chiefly as migrant wage laborers specializing in the repair of bunds and in harvesting. Indian moneylenders provided most of the agricultural credit, poor risks depended on Burman moneylenders, landlords lent to their tenants, and Chinese shopkeepers extended short-term loans to laborers. Burmans and Karens were owner-cultivators and increasingly became tenants to landlords of their own ethnic group, while Indians were tenants of Indian and later Burman landlords. By the turn of the century Burmans in ever greater numbers were laboring along with Indians in the fields and in the proliferating upcountry mills. Indians worked the delta steamers and the docks.

Every segment of the rice industry profited during the four boom decades before the closing of the frontier in 1910. Afterward, the stagnating technology and decline in yields per acre pushed cultivators deeply into debt. The final blow was the world depression which brought a downward spiraling rice price. By 1940, 65 percent of the land in Myaungmya district, and in the delta as a whole, belonged to Indian and Burman landlords who rented it to a transient tenant population.

Yet despite these powerful and obvious economic tensions, the violence of 1942 was not directed across class lines—dispossessed cultivators against landlords—but rather across ethnic lines.[5] We can understand this through the concept of the plural society which Furnivall developed to explain the disintegration of social life in the delta of lower Burma.[6]

5. Donald L. Horowitz, "Multiracial Politics in the New States: Toward a Theory of Conflict," in Robert Jackson and Michael Stein, eds., *Issues in Comparative Politics* (New York: St. Martin's Press, 1971), pp. 164–180, gives some perceptive arguments why economic grievances are seldom the basis of mass conflict in plural societies.

6. John S. Furnivall, *Colonial Policy and Practice: A Comparative Study of Burma and Netherlands India* (New York: New York University Press, 1956), esp. pp. 303–312.

He theorized that colonial rule and the unrestrained play of market forces throughout Asia and Africa had broken the traditional social cohesion and restraint on individuals. Within this context, a constellation of factors operated to bring about an influx of different ethnic groups, ethnically stratified economic participation, lack of internal social cohesion within ethnic groups, and individual pursuit of personal economic gain to the neglect of social values. Moneymaking was the primary motive of the Burmans, Indians, and British who migrated to lower Burma. In the stunted social life which resulted, most Indians and British did not raise families in Burma but looked abroad for home. Burman immigrants, too, in comparison to those in upper Burma or to the long-settled Karens, lived in social impoverishment, as evidenced by their infrequent community festivals, weak family ties, uncertain attachment to land, few monasteries and pagodas, and inclination to crime. In the plural society each ethnic group had separate basic institutions—kinship, religion, education, property, recreation—but no sense of loyalty to an overarching community.

The concept of ethnicity as a role, rather than as a specific set of cultural and physical traits, provides new insight into the nature of plural societies. In their work on the hill peoples of Burma and Thailand, Leach, Lehman, and Moerman have demonstrated the utility of regarding ethnic groups as roles and of viewing the relations among ethnic groups as a role system.[7] Briefly, ethnicity becomes salient only in social settings where more than one ethnic group is present. Like a role, one ethnic group is defined in relation to other ethnic groups, just as the role of tenant farmer is defined in relation to the role of landlord. When a new role is introduced, such as moneylender, it changes the preexisting role system and the particular role relationship between tenant and landlord. Similarly when an ethnic group enters or departs from the role system its movement changes the relationships among other ethnic groups. Thus, the meaning attached to a single ethnic group, the identity of a group, depends upon the current relation of

7. E. R. Leach, *Political Systems of Highland Burma: A Study of Kachin Social Structure* (London: G. W. Bell, 1964); F. K. Lehman, "Ethnic Categories in Burma and the Theory of Social Systems," in Peter Kunstadter, ed., *Southeast Asian Tribes, Minorities, and Nations* (Princeton: Princeton University Press, 1967); and Michael Moerman, "Ethnic Identification in a Complex Society: Who Are the Lue?" *American Anthropologist* 67 (1965): 1215–1230.

that group with other ethnic groups. In the study of a plural society, where an individual's ethnic identity tends to define the economic and political roles open to him, it is especially rewarding to view ethnic identity as a role relationship. The central theoretical contribution of this essay is the insight that the sudden elimination of the British role so wracked the prevailing role system as to create new and conflicting definitions of ethnic self for both Burmans and Karens. This rupture set the psychological preconditions for the unexpected outburst of communal warfare.

The rough schematic representation of three successive role systems shown in the chart provides a vivid overview of the changes. The higher level in each role system indicates the dominant ethnic group while the lines indicate the major relationships that established the role definitions.

During the first half of the nineteenth century the Burmans were politically and socially the dominant ethnic group in the delta. The arrow in the Mon circle indicates the process of Mon assimilation to Burman, which was completed in the delta by the twentieth century.

When the British established themselves in the dominant role in 1852, they radically changed the previous relationships among all indigenous ethnic roles. The defining relationship for an ethnic group was no longer its position vis-à-vis the Burman but vis-à-vis the British. The British erected the highest social barrier on the ethnic boundaries between the elite (British) and the mass (native). They quickly introduced a new role—Indian—by deliberately encouraging immigration. All ethnic roles became more salient and more sharply defined under the British system of ethnic labeling in the census, in education, and in parliamentary constituencies. American missionaries and British officials encouraged the rise of a common Karen identity, diagramed by the merger of the circles for the two major Karen tribes, Pwo and Sgaw. Taungthu Karens, who inhabited the hills bordering Thailand, continued to feel separate, in keeping with their physical isolation.

The role of Indian as a unitary ethnic identification was fostered by the colonial role system in Burma. Burmans did not distinguish between Hindus and Moslems, among castes, or among regions of origin. This unity of Indians which was so self-evident in the Burma delta was proving impossible to achieve in India, even by the efforts of as great a leader as Gandhi. The Burma role system changed the self-perception of

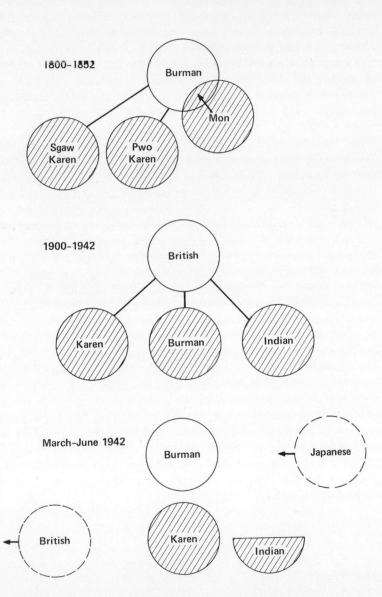

migrants from India, for they increasingly refused to provide their caste designations to the census taker, apparently in the belief that caste no longer had meaning.[8] Burmans disdained all Indians among them, whether they came as moneylenders, shopkeepers, or laborers, regarding them as drudges who drove down the Burman standard of living with the backing of the British. Burmans discounted Indians to such an extent that contemporary accounts and later reminiscences of the colonial period tend to ignore the presence of Indians.

The physical and psychic destruction of the British role in 1942 is indicated in the chart by the dotted circle headed off the page. Similarly, the Japanese are represented by a dotted circle entering the role system, vaguely known and not yet established in the dominant role. The circle representing the Indian role is sliced in half to indicate that half the holders of this role, some 350,000 people, were fleeing the country in terror after the Japanese bombing of Rangoon in December 1941. Indians were acutely conscious of how their role depended upon the British role of protector. Probably about one-third of the Indians in the delta joined those of Rangoon in trekking "home" to India, but the Burmese sources on which this essay depends are silent on the actions of Indians. By and large, the remaining Indians, like the similarly situated Chinese, devoted themselves to keeping out of harm's way.

All Indians who joined the conflict, possibly one-tenth of those remaining, took the Karen side. Economic roles would not explain this alliance, for Karens had suffered as much as Burmans from foreclosures by Indian moneylenders and from the competition of Indian laborers.[9] What brought the two minorities together against the Burmans was instead the similarity of the Indian-British and Karen-British relationships. There is no evidence that Burmans in Myaungmya attacked Indians, as some had in the heavily Indian district of Hanthawaddy and along their exodus route. In Myaungmya, the Burmans merely noted without over-

8. Adas, pp. 231–232, 342.

9. Here is an example of extreme animosity of a Karen witness to Indian moneylenders: "Chettiar bankers are fiery dragons that parch every land that has the misfortune of coming under their wicked creeping. . . . [T]he swindling, cheating, deception, and oppression of the Chettiars in the country, particularly among ignorant folks, are well known" (Burma, *Report of the Burma Provincial Banking Enquiry Committee, 1929-30*, vol. 1, *Banking and Credit in Burma* [Rangoon: Government Printing, 1930], p. 189).

ture or rebuff the presence of Indians in Karen bands. The overriding Burman concern was the new Burman-Karen role relationship.

The various Karen tribes have traditionally viewed themselves as people living in the context of other peoples. There is no record of their ever having established a state or kingdom. Rather, they have lived as constituent peoples of the Mon kingdom, the Burmese kingdom, and the Thai kingdom. In their myths as well, Karen tribes see themselves as one people among many. When mankind began, the primal father and mother ate 101 crabs to beget 101 children. Karens are simply the off-spring of one of these original children. This deeply rooted view of themselves as constituents of a multiethnic system dominated by others may have facilitated their quick identity change from subordinates in a Burmese kingdom to the most faithful subordinates in a British colony. A further change took place, a muting of distinctions among Karen-speaking tribes—particularly between the two basic plains-dwelling groups in the delta, the Sgaw and Pwo. Their common identity as Karens emerged in the nineteenth century after missionaries raised Karen consciousness, established the National Karen Association, and led some Karens in battle against Burmans during the Third Anglo-Burmese War.[10]

The Sgaw and Pwo have different legendary-historical roots to their grievances against Burmans. The Sgaw Karens possess a strong oral tradition recounting their oppression under the Burmese kings, and evidence from Pagan inscriptions agrees with their myth that Kyanzittha (1084–1112) forced migration of Sgaw Karens to the Pagan area where they were apparently treated as hereditary menials. As such, the Sgaw were excluded from the service classes, the basic political unit of traditional Burma through which people owed military service to the king and received recognition. The Pwo Karens, the larger and more self-confident group, had been recognized in the ancient Mon kingdom of Thaton as "the people who had the prior right." A Pwo Karen sense of lost great-ness stems from their belief in a legendary Karen kingdom that preceded the Mon kingdom, that preceded the Burman kingdom. Pwo Karens tended to see themselves as political leaders of all Karens in urging the

10. Donald M. Smeaton, *The Loyal Karens of Burma* (London, 1887), pp. 13–16, provides a missionary account of forging Karen identity; but the subject needs to be pursued by historians and anthropologists.

British to carve out a separate Karen state.[11] In daily affairs no latent fears surfaced. Karens simply preferred to deal with each other and regarded the Burmans with mild suspicion for being too quick-witted.

The conversion of a substantial minority of Karens from their previous animism and Buddhism profoundly changed the way they viewed their relationship to the Burmans. Perceiving in Christianity the fulfillment of an ancient prophecy about the return of a fair-skinned younger brother who kept the Golden Book, upwards of 220,000 Karens became Christians, compared to only 15,000 Burmans.[12] Karen Christians and Buddhists intermingled, feeling no strain of religious difference. Fully 50 percent of the Sgaw Karens in the delta adopted Christianity, as against only 10 percent of the Pwo.[13] A partial explanation lies in the Sgaw rejection of their past history and in the Pwo's deeper commitment to Buddhism. Pwo Karen villagers had been clients at the monasteries of first the Mon and later the Burmans.[14] Tradition tells that the first Karen permitted to join the Burmese monkhood, in the nineteenth century, was a Pwo.[15] Thereafter Pwo Karen built some monasteries of their own, though most remained clients of the Burman monastic system.

Christianity provided a shortcut both to a great tradition and to the modern world.[16] Prior to their acceptance of Christianity, Karens were illiterate, living on the periphery of a Mon and Burman Buddhist civilization which participated in the arc of Buddhism stretching from Ceylon to Japan. American missionaries adapted Burmese script for Karen languages so as to give them the Bible. Baptists, Catholics, and Anglicans from Europe and America established mission schools which provided instruction in English, the key to personal advancement in colonial Burma. Christians, Sgaw and Pwo, became national spokesmen for all Karens. Buddhists became educationally disadvantaged as their monastic schools became increasingly anachronistic. Burman Buddhists were no

---

11. Sir San C. Po, *Burma and the Karens* (London: Elliot Stock, 1928), is a classic example.

12. India, Census Commissioner, *Census of India,* vol. 11, pt. 1, p. 213.

13. Ibid., pt. 2, p. 255, enumerates 70,000 Sgaw as Christian and 26,000 Pwo.

14. F. K. Lehman, personal communication.

15. Theodore Stern, "Three Pwo Karen Scripts: A Study of Alphabet Formation," *Anthropological Linguistics* 10, no. 1 (January 1968): 2.

16. I am indebted to F. K. Lehman for this insight.

longer the central civilized people before whom Karens acknowledged their own peripheral position. The advent of the British and their Christianity made Burmans seem a backward people who must scramble to become modern.

Burmans held particular resentment toward Karen Christianity because they viewed Christianity as the key to British favoritism toward Karens. Not that Burmans resented Christianity per se, for the pervasive Buddhist tolerance accepted prominent Burman Christians as respected individuals, if with quiet regret that the converts were unbelievers and perhaps not truly Burmese. Burmans could easily view outspoken Karen Christians as representative of all Karens and individual Britishers who proclaimed their special affection for Karens as spokesmen of British policy. That only 20 percent of the Karens became Christians was obscured by the prominence of the Christian Karen leadership.

The Karen legend of Taw-mei-pa who will someday appear to lead his people to the promised land indicates a traditional yearning that would be expressed as political independence in modern terms. An independent Karen state is what Pwo Karen leaders wished the British would grant in that distant future when British rule would end. Karens had received separate headmen in large villages shared with Burmans,[17] separate electoral constituencies, separate representation at the London constitutional conference, and preferential recruitment to the army and military police, though never any promise of a state. For both political and social reasons Karens tended more and more to look to the British as their protectors from the Burmans. Karens took pride in the British calling them a loyal people and felt genuinely thankful for British protection from Burman domination. In summing up the benefits of colonial rule, a Pwo Karen leader remarked, "The British gave us justice, and the Americans gave us the Message."

Colonial rule had also altered drastically the meaning of being a Burman, for in destroying the independent Burmese kingdom and banishing the last Burmese king the British destroyed the central institution by which Burmans had related to other ethnic groups. It is indicative of their altered roles that, when the Burmans no longer had a king for the Karens to be loyal to, Karens attached their loyalty to the British monarchy. The Burmese monarchy had expressed the legitimacy of

17. Burma, *Report on Administration, 1922/23* (Rangoon: Government Printing, 1924), p. 33, mentions the headmen.

Burman rule, provided a model for the Shan princes in their relations to Karens and Kachins,[18] and furnished the drama of Burmese history. In emphasis of the monarchy's legitimacy, the last of the royal Burmese chronicles opens by placing the founding of the Burmese kingdom well before the birth of the Buddha. The inchoate Burman longing for a king was fleetingly fulfilled during the interregnum by the leader of the Burma Independence Army, Bo Mogyo, who was popularly believed to be the son of the Mingyun prince, but who was in fact a Japanese colonel.

Reaction to their role under the British as a causal force in the resurgence of Burman nationalism between 1920 and 1940 has been well detailed by Cady, Maung Maung, Trager, and Sarkisyanz.[19] We only need note here that other indigenous ethnic groups were peripheral to the nationalist movement. The British had excluded the peoples of the hill areas from the progressive doses of parliamentary government given the Burmans. In the delta the separate electoral constituencies for Karens who lived among Burmans resulted in neither Burman nor Karen leaders ever needing to build popular support across ethnic barriers. The most vociferous nationalists of the late 1930s, the Thakins, followed the pattern of ignoring Karens.

Attributing any hostility from other ethnic groups to a British system of divide and rule, Burmans believed that the British deliberately favored the Karens because Karens had swallowed the foreigners' religion. Burmans accused the British of awarding Karens a disproportion of posts in all government services. In fact, their overrepresentation in the army and military police stemmed from the British preference for recruiting hill peoples on the Indian model and from Karen willingness to accept discipline. Their overrepresentation in the education service was due to their mission schooling. In all other government services, Karens were underrepresented.

The profound differences just described between the roles of Karen

18. Lehman, "Ethnic Categories in Burma," pp. 99, 110.
19. John F. Cady, *A History of Modern Burma* (Ithaca: Cornell University Press, 1958); Maung Maung, *Burma in the Family of Nations* (Amsterdam and New York: Djambatan and Institute of Pacific Relations, 1956); Frank N. Trager, *Burma: From Kingdom to Republic* (New York: Praeger, 1966); and E. Sarkisyanz, *Buddhist Backgrounds of the Burmese Revolution* (The Hague: Martinus Nijhoff, 1965).

and Burman were somewhat muted by a religious similarity and a cross-cutting educational cleavage. These common values had significantly aided communication in normal times but proved of little use during the turmoil. Overwhelmingly Burmans in Myaungmya district were Buddhist, as were 79 percent of the Karens.[20] Although a shared Buddhist faith enabled Karens and Burmans to accept briefly the mediation of a Karen sayadaw during the escalation of the conflict, Burmans did not reciprocate by respecting pastors, who had stirred their resentment by frequent criticism of Buddhists as idol worshipers.

The educational cleavage divided the British-educated leadership of both communities from the villagers. Among the elite, educational credentials were more important than ethnic identity in establishing position. Lawyers, administrators, conservative politicians, and teachers—Burman or Karen—communicated easily and frequently, often on the basis of special friendships dating from joint attendance at Rangoon College. These Westernized intellectuals, the individuals most distraught and most humbled by the British retreat, quickly lost their followings.

Karen and Burman reacted in opposite ways to the retreat, epitomizing their discrepant role relations to the British and to each other. Karens were stunned, disbelieving that their protectors had vanished and hopeful that they would return after the monsoon, as promised. Burmans were euphoric, certain that the British were gone forever. The Burma Independence Army, proclaiming itself an army of national liberation, had been founded through the collaboration of a fiercely independent Japanese colonel, Suzuki Keiji, and a group of student nationalists from the Thakin party who called themselves the Thirty Comrades. At the beginning of the invasion the BIA received a tumultuous welcome. Crowds cheered, girls gave rice packets into which they had tucked coquettish notes, old women blessed the boys, and everyone passed along ancient prophecies of their coming and fantastic stories of their accomplishments. Some 25,000 youths from the village and town flocked to the columns of the BIA. As in previous nationalist movements, only Burmans joined. The BIA regarded itself as the military force assuring Burmese independence and creating a new Burmese government.

20. India, *Census of India,* 1931, vol. 11, pt. 2, p. 255.

Lawlessness broke out in every district with the sudden disintegration of government. Anarchy is not too strong a term to describe the conditions in the countryside. The hot season was at its height, a time in any culture when crimes of passion increase markedly. In Burma, February through May is also the time of idleness after the harvest and before the next planting. In March and April the reported rates for murder and assault typically rise to twice the levels in August, when the monsoon, planting labors, and Buddhist Lent have quenched passions.[21] In addition to the upward seasonal swing of crime, the secular trend since the turn of the century had pushed the reported crime rate in Burma higher than in any other territory under British rule.[22]

With the breakdown of transportation and communications all conflicts and solutions became local. Whether general lawlessness deteriorated into ethnic warfare depended upon whether Karens refused the new ethnic role which Burmans envisioned for them. The numerical balance between ethnic groups in each district provides a first-order understanding of the variation in scale of ethnic warfare.[23] Where Karens formed a sizable minority and thus felt capable of open opposition, Burmans viewed them as a threat. Where Karens were proportionately few, their safety lay in avoiding any provocation. Table 1 ranks districts by Burman-Karen ratio ranging from Thaton, where Karens outnumbered Burmans, to Tharrawaddy, where the ratio first rises above the national average of 14 to 1. As can be seen, communal warfare was most serious and prolonged in the districts where the ethnic ratio was nearest equality and dropped off as the proportion of Burmans rose. An exception is the southern part of Bassein, where warfare was light due to Sir San C. Po's negotiation of a compromise with the local BIA.

21. Burma, *Report of the Committee Appointed to Advise on Murder and Dacoity, 1926* (Rangoon: Government Printing, 1927), annexure Y gives monthly crime figures for each year, 1923 to 1925. Figures for 1937, aggregated by calendar quarter, indicate that the murder rate in the first half of the year was 50 percent higher than in the last half.

22. Furnivall, *Colonial Policy and Practice*, p. 138.

23. Ted Robert Gurr, *Why Men Rebel* (Princeton: Princeton University Press, 1970), develops useful paradigms for assessing the likelihood of political violence. Specifically ethnic patterns of violence are assessed by Philip Mason, *Patterns of Domination* (London: Oxford Press, 1970), pp. 54–65; Michael Banton, *Race Relations* (New York: Basic Books, 1967), ch. 4; and Pierre L. van den Berghe, *Race and Racism: Comparative Perspectives* (New York: John Wiley, 1967).

Table 1. Relation of Ethnic Balance and Ethnic Warfare

District[a]	% Burman	% Karen	% Indian	Burman-Karen Ratio	Intensity of Burman-Karen Warfare[b]
Thaton	26	53	6	1:2	Heavy
Maubin	64	30	4	2:1	Heavy
Myaung-mya	65	27	6	2:1	Heavy
Toungoo	66	21	7	3:1	Unknown
Bassein	71	23	4	3:1	Heavy in north, light in south central
Insein	70	11	13	6:1	Light
Henzada	86	10	2	8:1	Unknown
Pegu	75	8	10	9:1	Unknown
Hantha-waddy	73	7	16	10:1	None to light
Pyapon	81	6	10	13:1	Unknown
Tharra-waddy	90	5	3	18:1	None

SOURCE: The population statistics are from India, *Cenus of India, 1931*, vol. 11, pt. 1, p. 234.

[a]With the exception of Thaton and Toungoo, which lie in the Eastern Yoma, all districts are in the delta.

[b]As the description of events will show, the proportion of villages burned would be an appropriate indicator of the intensity of warfare, but because village burnings are underreported I have avoided presenting the illusion of accuracy that numbers would give and instead roughly classified the warfare in each district as heavy, light, or none.

In its terrain Myaungmya district is typical of the lower delta, that stretch of flat land laced with the many streams distributing the Irrawaddy river into the Bay of Bengal (see map). The salty marshes in the southern half of the district so discourage cultivation that population has always been sparse. The vast proportion of the arable land was cultivated with rice, some 1,900 square miles, while 580 square miles were planted to all other crops, and only 510 square miles were forested.[24]

24. The data on Myaungmya come from Burma, Census Office, *Burma Gazetteer, Myaungmya District*, vol. B (no. 13), (Rangoon: Government Printing, 1924), and the 1931 census.

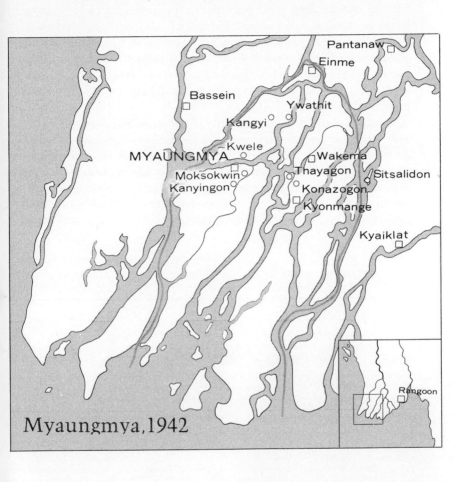

Myaungmya, 1942

Fully 95 percent of the district's population were rice cultivators, living in villages dotting the riverine network. There was no railway, no major highway, and no deep water port, but river steamers called at fifty-six towns and villages, with sampans and bullock carts supplying most local transportation. Sixteen settlements were considered towns, their populations ranging from 1,000 to 8,000, though these settlements were in actuality overgrown villages clustered around a market, a government office, or a few rice mills. Myaungmya inhabitants looked to nearby Bassein town for urban services.

As table 2 shows, the great majority of Karens in Myaungmya district were Buddhist, despite the impact of Christianity in highlighting ethnic differences. The even division of Indians between Hindu and Muslim was an impediment to Indian cohesion. The few thousand Chinese intermingled with the Burmans, working mostly as middlemen and shopkeepers in the towns. All thirty Englishmen were top officials, businessmen, or professionals in Myaungmya, the district capital, a

Table 2. Ethnic and Religious Composition of Myaungmya District

| | Population | | Religion | | | |
| | | | Myaungmya District | | | |
Ethnic Group	Myaung-mya District	Myaung-mya Town	Buddhist	Christian	Hindu	Muslim
Burman	288,400	4,700	288,000	400	–	–
Pwo Karen	101,000 ⎫		92,000	9,000	–	–
Sgaw	⎬	400				
Karen	16,000 ⎭		2,000	14,000	–	–
Indian	28,000	1,900	–	–	14,000	14,000
Chinese	7,000	600	2,000	5,000	–	–
Indo-Burman	100	100	–	–	–	–
English	30	30	–	30	–	–
Total	440,530	7,730	384,000	28,430	14,000	14,000

SOURCE: India, *Census of India, 1931,* vol. 11, pt. 2 (*Burma*), pp. 250, 280.

town slightly smaller than Wakema, the township headquarters in the more densely settled north of the district. In all sixteen towns Burmans predominated, Indians settled in considerable numbers, and Karens were rare.[25]

Two issues precipitated the clash that erupted in Myaungmya district between the Burma Independence Army and the Karens. First, the euphoric BIA defined any opposition from other segments of the population as a challenge to its legitimacy as a government. Second, the BIA confronted Karen soldiers with a demand for the surrender of their guns.

The first step in the breakdown of authority occurred on 28 February when the government ordered the evacuation of all civil servants from Myaungmya district to upper Burma, which the government expected to hold. The fleeing civil servants were predominantly Burman but included an Englishman as the head of the police and Indians as military policemen and jailers. Upon departure, the district commissioner set free several hundred convicts from Myaungmya jail. An ad hoc committee of town elders assumed responsibility for peacekeeping only to be thrust aside on 4 March by the arrival of a BIA column.

Heading the 400-man BIA contingent was Maung Maung, a Rangoon College student in rebellion against his civil servant father and later to have a distinguished military career as brigadier. Close to the Thakin leaders at the national level but without personal connections to Myaungmya, Maung Maung appointed a Free Burma Government composed of twenty-four local youths. Among these were sixteen Thakins, three BIA men, three teachers from the national school, a landlord, and a restaurant owner, but not a single Karen.

The youths thus catapulted into office by the BIA fervently believed that they were creating a national revolution. Indeed, just the fact of their seizure of office was revolutionary for Burmese society, which respects age. However, the policies which the BIA government followed on such crucial matters as agriculture and taxes were mere copies of the

25. India, *Census of India,* 1931, vol. 11. pt. 1, p. 58.

colonial ones. Their revolutionary urge could be satisfied in symbols.[26] BIA government pronouncements opened as proclamations of the Government of Independent Burma—a huge presumption considering the prevailing anarchy—and closed with the traditional phrase describing affairs of the royal court which Thakins had adopted as their slogan in the 1938 oil field strike, "Victory in the noble struggle." The most widely resented of BIA attempts to impose the symbols of authority was the demand that all colonial currency be submitted for overprinting with the seal of Free Burma. Resistance to this currency recall brought the replacement of the first BIA government, but by then the Burman-Karen conflict was open warfare.

About the beginning of April the Myaungmya government issued the first of a series of assurances to Karens. It is symptomatic of the Burman nationalistic preoccupation that none were in the Karen language. Apparently the Myaungmya committee did not reflect that Karens in the district, over 80 percent of whom spoke Burmese fluently, would prefer their own language.[27] The translation below of this widely circulated first leaflet will indicate the character of the succeeding twelve appeals for trust which continued the same benevolent tone.

Government of Independent Burma

Announcement No. 2

To the Karen People:

1. Friends, we believe that you understand from Burmese history that you and we Burmese are related by flesh and blood and have lived together and shared the same water.

2. In establishing the Government of Independent Burma, we have no intention whatsoever of unjust abuse or mistreatment even of those foreigners—Chinese and Indians—who are not of our blood. Each and every one, regardless of his race or religion, should be free to enjoy the privileges to which he is rightfully entitled. To defend these rights and to protect the lives and property of all

26. See my dissertation, "The Political Impact of the Japanese Occupation of Burma" (Yale University, 1966), ch. 5, for an analysis of the composition and actions of the Myaungmya committee.

27. Figures on bilingualism from the 1931 census, pt. 2, p. 234. Moreover, only about a third of Karen men were literate in any language; ibid., pt. 2, p. 218.

races, we have established the Government of Independent Burma.

3. We shall protect, as is our policy, the lives and property of those foreigners such as the Chinese and Indians who present no threat of enmity or opposition to us. Therefore, friends, kinsmen such as you—Karens, Chins, Shans, Palaungs, Danus, and Arakanese, etc.—natives of Burma—we urge you to have faith in us. We pledge to protect your lives and property even at the cost of forfeiting our own lives.

4. The Government of Independent Burma is presently striving for the peace and serenity of our citizens and to make possible peaceful trade as before. We are ruthlessly suppressing the danger from those ruffians, scoundrels, and bandits who lawlessly steal, plunder, fight, and torture.

5. Thus, if you should have any misapprehension that we will impose misery and suffering on you due to the differences in our race or religion, we sincerely urge you, from today, to banish that thought from your minds. We believe that religion is a right that everyone possesses. It is a natural law that everyone has the freedom to choose his own religion. Just because your religion is different we cannot consider you our enemies. Everyone who is not opposing the Government of Independent Burma is considered our friend. Without discrimination on the basis of nationality or race, we believe that those who work for the peace and prosperity of the country will be our friends.

6. In conclusion, we would like to make generally known that since we are assuring our protection to the life and material welfare of each and every human being, we believe that you, our friends, will give us your wholehearted cooperation for the sake of our country's peace and prosperity.[28]

28. Lutlattho bama pyi asoya kyeinyasadin 2 kayin amyotha apaungtho (Government of Independent Burma, Announcement no. 2, to members of the Karen ethnic group), updated but before 5 April. No extant leaflets are labeled announcement no. 1, but a likely candidate is an undated handwritten proclamation of Burma's liberation. *Delta News*, no. 3, 13 April 1942, p. 4, claims that a conciliatory message by Bo Kyin, commander of the delta regional pacification force, was dropped over villages on 11 April by a Japanese plane.

Particularly noteworthy are the references to ethnicity and religion. At the time this leaflet appeared there was no collective term for the natives of Burma other than *bama*, the common term for ethnic Burmans. Carefully avoiding this word, the BIA used the term for kinsman and then a partial enumeration of peoples to convey the concept now carried by the more formal term for ethnic Burmans, *myinma*, which has been adopted in an attempt to find an inclusive label for Burmese nationals. Note how the Burmans cast themselves in the central, protective role vis-à-vis each indigenous and foreign ethnic group just as the British had done. The leaflet discussed religious toleration using the unusual concept of a natural law guaranteeing freedom of religious choice. The term for nature in the leaflet was not the one conveying the Western meaning but rather one referring to the great world cycle of Buddhist cosmology.

There assuredly was a genuine desire for trust and acceptance behind these appeals, and the conciliatory tone clearly was rooted in the typically Burman view of the powerful as protectors. The Myaungmya Thakins were solidly in the tradition of Burmese kings, whose formal statements asserted the limitless character of the benevolent power and assumed a commonality of interests among all subjects. Since independence, Burmese governments have continued in this tradition of formal statements proclaiming the righteousness of government coupled with a tacit rejection of the legitimacy of any interest divergent from official policy.[29]

As the Burman tradition contained no notion of the desirability of limiting power, it becomes understandable that any Karen not totally submissive to the new government was considered one of the "ruffians, scoundrels, and bandits" from whom the BIA would protect the Karen people. Simultaneously with the appeals for brotherhood, the BIA government issued a curt order to Karen rebels. This surrender ultimatum of 4 April, so at variance with the appeals in tone and substance, may have been issued by a different faction of the Myaungmya government, but more likely it reflected a consensus that Karens must actively demonstrate their loyalty to the new Burmese order.

29. The Burma section of Roger Smith, ed., *Documents of Southeast Asia* (Ithaca: Cornell University Press, 1974), gives many assertions of the benevolence of government power.

The Order of the Government of Independent Burma
The Rebels Who Surrender to the Government Will be Pardoned

Karens note: Karens who will swear loyalty to the Burmese government, and will associate like brothers in friendship with Burmans as in the past, you should go to your respective government officer as soon as possible for official acknowledgment of your sworn-in status. Karen rebels who are still resisting must surrender their arms and rally to the government before the ninth waning of Tagu [8 April]. Any rebellion continuing after that date will be ruthlessly suppressed.[30]

A rumor, believed by some in the BIA, that Karens were attempting to establish a Karen state has not been supported by evidence.[31] There are no claims in the extent documents and only denials from knowledgeable Karens. Their feeling of extreme vulnerability following the departure of the British argues against the likelihood of such a venture. Karen villages did resist the symbol of BIA domination, refusing to fly the tricolor. Some villages flew a white flag, but so emotionally charged was the atmosphere that this traditional symbol of surrender may have taken on meanings of separatism to the BIA.

Guns quickly became a bone of contention between the BIA and the Karens. In colonial Burma careful British licensing had confined rifles to the army, shotguns as awards to trusted headmen, and revolvers to a few wealthy Anglophiles. Even the 400-man police force for Myaungmya district possessed only 140 shotguns and 50 revolvers.[32] Guns had

30. Lutlattho bama pyi asoya ameinsa (Order of the Government of Independent Burma) issued by the Government Organization of Independent Burma, Myaungmya, 4 April 1942. (Tagu 5th waning, 1303, all dates were stated by the Burma calendar.)

31. None of the BIA leaflets or internal reports from Myaungmya accuse Karens of attempting to establish a state. The only evidence of quasi-governmental action comes from Pantanaw, fifty miles northeast of Myaungmya, where the local BIA believed that Karen soldiers set up "military offices" which gave orders in land tenancy disputes and arrested bad hats. See DR 891 iii (a) Letter from the BIA Pantanaw administration to Bo Sein Hman, beginning of June 1942. Rumors of attempts to establish a Karen state were picked up by the government in exile in Simla, Burma (Simla), *Burma under the Japanese,* vol. 1, p. 17, and then repeated by Willard H. Elsbree, *Japan's Role in Southeast Asian Nationalist Movements, 1940 to 1945* (Cambridge: Harvard University Press, 1954), p. 160.

32. Burma, *Report on the Police Administration of Burma, 1938* (Rangoon:

such importance as a status symbol that even a gun without ammunition was coveted for its value in attesting its owner's prestige in the colonial system or the BIA man's power in the new order. When the BIA massed several hundred strong in Myaungmya they had only a score of guns among them. Desperate to acquire guns that would substantiate their claims as an army, the BIA put pressure on wealthy individual owners, headmen, and police officers, who temporized briefly and then surrendered their guns.

Karen soldiers straggling home from the front were the most obvious source of guns. The rapidly disintegrating Burma Rifles had numbered 8,000, including over 3,000 Karens. About 2,000 of the Burma Rifles were discharged at the beginning of the retreat in March to avoid their desertion, another 2,000 to 3,000 actually deserted en route, and the remainder—save 800 who elected to evacuate to India—were discharged at Mandalay on 25 April. No soldiers had been stationed in Myaungmya district during colonial rule. Karen deserters and dischargees streaming into delta villages may have numbered 700 by early April and 1,500 by mid-May. Their alarm over BIA attacks on the British and their fear of the Japanese, coupled with a condition of general lawlessness in the countryside, made Karen soldiers feel fully justified in keeping their guns. The BIA reacted to the widespread refusal to obey the 4 April surrender order by sending a search party of about 50 men to the Kwele village across the river from Myaungmya. The Karens repulsed them, killing one man.

At this point, the atmosphere became enflamed with news of village burnings and rumors of atrocities. Karens believed that the BIA of Myaungmya had publicly hacked to bits two Karens as summary punishment for alleged theft and rape.[33] Burmans in the BIA circulated rumors that Karens had killed pongyis. Burmans also believed false rumors, consonant with their view of the colonial ethnic system, that the Karens were following British instructions not to submit to a government by Burmans and that Karens were harboring British soldiers,

---

Government Printing, 1939), pp. 110–111, provides the most recent figures available.

33. Ian Morrison, *Grandfather Longlegs: The Life and Gallant Death of Major H. P. Seagrim* (London: 1947), p. 187. Punishment at this level of brutality was consistent with suppression elsewhere. His data appear to come entirely from Karen informants.

even parachutists, who would lead them in attacks on Burmans. Whether or not any of the atrocity rumors were true, they were believed as if true.

It is almost impossible to exaggerate the importance of rumor in 1942 Burma. Although people everywhere in time of trouble resort to rumor in trying to grasp uncertainty, in Burma, even when a free press prevailed under democracy, all segments of the public preferred rumor's earthy detail. Burmese take such delight in the face-to-face exchange of personal tidbits that rumor passing may be considered the national pastime.

Once begun, communal warfare has a built-in accelerator. In Myaung-mya everyone was automatically cast into partisanship by his ethnic identity. Neighbor against neighbor meant no place to escape the conflict. The simplest form of attack—village burning—created roving bands of refugees who easily became attackers themselves, having lost all material stake in tranquillity. In this expanding conflict, growing bands of refugees fled crazily across the delta, seeking shelter, searching for lost relatives, driven by fear.

The single most important factor intensifying the conflict was the absence of stable power structures. The BIA grew wildly, without central control, as in repeated fission units split and new commanding officers appeared. In these chaotic circumstances, freebooting officers pushed aside more responsible individuals and rebuffed half-hearted attempts at restraint. Where early BIA demands had been for guns, the symbol of a national army, the later demands were for personal glory and loot. Fear of the BIA propelled Karen villagers toward their own uncompromising leaders.

The ramshackle structure of power which the BIA threw together had conflict built into its joints. Maung Maung, having appointed the first government for Myaungmya, also appointed commanding officers for all the towns he toured, without establishing a hierarchy among them. After Maung Maung's return to Rangoon, Bo Ye Myint took command of the delta—while in Rangoon Bo Let Ya, Maung Maung's superior and one of the Thirty Comrades, proceeded to name more commanding officers for the delta and then pass responsibility for lower Burma to another of the Thirty Comrades, Bo Kyaw Zaw.[34]

After some shuffling, there were as of 1 May four commanding officers for Myaungmya district alone, each with an unruly personal following.[35] None of these officers could command another, and only one, Bo Kyin, worked with the BIA government of Myaungmya.[36] In response to many complaints on the acts of the first Myaungmya government, especially their recall of the currency for overprinting, BIA leaders in Rangoon directed Bo Kyin to appoint a new government for Myaungmya. This thirteen-man committee took office on 28 April, headed by Thakin Thein Pe, a serious and thoughtful nationalist from Wakema who had spent the year organizing peasant branches for the Thakin party in the lower delta and hiding to evade arrest by the colonial government. Four Thakins were carryovers from the first government; the new members consisted of Thakin Thein Pe and a leavening of elders, a Burman advocate, a Burman civil servant, and two Karens—Saw Pe Tha and U Ta Pe Lu. Unfortunately Bo Kyin's cooperation with the new Myaungmya government was sporadic, because in his attempt to oversee the whole delta he kept shifting his base between the districts of Myaungmya and Henzada.

Although the three other generals rejected the authority of the Myaungmya government, friction was minimized by the departure of two of them, Bo Htain Win and Bo Kyaw Win, from the district headquarters. Bo Htain Win, who had been appointed by Bo Let Ya, took his troops to Kyonmange, twenty miles away, where he became a law unto himself. Bo Kyaw Win, also appointed by one of the Thirty Comrades, Bo Set Kya, had no soldiers under his command because the officer he replaced, Bo Myint Swe, had taken his troops with him in defiance of orders. Thus robbed of soldiers by the personal nature of authority, Bo Kyaw Win made his empty claims to command from Kyaiklat, out of contact with other officers.

34. *Delta News,* no. 4, 18 April 1942, p. 4.

35. Examples of indiscipline are mentioned in "Regular Army," *Delta News* no. 5, 25 April 1942, p. 4, and DR 1859 iii (a) Myaungmya Army headquarters, Ten Regulations, 14 May 1942.

36. DR 891 iii (a) Thakin Thein Pe, Report from the Myaungmya Administration to Bo Let Ya, Rangoon, 2 May 1942, describes the four generals. This and other documents from the Defence Services Historical Research Institute, Rangoon, are preceded by the accession number.

The most dynamic of the four commanders in Myaungmya was Bo Myint, a fierce youth of about twenty-one and a native of the district, who had been appointed by Maung Maung after three years in Rangoon as a poorly paid reporter on a vernacular newspaper. A freebooter who inspired admiration and emulation in a circle of followers and struck fear into all others, Bo Myint packed pistols in his belt and had an unnerving manner of brandishing them to emphasize his points to subordinates, even threatening to shoot BIA administrators who challenged him.[37] In exceptional liberation from traditional forms of deference the young firebrand enjoyed ordering about his former high school teacher, a Thakin of national reputation who had been a newspaper editor in Rangoon, and added to his reputation as a swashbuckler by keeping two Karen girls in the house he had appropriated.[38] The traditional role which Bo Myint filled was that of the dacoit leader who leads his personal band in looting raids on villages and evades the law by daring and cunning. In the absence of government, Bo Myint easily confiscated valuables from the well-to-do of all races and from Karens who were burned out. His avaricious appetite quickly grew beyond the supply of gold and jewelry to watches, radios, pianos, bicycles, and even a lathe—all of which were shipped off to Rangoon for disposal. Torture and imprisonment were the fate of any subordinate who failed to deliver his quota of cash from a village raid.[39] In all, his men took an estimated R400,000 worth of property.[40]

More serious were his acts against Karens in total disregard of the conciliatory leaflets issued by the Myaungmya government. To retaliate for the burning of one Burman village on 1 April Bo Myint led the BIA in the burning of five Karen villages.[41] At his whim any Karen might be arrested and given a trial, a mockery of justice in which the accused

37. Interview with a member of the Burma Independence Army administration.
38. DR 891 iii (a) Information from Myaungmya headquarters, 3 July 1942.
39. DR 891 iii (a) Testimony of a BIA soldier at the court-martial of Bo Myint, 9 July 1942.
40. DR 891 iii (a) Testimony at Bo Myint's court-martial by Thakin Htun Maung, keeper of army stores; Information from Myaungmya army headquarters, 3 July 1942; Letter to the BIA commander from an Indian engineer, 13 June 1942; Bo Myint's confiscation order of 16 May 1942; and Letter of Thakin Thein Maung to Bo Kyaw Zaw, Rangoon, 23 June 1942.
41. *Delta News*, no. 4, 18 April 1942, p. 4; and DR 531 iii (a) Directives from Myaungmya District Administration to township officials, 10 April 1942.

was denied the right to testify, cross-examine, or call witnesses.[42] Bo Myint admitted to killing ten men, but a loyal subordinate attempted to justify his execution of about one hundred.[43]

His coterie of thoroughly trusted companions numbered about seven.[44] This highly personal following broke up in early June when, on the pretext of illness, he passed command to one of his lieutenants, Bo Thi. About 150 BIA members resigned outright. Actually Bo Myint was fleeing Myaungmya on learning that the BIA was about to arrest him.[45]

On the Karen side as well, established leaders were pushed aside by parvenus. At the beginning of April eleven respected Karen leaders met in Myaungmya with the BIA government to constitute a peace committee and issued this leaflet.

Announcement from the Karen Leaders

To all Karen people, that they may hear and know, it is hereby announced:

Members of all races in the territories conquered by the great Burma Independence Army are being governed so that they may live in peace and prosperity, whatever their religion or social status may be. We Karens are aware that we are enjoying the protection and benefits promised us in the Burmese Government Administrative Announcement number 2. The matter of special urgency is this—Do not harbor in your towns and villages those who are yet sworn to British loyalty and who remain a source of disturbance to the great Burma Independence Army. Instead, you should capture them or inform the great Burma Independence Army's administration of the whereabouts of those retreating British soldiers, former employees

42. DR 891 iii (a) Letter of Thakin Thein Pe to Bo Let Ya, 2 May 1942; Information from Myaungmya army headquarters, 3 July 1942; and Letter to BIA headquarters, 19 June 1942, from Thakin Htun Maung, keeper of army stores.

43. DR 891 iii (a) Testimony of Bo Myint, 9 July 1942, and Testimony of Bo Thi, personal assistant to Bo Myint, 22 June 1942. Other estimates of executions are Thakin Tun Maung of 40–50 in his letter dated 16 June 1942; and Morrison, p. 189, of 47 Karens and 50 Indians.

44. DR 891 iii (a) Letter for court-martial testimony from Thakin Tun Maung to BIA headquarters, 19 June 1942.

45. Letter from Myaungmya military headquarters, Bo Mya Maung to Rangoon BIA headquarters, 9 June 1942.

of the British, and members of the white-faced races. We, the under-
signed patriotic Karen leaders, bid you do this.[46]

A disproportionate number of those who signed were from the Sgaw
Baptist community, which could claim only 8 percent of the district's
Karens, and the education profession of several testifies to the impor-
tance of the mission school system in the creation of the Karen elite.
We do not know whether the signers included all of the most influential
Karens then present in Myaungmya town, but we do know that both
Karen members of parliament signed. Saw Pe Tha, the most prestigious,
was the Minister of Justice, who just fled home to Myaungmya with his
English wife. Thakins in the Myaungmya government were apprehensive
of his sophistication and his ties to the armed group gathering in
Kanyingon village.[47] Table 3 gives the background of all eleven who
signed. The fact that these leaders, among the most highly Anglicized of
Karens, were urging the betrayal of British soldiers was a powerful act
of disloyalty to their former masters, because at the time both Karens

Table 3. Background of Signers of the Conciliation Leaflet

Name	Karen Group	Religion	Other Data
U Kan Aye	Pwo	Buddhist	Landowner, M.P.
U Po Nyein	Pwo	Buddhist	Father of Aung San's wife
Saw Pe Tha	Sgaw	Baptist	Lawyer, M.P.
U Ta Pe Lu	Sgaw	Baptist	School inspector
Saw Tha Aye	Sgaw	Baptist	Educator
U Kra Su	Sgaw	Baptist	—
Saya Shwe Ba	Pwo	Baptist	Educator, repre-sented Karens at Round Table
Saw Mya Htin	Sgaw	—	—
U Po Shwe	Pwo	—	—
U Kar Ti	—	—	Unidentified
U Naing Gan	—	—	Unidentified

46. Kayin kaungsaung lugyimya kyeinachet (Announcement by Karen leaders),
printed in Myaungmya (undated) and Wakema, 5 April 1942.
47. DR 891 iii (a) Thakin Thein Pe's letter, 2 May 1942, confirmed by an interview with a member of the Myaungmya government.

and Burmans believed the false rumors that substantial numbers of British soldiers had stayed behind to continue the war against Japan. Clearly the leaders were willing to contravene the old Karen-British relationships, the underlying cause of Burman hostility, as the price for peaceful entrance into the new role system among ethnic groups. The appeal failed, however, to offer the critically needed guidance on the emerging issues of village burnings and control of guns.

The village burnings brought forward restless new leaders, and a familiar problem in Karen villages, the inability of the elders to restrain headstrong individuals, became exacerbated during the turmoil. The social isolation of the Karen villages frustrated attempts at conciliation by the town-based moderates. Buddhist Karens were not linked to supravillage organizations, while Christians were divided among Catholics, Baptists, and Anglicans. By the end of April only two Karen villages into which refugees had crowded continued to follow moderate leaders—Kanyingon, faithful to Saw Pe Tha, and Sitsalidon, where a local Buddhist landowner named U Kan Aye still held sway.

During April thousands of refugees flocked to the leadership of Shwe Tun Kya, headman of a Pwo Karen village near Einme. A Buddhist aged about thirty-five, Shwe Tun Kya had recently been convicted of a criminal offense but was released from Myaungmya jail with hundreds of other offenders during the retreat. Taking upon himself the avenging of the victims of the village burnings, Shwe Tun Kya developed a deep hatred of all Burmans and by his actions became widely regarded as the man of the hour.[48] Two villages near Einme were virtual armed camps of his refugee followers.[49] The larger one, Ywathit, had a population base of 1,200 Buddhist Karens with a scattering of Christian Karens and 100 Indians. The smaller village, Tagundaing, swelled from 400 Buddhist Karens to about 6,000 Karens and 2,000 Indians.[50] Flocking to Shwe Tun Kya were Christians as well as Buddhists, Sgaw and Pwo, refugees from within the district and from nearby. Most of the Indians were probably migrant laborers who lacked other refuge. So overtaxed were the resources of Tagundaing that raids were conducted as much for food and building materials as for retaliation.

48. Interviews with three Karen leaders from the delta.
49. *Delta News*, no. 4, 18 April 1942, p. 4.
50. DR 891 iii (a) Thakin Thein Pe, Report from the Myaungmya Administration to Bo Let Ya, Rangoon, 2 May 1942.

Shwe Tun Kya's leadership style fit the traditional Burmese pattern of messianic leaders. Added to his earlier fame for amorous prowess was a new emphasis on warrior prowess suggested by his name, Magnificent Shining Tiger. In his passion for charms of invulnerability Shwe Tun Kya bore tattoos all over his body and wore a belt of human hair with a skull.[51] Rumors that bullets bounced off his chest and that he could bring down an airplane by pointing his finger at it were the same as the rumors simultaneously spread about the Thirty Comrades. Shwe Tun Kya carried small balls of gold and silver in his mouth to insure eloquence and, wherever he went, drew an enthusiastic Karen following. The BIA administration in Pantanaw reported, "Karens believe in Shwe Tun Kya and in his strength as though he were a *nat* or Thagya Min."[52]

Among others who led burning raids was the eccentric San Po Thin, a member of a landowning family of Bassein who had studied abroad, dabbled in music, but not yet found his career before joining the colonial army at the age of thirty-seven in 1940. After the army's rout from Tenasserim, San Po Thin returned to the delta to gather a following called the Taw-mei-pa association.[53]

Even the Karen cabinet ministers in the new BIA administration could not regain authority with Shwe Tun Kya's followers. Two Burman members of the administration traveled to Bassein seeking the assistance of the most prestigious Karen, Sir San C. Po, who promised to tour the troubled areas advising cooperation with the BIA but was unable to go.[54] Thus Karen and Burman moderates were both unsuccessful in trying to divert followers from the bands gathered by colorful extremists. Every village burning created refugees, with Karens fleeing to a few village strongholds and Burmans fleeing to Myaungmya town. Yet neither side possessed a preponderance of force to inhibit the attacks of the other side (see table 4). As Thakin Thein Pe recognized, each side had stronger offensive than defensive capabilities:

Our armed forces . . . cannot carry out positional warfare. What

51. Morrison, p. 190.

52. DR 891 iii (a) Letter from the eleven-member Pantanaw administration to Bo Sein Hman, dated beginning of June 1942. Thagya Min is king of the spirits (*nats*).

53. Morrison, pp. 190–201.

54. *Delta News*, no. 5, 25 April 1942, p. 1, "Karen Revolt Quiets Down."

Table 4. Estimated Strength of Karen Bands and BIA as of 1 May 1942

Location and Leadership	Manpower	Firepower
Karens		
Tagundaing (Shwe Tun Kya)	8,000 refugees n.e. active men[a]	20 rifles 2 machine guns 60 other guns
Kanyingon (some influence from Saw Pe Tha)	4,000 refugees 1,000 active men	60 rifles 60 other guns
Inma and Taguseik (in contact with Sir San C. Po)	10,000 refugees 4,000 active men	200 rifles
Sitsalidon (weak influence of U Kan Aye)	n.e.	100 rifles
BIA		
Myaungmya	6,000 residents 3,000 refugees 600 BIA	40 rifles 100 other guns
Wakema	9,000 residents n.e. refugees 400 BIA	8 rifles 10 muskets 30 shotguns

SOURCE: DR 891, iii (a), Thakin Thein Pe's letter of 2 May 1942; India, *Census of India, 1931*; and DR 531, iii (a), Independent Burma Government, General District Administration in Myaungmya, 10 April 1942.
[a]*n.e.* = no estimate.

they can do is to raid Karen villages and then return to town to defend it.... [Then] Karen forces maraud Burman villages again.[55]

While probably overstating the number of active Karens, Thakin Thein Pe is correct on the general configuration—the BIA was less armed and there was a common severe shortage of guns. We may suppose that every rifle in the Karen villages was possessed by a soldier returned

55. DR 891 iii (a) Letter from Thakin Thein Pe to BIA headquarters, 2 May 1942.

from the colonial army. That Shwe Tun Kya's followers had fewer rifles than those villagers in contact with Sir San C. Po and U Kan Aye may indicate a preference among soldiers for the established leaders rather than the charismatic hero. Thakin Thein Pe had no fear of Sitsalidon, for that refugee village was under the leadership of a former district commissioner who would fight only in defense of the village. The real danger of attack on Myaungmya would come if the aggressive band of Shwe Tun Kya combined with the strength of Inma and Taguseik.

Why did social disintegration proceed so far and so quickly as to erupt in an unexpected communal war? The reason why the local Westernized elites lost control cannot be stated solely by reference to the lack of central government which made irrelevant their Rangoon connections and English skills. A more fundamental explanation lies in the nature of personal status relationships that forms the basic social structure not only in Burma but throughout Southeast Asia. The fundamental orientation of each individual is not to a corporate group but to the web formed of one-to-one (dyadic) relationships with every other individual he knows. Leaders who arise in such a system have a number of clients who are personally bound to them and who in turn may have clients of their own. The structure of authority thus constructed is totally different from that of a formal organization which attracts members on the basis of common traits.[56] Dependent as it is on the exchange of service and patronage maintained through face-to-face relationships, it is never more than one layer deep—a patron can reach his client's followers only through that client, their leader.[57] As a result, the pyramid of power is very unstable. Even within a single layer the relationship is fluid, for individuals may shift allegiance from one leader to another in pursuit of personal benefits. But though power may shift, goals do not, for it is not possible for an alternative set of leaders to capture a patronage network as young turks may seize control within a

56. This has been shown in an outstanding systematic presentation, Carl Landé, "Networks and Groups in Southeast Asia: Some Observations on the Group Theory of Politics," *American Political Science Review* 67, no. 1 (March 1973): 103–127.

57. L. M. Hanks, "Entourage and Circle in Burma," *Bennington Review* 11, no. 1 (Winter 1968): 32–36, 41–45; and James C. Scott, "Patron-Client Politics and Political Change in Southeast Asia," *American Political Science Review* 66, no. 1 (March 1972): 91–113.

modern organization. Nor can followers restrain leaders by appealing to group goals, for the leader has formed his network on the basis of personal and often different ties to each follower, setting his own goals. The colonial experience had left this system of networks intact. Indeed, to the extent that colonial rule had eroded values and created greater economic differentiation and uncertainty, it encouraged people to seek identity, protection, and advancement through attachment to a more powerful individual. Nor, for all the talk of national goals, party-building, and disciplined organization, did networks give way to modern organization in the postcolonial period. Dyadic relations have persisted as the basis of power, and in this lies the persisting inability of Burmese leaders to build stable and effective political organizations.

From this perspective we can see that the BIA in the delta was not an organization, much less an army, but a number of personal followings gathered by individual commanders. The Myaungmya independent government was not an administrative hierarchy which could obtain compliance from citizen or soldier. It was a loose collection of individuals, none of whom could assure the subordination of any of the four commanding generals. Neither would one general accept orders from another, nor would troops remain when their personal commander departed.

To the Myaungmya events we must add the element of crisis. In time of danger, men tend to turn toward charismatic leadership, the most intense form of personal authority.[58] The blind faith of the followers of a charismatic leader is born of hope, and indeed that hope may rise from despair. The shaken Karens—Pwo, Sgaw, Buddhist, Christian—found hope in their attachment to Shwe Tun Kya. Personal and communal survival became the bond of attachment, making trivial the previous attachments to established Karen leadership based on such relations as teacher-pupil and landlord-tenant. When Shwe Tun Kya became savior to the fearful, the reasoned appeals for moderation from former leaders could not compete. Bo Myint also had a charismatic appeal and his followers, assembled within a month of appearance, were too intoxicated by loot and the emotional satisfaction of pro-

58. The theory that long-run social disequilibrium and a precipitant crisis will dispose people toward charismatic authority has been persuasively argued in Ann Ruth Willner, *Charismatic Political Leadership: A Theory*, Center of International Studies Research Monograph no. 32 (Princeton, 1968).

moting glory for Burma and for themselves to heed the call for moderation by members of the BIA government. Restraint was going to have to come from the preponderance of outside force.

The Burmese authorities in Rangoon could not intervene effectively to still the conflict. The BIA of Myaungmya began as early as April to appeal to BIA headquarters in Rangoon for assistance and advice. Unfortunately, the national BIA leaders, caught up in the euphoria of their liberation campaign, were giving little thought to the delta. Bo Let Ya, who had nominal responsibility for the area, maintained a file of reports and pleas,[59] requested Saw Pe Tha to calm the situation, and sent a conciliator to the area. His choice of U Pannawuntha for this task was particularly fortunate, for in an ethnic conflict whose lines had been sharply drawn, allowing little space for a neutral third party, this Karen sayadaw automatically gained Burman Buddhist deference to his position as head of a monastery and won Karen acceptance by virtue of his ethnicity and religious stature. Nevertheless, as a hill Karen from Thaton who had dwelt in a Rangoon monastery and come to know the national Thakin leadership, U Pannawuntha lacked personal connections to Myaungmya.[60] He labeled himself a Burmanized outsider when he spoke Burmese more fluently with the plains Karens than he spoke Karen.[61] Fluency in Karen is a strong element in Karen self-definition. An illustration from prophecy is that the messiah, Taw-mei-pa, will appear suddenly and touch a person quickly to startle him. If the surprised person exclaims in Karen, he belongs to Taw-mei-pa's people, but if he exclaims in Burmese he is not a true Karen. U Pannawuntha's appeals were written in Burmese.

Announcement of the Karen Leader, Sayadaw U Pannawuntha, Regarding the Country's Peace and Tranquillity

Karen people, my disciples: We have just achieved our independence. Yet there is news that we are divided in mind and spirit from

59. DR 891 iii (a).
60. Interviews with Bo Let Ya, 28 July 1962, and Bo Kyaw Zaw, 15 September 1962.
61. Interview with a Karen leader who toured the delta.

our comrades in adversity and in fortune, the Burmans. This is terrible. Ignorant people spreading rumors have caused this situation, I as sayadaw know. Hence I shall soon make a formal tour of your villages, towns, and cities in order to resolve these matters and to promote united efforts in your political affairs. Meanwhile, report to me your complaints and your wishes. In the intervening time before my arrival, do not go against my wishes by fighting to death and destruction among yourselves. Live in harmony with one another.

I am taking all the above action for the sake of the peace and tranquillity of everyone. At such an important time as this, prior to my arrival, tolerate one another's misunderstandings and misconceptions. This I strongly urge you.

U Pannawuntha

Temporarily at Myaungmya[62]

The urgency of this mid-April plea for tolerance underscores the extremist temper of the times. Although the sayadaw succeeded in persuading Bo Myint to call off his ten-day siege of the large Karen village of Kangyi,[63] the accommodation proved to be only temporary and unsupported by further mediation from Rangoon.[64]

When Bo Let Ya left Rangoon with the northern expedition on 7 April, responsibility for the delta fell to Bo Kyaw Zaw for the BIA and remained with another of the Thirty Comrades, Thakin Tun Oke, for the BIA committees of administration. Both were otherwise engaged, the one in training officers for a mushrooming army, the other in drafting unenforceable but procedurally correct regulations for the whole country. Colonel Suzuki, who as founder of the BIA might have taken early action, was engaged on a dozen fronts. The focus of his hectic activity was to stake out Burmese independence against the encroachments of the Japanese army, for Suzuki saw himself bringing a special present to the Japanese emperor in the form of a willingly allied Burma.

---

62. Hsayadaw u pannawuntha kayin amyotha gaungsaunggyi i tainpyi nyeingyan thayayei kyeinya sadin (Sayadaw U Pannawuntha's Announcement) Myaungmya, undated (mid-April).

63. *Delta News,* no. 5, 25 April 1942, p. 4.

64. DR 891 iii (a) Pantanaw, Appeal to Karens and Burmans for Peace, no. 2, 16 June 1942, shows the sayadaw continuing his lonely attempts.

Since the plans of the Japanese army diverged greatly from Suzuki's, he directed his attention to combating them. Concerning the delta in April, he merely dispatched a close comrade, Colonel Kimata Toyoji, to seek Burman-Karen conciliation.[65]

Colonel Suzuki, Bo Let Ya, and Thakin Tun Oke shared the misperception that British soldiers had parachuted behind the lines to foment trouble by using the Karens. Thakin Tun Oke considered the Karens to be in rebellion, favored the death penalty for their continued possession of guns, and wished to impose BIA law and order at any price.[66]

As the likelihood increased that each side would try to enlist Japanese soldiers to suppress the other, Thakin Thein Pe voiced this danger in again appealing for Rangoon's intercession.[67] By 25 May a handful of Japanese soldiers had established themselves in Myaungmya and their commander, Kakeihi, issued a stern order that all killing, burning, and rebelling stop immediately, whether by Karens, Burmans, or Indians.[68]

It would have taken more than his order to stop the slaughter that was about to begin. Some Karens believed that the BIA of Myaungmya had issued two leaflets urging the extermination, first, of all Karen Christians and then of all other Karens.[69] In this highly charged atmosphere, Shwe Tun Kya and San Po Thin proposed to attack the Burman stronghold of Myaungmya town. On the morning of 26 May

65. Interview with Colonel Suzuki. Like other Japanese soldiers in Suzuki's secret organization, Colonel Kimata had a pseudonym, Colonial Iijima, and he also was nicknamed Lovable (Bo Chit) by BIA men.

66. Interviews with Bo Kyaw Zaw, Colonel Suzuki, and Thakin Tun Oke.

67. Thakin Thein Pe, Letter to Burma Independence Army headquarters, 2 May 1942.

68. Gyapan sitbogy kakeihi i sit upadeiaya kyeinyagyet (Japanese Officer Kakeihi, Military Law Announcement) Myaungmya, 25 May 1942. The accepted date for the Karen attack on Myaungmya is 26 May, but the contemporary newspapers do not give the precise date. Morrison, p. 188, is probably the source based on his 1946 interviews. Unfortunately participants' memories are often unreliable on precise dates.'If the attack took place on 26 May, then Kakeihi's strict order was disregarded. If the attack were on the 24th or 25th Kakeihi's order was a response to the slaughter.

69. Burma, *Frontier Areas Committee of Enquiry, 1947: Report Presented to His Majesty's Government in the United Kingdom and the Government of Burma* (Rangoon: Government Printing, 1947), p. 2, appendices, pp. 165–169, and interviews with two Christian Karen leaders who presented the leaflets to the committee. The committee did not record their contents and subsequently they were lost.

about 300 Karens and 200 Indians moved in from several sides while town Karens hid in fear. The BIA leaders lacked the level-headed Thakin Thein Pe, who had gone to Rangoon for help, and felt weakened by the absence of a large BIA force which had just left on a punitive expedition to Moksokwin village about seven miles away. In fear, the Myaungmya BIA asked for help among the 3,000 Burman refugees camped on one side of town and immediately several hundred responded, brandishing sticks and knives and shouting the nationalist slogan "Dobama" as they charged the Indians who were attempting to set the town ablaze. Even pongyis joined the fight, setting fire to a rice mill that sheltered Karen snipers. On both sides, mobs armed only with primitive weapons ran in front of the few men with guns. The defenders of Myaungmya held an exaggerated view that this was the ultimate battle in which it was kill or be killed.

As soon as the attackers were repulsed, frenzied refugees and BIA men stormed the Catholic church, which they regarded as the center of Karen conspiracy, and slaughtered every town Karen who had taken refuge there.[70] Otherwise reasonable Thakins read Karen plots into innocuous events: a van parked at the church the night before was an arms delivery vehicle; food prepared in the church was a victory banquet. They believed rumors that Saw Pe Tha had played a double game: public appeals for Karen submission and secret encouragement of Karen rebellion. Thus when the mob turned upon the Karen quarter of Myaungmya and slaughtered residents, Saw Pe Tha and his family were among them.[71] Led by Bo Myint, vindictive Burmans jailed the remaining Karens and for the next two weeks shot them in batches. In their fear of a second Karen attack, BIA leaders fortified the town with bamboo stakes. Some officers of the BIA marked up a map of the delta, indicating Karen villages, in the hope that the Japanese would bomb them.[72]

The most ruthless suppression of Karens was carried out by the iron-

70. Using Karen accounts, Morrison estimates 152 were killed, while Thakins estimated 50 killed.

71. Morrison, pp. 188–190; Dr. Ba Maw, *Breakthrough in Burma: Memoirs of a Revolution, 1939–1946* (New Haven: Yale University Press, 1968), pp. 189–190; interviews with Thakins present. Dr. Ba Maw's account of the conflicts describes many more deaths than the contemporary newspapers and my interviews.

72. Interview with one of the BIA participants.

willed Colonel Suzuki, who knew little of Karen-Burman relationships and admitted that he could not distinguish a Karen from a Burman. Simultaneously, rumors had reached Suzuki in Rangoon that Karens had decapitated his comrade Kimata and that Karens were about to kill all Burmans in Myaungmya town. The vengeful Suzuki acted on his own in ordering a battalion of BIA troops aboard steamers and immediately sailing for Myaungmya via Wakema. Suzuki informed his BIA troops that they would be resting several days at Wakema, but at midnight he aroused them and steamed to Thayagon, a large Karen village containing many refugees. Suzuki had his BIA troops surround and set fire to the village. As people attempted to flee, the BIA hacked them all to death by the light of their burning homes. Suzuki repeated the slaughter at the neighboring village of Kanazogon. Saw Bu, a respected Sgaw Baptist, hurriedly sought Suzuki's mercy for Karens. Only his total abasement prevented further slaughter.[73]

Saw Bu honored his word to gather thousands of Karens to hear Suzuki, who impressed upon them the necessity for obedience to the BIA government while BIA men trained their machine guns and rifles on the audience. His orders bolstered BIA claims by requiring Karens to surrender their guns, to travel only with the BIA tricolor, and to surrender all lawbreakers to the BIA.[74] Suzuki apparently released the Karens still held in the Myaungmya jail, but his threats toward Karens continued unabated, as evidenced in this speech of 2 June to a gathering of 1,500 Karens and Indians:

> We have come to your region to advocate peace. We cannot understand why Karens have fought and killed Burmese, destroyed their property, and burnt down villages. It is like chickens from the same yard fighting among themselves. Our Burma Independence Army, with the help of the Burmese, is establishing and nurturing a new Burma. By "Burmese" I mean to include all those born in Burma— the Burmans, Karens, Shans, Chins, etc. of the indigenous races.

73. Interview with Colonel Suzuki, who recalled counting over 1,000 bodies afterward. Bo Kyaw Zaw and Bo Than Daing were Suzuki's second in command. Dr. Ba Maw's parallel description, p. 189, is also based on an interview with Suzuki.

74. DR 1398 iii (a) Burma Independence Army Central War Office (temporary) Myaungmya. Bo Mogyo's pacification order no 1, 4 June 1942, printed in Wakema.

Karens are not different from Burmese, they are one and the same. Everyone without exception from the indigenous races may join and serve in the Burma Independence Army. The Burma Independence Army's sole objective is to combine the Japanese Emperor's Army with ours in order to expel our enemies—the British and Americans and the Chinese insurgents. In accordance with this aim we have already forced the enemies and insurgents to flee panic-stricken from Burma. Only if there is peace and security in the country can we carry out administration throughout the country in accordance with our plans. Therefore, all fighting and killing must be halted immediately. If you are of the opinion that your strength is complete enough to rival and combat ours, notify us. We will destroy you completely, not even sparing your women and children. You have heard how we demolished Kanazogon, Thaya-gon, and other Karen insurgent villages in the Wakema area. Those who do not submit to our authority and power will likewise be utterly and completely destroyed. If you yet wish to pit your strength against us, we shall allow you to leave Burma to join your old mentors the British. We have allowed 200 Indians who did not wish to be under our rule to return safely to India. Should you not wish to depart from Burma you must join with us in our efforts to establish a new peaceful and tranquil Burma. You are forbidden to fly white flags in your villages, to burn down villages, or to fight and kill Burmese. We clearly and definitely guarantee in public announcements that you will be given equal privileges with the Burmese and that we will fully protect your lives and property. You may worship in freedom any religion you please; but we must sternly prohibit you from any projects in liaison with the British and Americans. At this time there are not many of your people serving as soldiers in the Burma Independence Army, and thus Burmese soldiers must be posted to protect your towns and villages. From this day onward strive to the best of your ability to join the Burma Independence Army. Then only will the Burma Independence Army have Karen soldiers to assign to the defense of your villages. Do not give further aid or encouragement to Karen insurgents. If they should come to attack your villages, do not fight back in self-defense, but send couriers in all haste to either Wakema or Myaungmya to notify the Burma Independence Army, which

will then give you the necessary assistance. In the future if we hear
or see you giving encouragement to Karen ruffians and scoundrels,
we shall eradicate you without mercy, leaving no roots as when
cutting down the bamboo. We wish to meet and hold discussions
with every representative leader from Karen villages in the Myaungmya district to give them instructions and orders. For this purpose
we wish you to send those representatives to us. We shall dispatch a
boat for them.

For your part, distribute this announcement to nearby villages. I
shall give orders to my Burma Independence Army soldiers not to
harass you further. You may now return to your villages without
fear, in peace.[75]

This speech was fiercer than extant Burman leaflets, just as his night
attack on Thayagon was more vicious than any reported Burman attacks, yet Suzuki has escaped blame for suppressing Karens. Two possible explanations are that contemporaries did not know of his role or
that selective memory has erased the knowledge. Throughout the campaign Suzuki used only his Burmese nom de guerre, Bo Mogyo (Thun-
derbolt). Rumors proclaimed Bo Mogyo to be a Burmese prince returned
from exile. The many communications from the various BIA committees to Bo Mogyo as commander in chief show no recognition that
the commander in chief was Japanese—an incongruity either unsus-
pected or ignored in the fervor of Burmese nationalism. Moreover, because events in Myaungmya have never previously been sketched, the
slaughter by the BIA under Suzuki's command has not been distinguished from the attacks by Bo Myint's BIA nor from the reconciliation
attempts of the BIA administration of Myaungmya. Alternatively, it is
possible that the widespread Burman-Karen fighting of 1949 so colored
recollections that the 1942 conflict became, in selective memory, a
simple precursor in which Suzuki played little or no part.

Upon leaving Myaungmya on 5 June, Suzuki installed Bo Hla Pe as
the district BIA commander.[76] but the rule of the Burma Independence

75. *Delta News,* no. 11, 6 June 1942, p. 4, reporting a speech of 2 June near
Htawkalo village rice mill. There is no corroboration available for several of
Suzuki's assertions: whether 200 Indians emigrated in the wake of battle, whether
any Karens joined the Burma Independence Army, and what was the precise name
or location of Konazogon.

76. DR 891 iii (a) Testimony of Bo Hla Tin in the court-martial of Bo Myint.

Army was over. Three days earlier the Japanese commander in chief for Burma had laid down the policy for the BIA: it must withdraw from all administration and undergo complete reorganization.[77] The varying speed of communication and the presence of Japanese troops probably account for the great discrepancies in obedience to his order. Bo Hla Pe ordered Bo Myint's arrest to prevent the Japanese from arresting him.[78] Bo Myint escaped from custody on the steamer back to Rangoon but was recaptured and court-martialed in Rangoon on 9 July.[79] During the proceedings Bo Kyaw Zaw interceded to ask the BIA judicial department to release Bo Myint and close his case temporarily.[80] Whether the court-martial resumed is doubtful, for one next hears of Bo Myint a year later when as a ranking officer at the main training camp he caused substantial discipline problems.[81]

Elsewhere in the delta, erratic battles and burnings raged through the end of June. BIA troops from Myaungmya helped suppress Karens in the Pantanaw area.[82] By 11 July a Burman career civil servant posted to Myaungmya as district commissioner joined with two Karens, three Burmans, and two Indians to order restitution of property.[83] Individual Thakins were drawn to Rangoon largely in the vain hope of subsequent government appointment. Slowly and erratically the Westernized and landowning elites resumed control in the delta, encountering overwhelming problems of suffering and hatred.

During the remainder of the Japanese occupation, efforts at reconciliation fostered an ethnic truce in the delta but provided no basis for

77. Japan, Rikugun, Biruma Homengun (Army, Burma Area Army), *Biruma Gunseishi* (History of the Military Administration in Burma), (Tokyo: Gunmu-Kyoku at the request of Mori no. 7900 Butai, September 1943), app. 26, "Address of the Commander in Chief to Burmese Dignitaries, 2 June 1942."

78. DR 891 iii (a) Letter to Bo Kyaw Zaw from Myaungmya administration, 14 June 1942.

79. Order from the BIA Central War Office, 24 June 1942.

80. DR 891 iii (a) Order of Bo Kyaw Zaw, undated.

81. DR 29 iii (b) Confidential letter of Bo Taya at Kabalu, 15 June 1943.

82. DR 891 iii (a) Four letters and peace appeals from the Pantanaw BIA administration, from the beginning of June to the 20th, 1942.

83. *Delta News*, no. 16, 11 July 1942, p. 3.

long-term harmony. Mass organizations mobilized tens of thousands of young Burmans to nationalist politics, yet largely ignored Karens. The few Karens recruited into the Burma National Army, successor to the BIA, were assigned to a separate battalion which never got the political indoctrination given the rest of the army. Only one group, the Central Karen Organization, had a mandate to "bring about a speedy solution of all problems connected with the Karen citizens of Burma."[84] Appointed by Dr. Ba Maw, wartime head of government, the roster of this committee reads like a prewar who's who, composed overwhelmingly of Christian moderates. No Karens who had led armed bands joined the organization. Officially, the organization concentrated on public relations, producing statistics of good will tours, speeches, and pamphlets which deluded Burman leaders into the belief that the organization had accomplished reconciliation. Informally, members of the Central Karen Organization served as channels by which Karens sought favors from government, thus perpetuating the colonial pattern of separate access for ethnic groups. The organization lost its credibility by enthusiastically recruiting laborers for the Sweat Army, only to learn with the public of the killing conditions under which these workers were forced to construct the railway to Thailand. The organization fell into a decline, demoralized by the labor recruitment and the disgruntlement of its members over the lack of salaries.

Concerted efforts by Burmans and Karens achieved for Myaungmya and the delta as a whole a relatively peaceful second interregnum in 1945.[85] A power vacuum recurred when the Japanese evacuated in early April, and the British did not reoccupy Bassein until 25 May nor Myaungmya, Maybin, and Pyapon until July.[86] The crucial difference was that the disciplined Burma National Army had recruited a battalion of Karen regulars and stationed it in the delta. Moreover, General Aung San's stern proscription of communal strife became known and re-

84. Personal interview data agrees with testimony from 1947. See Burma, *Frontier Enquiry Commission,* testimony of U Nu. However, F. S. V. Donnison, *British Military Administration in the Far East, 1943-1946* (London: Her Majesty's Stationery Office, 1956), pp. 100–111, repeats rumor of extensive communal trouble during 1945 but offers no data.

85. Ibid.

86. Bo Tin Maung, Diary and interview; DR 1200 iii (c) The Views of Defense Minister Aung San on Racial Affairs, 19 February 1945.

spected among the ranks;[87] Thakin Soe as leader of the Communist resistance in Pyapon also urged racial harmony;[88] and civil servants maintained their local posts after the Rangoon government had fled. The extremist leaders were absent: Bo Myint posted outside the delta, Colonel Suzuki long since reassigned to Japan, and Shwe Tun Kya killed by the Kempeitai as a British agent. Burmans and Karens shared a weary relief that the British return was ending the privations of war.

The long-run failure of the attempts at reconciliation reflects both the gravity of the 1942 clash and the subsequent low priority Burmans placed on conciliating Karens. The 1942 warfare both foreshadowed the Karen rebellion of 1949 and was itself a contributing factor in that persisting tragedy. The absence of community which had characterized Burman-Karen relations under colonial rule degenerated into open hostility after the war as Karens struggled to gain political recognition. In brief, Karen leaders had in 1946 unsuccessfully sought in London continued special protection for their community. Aung San's 1947 delegation to London which hammered out the details of independence excluded minority representatives. When the leading Karen resigned from the cabinet in protest, he was replaced by the eccentric San Po Thin. Subsequently the Panglong agreement gained the adhesion of Shans, Kachins, and Chins, but the Karens, who attended merely as observers, felt unconsulted. The Frontier Enquiry Commission heard strong Karen testimony in favor of a separate Karen state, but Burman leadership opposed the idea. When the Karen National Union, the leading Karen organization, boycotted the elections to the constituent assembly, Burmans found Karen placemen to run.

The British withdrawal at independence left an authority vacuum in which rebellions flourished—by the Communists of Thakin Soe, by the Communists of Thakin Than Tun, by the Muslim Mujahids in Arakan, and by the White Flag People's Volunteer Organization composed of former Burman soldiers. In these chaotic circumstances, Karen extremists also attempted to set up a separate state in Papun, revolted in Karenni, and occupied Moulmein and Thaton. Karen National Union leaders disavowed these rebellious acts and forced those responsible to

87. Kayin bama thweisiyei sweingwei thi (Karens and Burmans Are Blood Brothers), June and December 1944 issues seen.

88. Burma, *Financial and Economic Annual, 1943* (Rangoon: Bureau of State Printing Press, 1943), p. 20.

retract their calls to rebellion, while the Burmese cabinet moved toward a compromise by setting up a Regional Autonomy Commission. However, PVO bands attacked Karens in the name of the government, and Karens responded by establishing the Karen National Defense Organization for defense and counterattack. As in 1942, the outbursts of local clashes which Rangoon could not control spiraled into a communal war.

A new physical ingredient was the widespread availability of modern arms, which made the fighting more deadly. The important new psychological ingredient was the memory of the 1942 conflict.[89] It appears that many Karens as well as Burmans were spurred to an uncompromising stand in 1949 by memories of the earlier strife. As an example, Saw James Tun Aung, a police officer in colonial Burma, considered himself a moderate until he toured the delta with Shwe Tun Kya. In his horror at the devastation, he resolved to dedicate his life to Karen separatism and later became a KNU leader. Karens tended to blame the Burman national leaders of 1948 for the tragedy of 1942. Even Karens who knew that Suzuki had razed Thayagon believed that Burmans had tricked him into it. On the Burman side the PVO leaders who attacked Karens were more likely than the abstainers to have previous experience as BIA men in the delta clashes. One case is Bo Sein Hman, the BIA leader who in 1942 sacked Karen villages in the Pantanaw area and in January 1949 precipitated rebellion by burning and slaughtering a village in the Taikyi area.

In retrospect it seems that the abrupt wrenching of the colonial ethnic system and the absence of authority in 1942 brought on the ethnic warfare. During the twentieth century there were no precursors of the conflict, and no discernible trend of growing hostility. Rather, Burmans and Karens focused on their relations with the British as the dominant ethnic group and had relatively little concern for each other. In the uncertain days following the British evacuation, radicals of each ethnic group attracted sizable followings, on the one side to assert a new order and on the other to survive the crumbling of the old order. Once the village burnings and slaughter occurred, these tragedies alienated Karens from Burman causes. Since mobilization to nationalist politics progressed rapidly among youth during the war, this alienation meant that

89. Ba Maw, *Breakthrough in Burma*, pp. 192–196, recounts an interview held circa 1960 with a Karen who dated his separatist conviction to the wartime tragedy.

Karens were mobilized separately from Burmans—a separate leadership, a greatly expanded following, a separate political cause. The newly politicized Burmans backed the Burman leadership to win political independence. Because independence came only six years after the delta tragedy, Karen memories and fears made them reluctant participants in Burma's independence. This separate political mobilization of the Karens created a rebellion which not only threatened the existence of the Burmese government for four months but has continued to harass successive governments for more than twenty-five years.

Contributors

DOROTHY HESS GUYOT, Associate Professor at the Rutgers University School of Criminal Justice, specializes in the cross-cultural study of political and organizational change, an interest which has already led to field research in Burma and Japan on the political impact of the Japanese occupation of Burma, in Malaysia on land policy, and in Troy, New York, on administrative evolution in the police department.

EDILBERTO C. de JESÚS, Associate Professor of Business History at the Asian Institute of Management, did graduate work at Yale University before returning to the Philippines to begin his academic career. Paralleling his interest in economic history has been a special concern for the Philippine cultural heritage which has resulted in articles on the novelists Nick Joaquin and N. V. M. Gonzales.

JOHN A. LARKIN, Associate Professor of History at the State University of New York at Buffalo, was coeditor with Harry J. Benda of *The World of Southeast Asia: Selected Historical Readings* (1967). In addition to his general interest in the region, Larkin has been a particular advocate of the use of local history for understanding Southeast Asian society, arguing for this in seminal articles on Philippine local and rural history and in the major work, *The Pampangans: Colonial Society in a Philippine Province* (1972).

RUTH T. McVEY, Reader in Southeast Asian Politics at the School of Oriental and African Studies, University of London, was editor of the book *Indonesia* (1963), and her numerous studies of Indonesian Communist history include *The Rise of Indonesian Communism* (1965). Her general interest in social and ideological change is reflected in writings ranging from cultural aspects of nationalist thought to the development of postrevolutionary military organization in Indonesia and the ideological impact of socioeconomic change in rural southern Thailand.

ONGHOKHAM, Lecturer in History at the University of Indonesia, was already well known in his country as an authority on the problems of the Indonesian Chinese minority when he came to Yale University to take his doctorate. He has devoted himself to research on Javanese culture and social history as well as the history of the Java Chinese, and in his writings has particularly endeavored to make his understanding of these subjects available to the wider Indonesian reading public.

ADRIENNE SUDDARD, Editor of Southeast Asia Studies Publications at Yale University from 1963 to 1975, has edited over forty books on Asian subjects.

HEATHER SUTHERLAND, Reader in Non-Western History at the Free University of Amsterdam, is an Australian whose interest in social and intellectual history has ranged from studies of Indonesian literary movements to the transformation of Malay institutions in the early twentieth century and local history in southern Celebes (Sulawesi). Her most recent publication is *The Making of a Bureaucratic Elite: The Colonial Transformation of the Javanese Priyayi* (1978).

Index by Adrienne Suddard

237